Digital Typography Sourcebook

Marvin Bryan

WILEY COMPUTER PUBLISHING

John Wiley & Sons, Inc.

New York • Chichester • Brisbane • Toronto • Singapore • Weinheim

Publisher: Katherine Schowalter
Editor: Tim Ryan
Managing Editor: Micheline Frederick
Text Design & Composition: North Market Street Graphics

Library of Congress Cataloging-in-Publication Data:
ISBN 0-471-14811-3

Printed in the United States of America
10 9 8 7 6 5 4 3 2 1

To Phyllis, who is just my type.

About the Author

Marvin Bryan is an authority on typefaces and has written 17 books on related subjects including typography, graphic design, and desktop publishing. His work has been translated into many languages—including French, Spanish, Portuguese, Italian, and even Thai—and distributed throughout the world. He is also a former columnist and contributing editor for major computer magazines and the author of hundreds of feature articles.

Acknowledgments

I am especially indebted to Tim Ryan for suggesting this book and to him and Micheline Frederick for shepherding it through the publishing process.

Many people gave generously of their time and resources in helping me complete the project. Among those to whom I owe heartfelt thanks for assistance above and beyond what any reasonable person might expect are these executives and top professionals: Stefan Wennik, Jon Guerringue, Renée Risch, Sonya Schaefer, and Henry Mikiewicz. Special thanks too to Robert Givens, Allan Haley, Sumner Stone, Charles Bigelow and Kris Holmes, Russ McCann, Cynthia Hollandsworth, Ed Benguiat, Dennis Pasternak, Matthew Carter and Cherie Cone, Michael Bellefeuille, Danielle Kenney, Rachel Schindler, Harry Parker, Sam Berlow, Louise Domenitz, Julia Bradley, Kellie Bowman, Renée Platt, Judith Frey, Brock Bohonos, Tammy Wing, Bruce Frame, Chuck Moozakis, and a host of others—in no particular order.

Introduction

This book tells you all about the digital typefaces that are available for your personal computer. You may call them fonts. Whether you call them typefaces or fonts, this book will show you how to make the best use of digital typography in your work. You'll also get a look at the latest products from some of the world's leading designers. And software executives have given me access to secrets about their programs that help you use, alter, or even create typefaces. The result is information you won't find anywhere else.

Moreover, with the book you get a hybrid Macintosh/PC CD-ROM that's fastened to the inside back cover. This CD-ROM contains free typefaces from major vendors that are worth more than the price of the book, plus demonstration versions of the leading programs that let you use, modify, and create type.

In the days before Windows and the Macintosh, a few eager computer users experimented with switching to different typefaces—even though they couldn't see the results until they printed their documents. But most didn't bother to switch. There were few of those bitmapped typefaces available, they were relatively expensive, and they were hard to install and use. So what if the output looked as if it had been produced on a typewriter? Personal computers were just a form of electric typewriter anyway, weren't they?

Of course, the personal computer always did more than typing. But the people who primarily wrote documents instead of using a spreadsheet or a database had no reason to think much about those extra capabilities. However, when the screen turned graphic—when you could actually *see* what you were creating, the world of personal computing was changed forever.

Now you can choose among thousands of fine digital typefaces that you can display and manipulate on your screen and you can print them out along with photos and illustrations on pages that look as if some professional printshop had produced them.

With this awesome power at your disposal, shouldn't you know all about those typefaces and how to use them? Why shouldn't you share in the fun and excitement and—yes—the increased readership you'll have for your documents, whatever their purpose?

That's what this book is about—learning about typefaces and using them like a pro. But even if you're already a pro at using type, this book is for you, too. You'll become acquainted with many designs and sources you wouldn't otherwise encounter. You'll pick up tips about subjects such as layouts and special-effect utilities, too. Through hundreds of examples, you'll see what works and what doesn't in Windows and on the Macintosh.

HOW THIS BOOK IS ORGANIZED

The *Digital Typography Sourcebook* is organized into 16 chapters, plus a type-specimen section where you can examine the features of nearly 400 designs and an appendix that tells you where you can obtain them.

In writing this, I assumed that you know the basics of how to operate a PC running Windows or a Macintosh, but that you may not be familiar with all the special terms used in the design and publishing worlds to describe type and how it's used. Every time I introduce one of these important but unfamiliar words, you'll see it highlighted in italics, and it'll be defined right there. I won't leave you behind. The illustrations will demonstrate point after point. You won't have to use your imagination—which you can save for your own projects.

Typefaces are not created in a vacuum by faceless corporations. They are all drawn by real human beings with a story to tell. When you look at many of these designs, you're looking at history. The inspiration for some came from the inscriptions of ancient Rome—for others, from Napoleon's campaign in Egypt. The idea for one came to the artist while he was looking at the label on a beer can in Paris. You'll read these stories and more. You'll also learn designers' names, because the times they lived in and their personal styles will tell you what to expect when you see one of their names attached to a typeface.

Each typeface is identified at the spot where it's shown, with its source, so you'll not only become familiar with great designs, but you'll also know how to acquire them. I explain both the good and bad characteristics of the faces and suggest specific uses. For easy reference, all the typefaces are set in bold.

Every chapter ends with a summary, which may be just that, or it may be a brief commentary on the subject of the chapter or advice relating to that topic. Now let's take a quick look at what each chapter contains.

WHAT'S IN EACH CHAPTER

This section gives a short synopsis of the information you can find in each chapter of this book. Okay, here we go.

Chapter 1 Why Type Matters

Before you can get too excited about using a variety of typefaces, you need to know just why that's important—exactly the subject of this chapter. I'll show you a series of "before and after" examples; again and again, you'll see a document presented with a bad choice in typefaces, then with more appropriate designs. I start with a fairy tale as it would look in a plain, typewriter-like typeface, then show you how much atmosphere and reader interest the right types can add. Other examples are analyzed and corrected: a billboard for a dude ranch, a warning sign, a slogan about the world of the future, a logo for a resort, and a fashion ad with too many typefaces. The discussion ends with a display of novelty types that suggest specific subjects.

Chapter 2 The Kinds of Typefaces

Welcome to a whirlwind tour of type. You'll learn the difference between a *font* and a *typeface,* what *lowercase figures* are, how the terms *uppercase* and *lowercase* originated, and the difference between *proportional* and *nonproportional.* Once you have this information under your belt, you'll learn about the major categories into which typefaces are divided and which categories are most suitable for particular kinds of documents. To begin with, typefaces with *serifs* are separated from those that don't have those little lines or nubs sticking out from their main strokes. Then you'll investigate several other major divisions. The chapter finishes with an explanation of all the formats used for creating type, such as PostScript, TrueType, and GX.

Chapter 3 The Anatomy of Characters

In this chapter, you'll find the names of the various parts and attributes of characters: words like *spur* and *ear* and phrases such as *inclined stress* and *x-height*. You're not being presented with this new vocabulary just so you can amaze your friends or have something to study on cold winter nights. Familiarity with these characteristics will help you *identify* typefaces. Why do you need to do that? Frankly, nearly everyone encounters situations where he or she must revise a document created by someone else; in order to do that, he or she must be able to make a positive identification of the typefaces that were used and will be needed again. This detective work is accomplished in most cases by comparing the shapes of specific parts of characters—so you must know those parts by name. This vocabulary section is followed by an in-depth discussion of special characters—what they're for, how to find them from your keyboard, and how to use them; a test where you can try to spot the differences between two similar designs; and enlightenment on terms like *justification, kerning, tracking*, and *em dashes*.

Chapter 4 Old Style Typefaces

In Chapter 4 you'll get into the specifics of the first typeface category to be considered—Old Style. But first, there will be more information about serif typefaces in general so you can see where the category fits in. Then you'll learn about the so-called Venetians, the oldest group within the classification; for this, I'll take you back to fifteenth-century Italy. After that trip, your time travel will continue into later years to cover the remaining kinds of Old Style designs. A practical interlude will show you how appropriate various faces in the category are for use in a soda fountain ad. Next, I'll show you how a major digital type house has organized its own additional Old Style classifications. The chapter is completed with two examples of positioning type so it helps to tell a story.

Chapter 5 Transitional Typefaces

After a short explanation of the history and characteristics of the Transitional category, I'll show you interesting and useful examples, both old and new. This classification—as its name implies—embraces designs that bridge the gulf between two different groups. It mixes Old Style traits with those of Modern, another category that was developed later. However, since today's designers often create a new design by melding elements of both Old Style and Modern, a Transitional typeface shown in this chapter may have been designed early in the eighteenth century or as recently as yesterday.

Chapter 6 Modern Typefaces

They call this category Modern, although its first member was created in 1784. This style has descended from the precedents established late in the eighteenth century by two pioneer printers named Didot and Bodoni. In particular, many typefaces today bear the name Bodoni, although the designs differ in many respects from each other. All these developments are chronicled here. You can see and compare different Bodoni types in several versions of the same document, which recounts details of the man's life. Then I'll show you numerous other designs in the Modern tradition that may fit your needs.

Chapter 7 Slab Serif Typefaces

Some think the Slab Serif types were inspired by the antiquities of Egypt or Napoleon's invasion of that country. Whatever the inspiration, they appeared in profusion on handbills and posters early in the nineteenth century. You can explore several variations in these pages. For example, most of the time-honored typewriter typefaces belong in the Slab Serif category. You'll also learn to recognize Slab Serif groups such as Egyptian, Humanist, Geometric, and Clarendon.

Chapter 8 Other Serif Typefaces

Here we round up other serif categories with intriguing names: Latin, Flareserif, Engravers', and Incised. The potpourri of samples includes intriguing designs with little flags sticking out from the main strokes or strokes that flare at the ends, plus types that imitate engraving or ancient inscriptions. You might like to find some of these in your Christmas stocking.

Chapter 9 Sans-Serif Typefaces

Well, sans-serif typefaces are simply those without serifs. So the category is large. You'll find out about Grotesque, Humanist, and Geometric varieties. Through the vehicle of an announcement for an imaginary university, you can evaluate how different types in these groups work in a typical situation. The Bauhaus philosophy is explained; early in the twentieth century, instructors at this famous German school were firmly convinced that sans-serifs were the wave of the future. You'll see sans-serifs with fascinating alternate characters, designs that suggest periods in history, and the latest in contemporary sans-serifs.

Chapter 10 Script Typefaces

Yes, script typefaces look like handwriting—more or less. The groups include Brush script, Calligraphic, English roundhand, Chancery, Formal, Monolines, Freehand, and more—all described here. Examples show off the designs in a variety of settings.

Chapter 11 Blackletter and Uncial Typefaces

Uncial typefaces are based on the handwriting of medieval scribes; you may have to read this chapter to find out what they look like. Blackletter types are derived from the handwritten university textbooks of the twelfth century; everybody has seen them as "Old English" diploma lettering or in the names of church newsletters or newspapers or as the official type style of Germany before World War II. You'll discover in this chapter that the blackletter category is configured into several groups and has special characters that must be used in specific ways if you're printing words in the German language. Finally, you may be surprised to see brand new blackletters recently introduced by today's artists.

Chapter 12 Display and Novelty Typefaces

This is a fun category—and more varied than you could possibly imagine. I'll show you types that look like graffiti and one that retains the guidelines that the artist used to draw it. You'll see some overused display faces you might want to avoid, followed by tips on altering these tired designs so they'll look different. I'll recommend little-used faces that you might want to adopt immediately. Wild novelty types are included too, as well as amazing special-purpose designs for crossword puzzles, maps, chess games, writing music, labeling audio tapes, writing down human speech, and more.

Chapter 13 Typeface Utilities and Special Effects

Whether you use a PC or a Macintosh, you'll be delighted to read about the powerful typeface-related utilities that are available to you. You can find and insert special characters effortlessly, print out a display of any design's complete character set and access key combinations, learn all the benefits of Adobe Type Manager and Type Reunion, organize your typefaces into groups that will appear on your Font menu only when you need them, create a large initial capital letter on a paragraph automatically, and generate hundreds of special effects. Among the special-effects utilities in the spotlight: Bitstream Mini-Makeup, Adobe Acrobat, Letraset Envelopes, Illustrator and Freehand filters, PageMaker masking effects, Type Twister, and TypeStyler. Other goodies are: typefaces with special effects built-in and details on creating instant borders with Letraset's BorderFonts.

Chapter 14 Creating Your Own Characters and Typefaces

Get acquainted with programs that can quickly modify typefaces for you, as well as those that give you the power to design your own from the ground up. Shown at work are: Adobe's Font Creator making Multiple Master variants, FontChameleon creating new designs from old, plus Ikarus M, Fontographer, and FontLab, which are used by the professional typeface designers. There's more: Kernus and FontFiddler for modifying or replacing *kerning tables*—the information included in type files that tells programs how far apart to space character combinations.

Chapter 15 Using Type in Layouts

Look in this chapter for practical solutions to typical creative problems that occur when type is combined with other elements in page layouts. You'll see how to make clip art and type combine to simulate an original drawing. A series of figures shows different ways to combine special effects with type in a single layout. A modern movie poster uses type superimposed over a dramatic photo. Examples demonstrate the effective use of *white space*. You'll learn about *watermarks* and *runarounds* and how they can add to the impact of your pages. Additional topics include: using a unique type family to the fullest, matching the layout to the era, making novelty faces work, using concentric circles, and improving your word processing documents.

Chapter 16 Building a Library

I offer tips on creating your own type library: discussions of shareware and mail order, locating special typefaces, the advantages of a CD-ROM drive, a summary of the major type sources, comments on the changing industry and its effect on you, and advice on what to buy.

The Type Specimens

This section demonstrates nearly 400 typefaces through the use of one sample sentence: "Quickly the Paul Yusef Zebra vented its wrath on groom John Knox." All the letters of the alphabet are represented to give you a fairly representative idea of the various styles. A complete alphabet listing for each typeface along with the sample sentence is included on the accompanying CD-ROM.

THE BOTTOM LINE

The bottom line is that *The Digital Typography Sourcebook* gathers in one place the up-to-date information you need in order to acquire and use type with outstanding results. So move on to Chapter 1 now and expand your horizons.

Contents

15 Using Type in Layouts

16 Building a Library

1

Why Type Matters

People who use typefaces fall into several categories. At one extreme we might find a man who writes to his friends on an old typewriter that offers only one built-in typeface in one size. If he changes the ribbon periodically and keeps the metal characters clean, he can be sure that his words will be legible. He may claim to be completely satisfied. He may even say, "If you can read the message, what more do you need?" At the other extreme might be a publishing professional who has thousands of computer typefaces at her disposal but often can't find one that, in her opinion, perfectly represents the thought she wants to express.

You probably fall somewhere between these extremes. Most computer users are accustomed to having at least a few typefaces available—perhaps a couple of sturdy faces that are appropriate for long paragraphs of text, plus a few "fancy" display faces for headings and special occasions. The fact of the matter is that the more you learn about type and the more typefaces you acquire, the more you're likely to realize that each design makes a slightly different impact on the reader and that every day you may edge inevitably closer to the point of view held by the anonymous lady I used as an example in the previous paragraph.

Of course, when you really do come down with "typeface fever," you must temper your passion for more and more type with the practical side. You can only buy as much type as you can afford and have room to store. Therefore, you should make your new acquisitions wisely. Hopefully, this book will help you do so.

HOW TO LOSE A JOB IN THE TYPEFACE INDUSTRY

Here's a true story that emphasizes how people feel who work with type for a living.

One of the software executives I know is the president of a company that manufactures and sells a CD-ROM full of typefaces. Recently, a friend urged this executive to interview a man who—according to the friend—had a background in marketing software and was the perfect candidate to work as a salesperson for the firm. The president agreed to an appointment. The first thing he told the would-be employee was that the company's principal product is this CD-ROM containing 500 typefaces. The applicant was amazed and asked, "Why do you need so many?"

Well, out of politeness the president continued the conversation for a few more minutes before terminating the interview, but—in actuality—the candidate lost any chance of obtaining the job by having asked that question. To get anywhere in the type business, you must fervently believe that one never has enough typefaces—indeed, that with 10,000 typefaces available, it might still be impossible to find one that would produce the exact impression wanted in a particular document. Furthermore, many of the folks in the industry are convinced that this passion for typefaces is something you're born with—not a skill to be learned.

I don't agree with that point of view. Of course, people can learn to love typefaces. However, if they *never* acquire this all-consuming desire, it's obvious that they have ice water running in their veins and may have been built from surplus electronic parts rather than born to humankind.

SEEING IS BELIEVING: A FEW EXAMPLES OF TYPE AT WORK

If your acquaintance with type has been brief, it may be hard for you to imagine how much better a document can look when the proper type selections have been made. So, at this point I'll borrow an idea from plastic surgery brochures and show you a few "before and after" snapshots.

Telling a Fairy Tale in the Right Setting

If your parents read you fairy tales when you were little, it probably helped for you to be cuddled up in bed with the lights dimmed and the mysterious stars twinkling outside your window. The right atmosphere can make those stories more real and exciting. "They really could have happened," you might have said to yourself. In the same way, when you became old enough to read the printed pages for yourself, the type styles and design of the books probably added to your belief that something magical was contained in those words.

Now take a look at Figure 1.1, our first "before" example. Here you can see the beginning of a fairy tale I've called *The Tailor's Story*. The words are readable. They could well have been put on paper by the typewriter user I described in the first paragraph of the chapter. In fact, the typeface is **Courier,** which was originally designed about 50 years ago by Howard Kettler of IBM, specifically for use on typewriters. The version you see here was created a little later by the famed designer Adrian Frutiger and offered to the public when IBM

```
                    The Tailor's Story

     Once upon a time, in a land far away, there lived a poor
man who earned his living as a tailor.  He sewed magnificent
garments for the king and his friends, but he received very
little money.
     However, one day those circumstances were to change.  He
met an elf in the forest who promised to make him a rich man.
All he had to do in return, the elf said, was to sew a suit of
clothes with cloth spun from moonbeams.
     "Where will I find such a cloth?" asked the tailor,
worried.
     The elf nodded his head wisely.  "You will know it when you
see it."
```

1.1 A fairy tale reproduced on a typewriter provides little magic.

introduced its Selectric typewriters. It's still available for typewriters today and is a standard item on most personal computer systems. If you want to use a design that looks as if it was produced on a typewriter, **Courier** is a good choice.

But why is this page unappealing? Because, you see only the words; the type presents no mood or personality at all. The title is in the same dull typeface and size as the story itself. In fact, the characters don't even seem to cluster together into words very well because this typeface is *monospaced* or *nonproportional,* which means that each character takes up exactly the same amount of space horizontally, whether it needs it or not.

There are even more reasons for the apparent lack of cohesion. Each paragraph is indented a full five spaces and there are two spaces at the end of each sentence. These typing conventions can be useful in helping the reader detect sentence endings and the beginning of new paragraphs when those individual characters are so widely spaced, but the effect is still somewhat jarring. Furthermore, even the quotation marks tend to separate words and thoughts rather than bring them together—because these quotation marks are not the "curly" kind that would seem to enclose the words spoken by the characters. The quotation marks are "all-purpose, straight up and down" symbols intended for use both at the beginning and end of a quotation. In fact, throughout the English-speaking world the same marks are also used in combination with numbers to designate inches.

Contrast this page with Figure 1.2. In this "after" example, I haven't tried to make the page more appealing by adding a marvelous drawing of the elf talking to the tailor in the forest. I haven't even surrounded the text with a decorative border. Those improvements would have constituted cheating to make a point. So I've enhanced the fairy tale only by selecting more appropriate typefaces.

In our make-over of the page, we see the title in a typeface called **Goudy Text.** This is really one of those Old English styles—the blackletters—except that the capital letters are not the intricate characters you'd expect. Designer Frederic Goudy provided an alternate set of capitals he named Lombardic, which I've used here. Their appearance is ideal for a fairy tale; they remind us of some far-off time and

---

The Tailor's Story

 NCE UPON A TIME, in a land far away, there lived a poor man who earned his living as a tailor. He sewed magnificent garments for the king and his friends, but he received very little money.

However, one day those circumstances were to change. He met an elf in the forest who promised to make him a rich man. All he had to do in return, the elf said, was to sew a suit of clothes with cloth spun from moonbeams.

"Where will I find such a cloth?" asked the tailor, worried.

The elf nodded his head wisely. "You will know it when you see it."

1.2 A wise selection of typefaces sets the proper mood for the reader.

place, but without a formal or religious aura. See both versions of this Monotype typeface in Chapter 11, which covers the blackletter category.

Incidentally, you'll find Frederic Goudy's name attached to a multitude of type designs. He was born in 1865 and completed his first typeface in 1896. He continued to create beautiful type designs until shortly before his death in 1947. As might be expected, his work usually reminds us of the period in history in which he was active. Consequently, you'll probably find one of his 123 faces an excellent choice when you want to capture the elegance and style of his era.

The text of our fairy tale begins with the use of a *drop cap*, a large, ornate initial capital letter that is "dropped" into a paragraph. These special characters were used in the beautiful manuscripts produced in monasteries even before the invention of printing. This particular letter was designed by Marwan Aridi and is a part of Initial Caps Clip Art, three packages of three alphabets this artist created for Adobe both in color and black-and-white versions. My use of the drop cap is in line with the tradition of employing decorative initial capital letters in books of fairy tales. Needless to say, they must be used sparingly—at the beginning of a story or chapter but certainly not at the beginning of each and every paragraph.

However, you can use drop caps in many kinds of documents, to add a decorative touch, even if the capital letter is simply the typeface seen in the main text except in a larger, bold format. For example, the popular desktop publishing programs Adobe PageMaker and QuarkXPress both provide a utility that can convert the first letter of a paragraph into a drop cap automatically (see Chapter 13).

Following the drop cap inserted into our fairy tale, I've honored another tradition. Usually, we capitalize the remainder of any word starting with a drop cap—often, as here, it's an entire phrase. This practice provides a graceful transition from the huge beginning letter to the smaller text that follows.

Using a publishing term, the *body copy* that follows—the main text of the story as distinguished from titles and subheadings—is set in Monotype's **Dante** typeface, designed by Giovanni Mardersteig in 1954 and inspired by fifteenth-century Italian types. **Dante** is strong, graceful, traditional, and highly readable—excellent qualities for type that is to be the medium for bringing us a fairy tale. Like **Goudy Text,** **Dante** is a *proportional* typeface; each character occupies only as much space on the line as it needs. Therefore, words seem to cluster as natural groupings of characters. The paragraph indentations are two characters in depth rather than five, quotation marks are the "curly quotes" we normally see in books and magazines, and you'll find only one space after the end of each sentence. Since the characters are proportional, this spacing does not result in any confusion. By the way, almost all printed materials you'll see in this modern age do feature proportional typefaces—for all of the good reasons I've mentioned. Nearly all of the faces displayed in this book are proportional as well. (You'll read more about proportional versus nonproportional in the next chapter.) Now, isn't our "after" fairy tale page better than the "before" version?

Promoting a Dude Ranch the Right Way

For our next example, let's visit a Western dude ranch. Imagine we need a billboard that will attract the proverbial Eastern tenderfoot to our spread. This means we'll want to use display typefaces that will get our message across. In addition, we'd better add some artwork. For that purpose,

1.3 A billboard for a dude ranch—ruined by a poor selection of typefaces.

what could be more fitting than the fine study of an old cowpoke displayed in Figure 1.3? This drawing is actually a piece of clip art from Dynamic Graphics, a company that distributes hundreds of quality images each year through its monthly clip-art services called Electronic Clipper and Designers Club. But the typefaces shown in that same figure don't look quite right, do they?

The top typeface is named **Gatsby,** which might tip you off that it was intended to remind us of the Roaring Twenties, not the wild West. Indeed, **Gatsby** (sold by Casady & Greene) was named in honor of the pivotal character in a novel about the 1920s written by Jazz Age novelist F. Scott Fitzgerald. The design is deliberately reminiscent of the Art Deco style of architecture and decor, which is based on geometric principles; it predominated in Europe and America between 1925 and 1940. Furthermore, **Gatsby** is very light, refined, even delicate in appearance—altogether a bad choice for a billboard plugging a dude ranch.

How about the other typeface? This is also from Casady & Greene and is called **Regency Script.** The Regency period in eighteenth-century France was noted for ornate designs and frivolous, spoiled noblemen—again rather far removed in spirit from the rugged outdoor life of the U.S. mountains and plains.

Compare this billboard with Figure 1.4, where Casady & Greene's **Prelude** heads the image, a bold script that almost looks like the coils of a lasso. The other typeface is **Playbill,** a popular Stephenson Blake typeface sold by Bitstream and other vendors that reminds you immediately of the lettering in newspaper ads and posters from the early Western settlements. The total effect of this billboard—with appropriate typefaces—is exactly what you'd want.

After thinking about it, we must realize that typefaces can either fight against our message or enhance it. The designs that are not right might be perfect choices for other jobs. We must simply be careful that our selections don't remind the reader of a lily pond when our subject is cactus.

Selecting a Design That Means What It Says

When you want to drive home a point, don't pick a typeface that whispers when there's a need to shout. You might think that a casual contemporary face would be all right for almost any modern message. After all, we live in a modern age—right? Not so.

Figure 1.5 shows two signs. The one on the left uses an attractive 1995 Letraset typeface called **John Handy Plain** (based on the personal handwriting of its designer, Tim Donalson). You might glance at this design appreciatively as you walked by. But in a public notice, would the words really register? In contrast, the typeface in the right-hand sign issues a stern and insistent message. It means business. It almost seems to say, "Ignore me at your own peril." This "pushy" design is **Helvetica Inserat,** a strong **Helvetica** display variant from Linotype-Hell, designed by Max Miedinger in 1966. *Inserat* is a German word for *advertising;* this face will attract attention in ads or anywhere else it's used.

Matching the Type to the Illustration

You can get by with using a more or less neutral typeface in conjunction with almost any drawing or photo. But you'll be better off if the type adds to the total effect. In Figure 1.6, a slogan wraps partially around another clip-art drawing from Dynamic Graphics. This symbolic drawing is contemporary—a human eye that reflects the continents of North and South America. I've added special effects to the typeface by selecting one of the many type manipulation

1.4 The same billboard with typefaces appropriate to the subject.

1.5 Use a strong typeface when you don't want your message to be ignored.

options offered in Broderbund's TypeStyler utility, but the type itself is still a design that was created in 1896 by an architect named Bertram Goodhue. It's called **Cheltenham;** the version that appears here is **ITC Cheltenham Condensed,** which was produced by Tony Stan for International Typeface Corporation (ITC) and licensed by them for sale by many digital type houses. (The word *condensed* simply means that the designer made the characters narrower than the regular face, in order to let the user squeeze more characters onto each line.) Although the changes Stan made to **Cheltenham** in 1975 could be said to have "brought the design up-to-date," its nineteenth-century roots are still very much in evidence. So why use this venerable design in combination with a modern drawing to present a slogan about the world of the future? It's a poor fit.

Figure 1.7 demonstrates how much more effective a modern drawing can be when presented in conjunction with a comparable typeface. The type is **Lynz,** an excellent choice if you want to talk about twenty-first-century matters. The Image Club staff produced it in 1991.

1.6 A modern symbolic drawing mismatched with a nineteenth-century typeface.

1.7 The image corrected, with the modern drawing and typeface in harmony.

Using Type Alone to Create a Memorable Logo

A *logo* is a symbol used to represent a product, company, or some other entity—even an idea or practice, such as recycling or Smokey Bear, who warns visitors to national parks about the hazards of forest fires. The symbol can consist solely of artwork, type, or a combination of the two. If you need a logo and can't afford to pay an artist to produce a distinctive design for you, you can often make do by settling on a type style suitable for the cause and, perhaps, arranging the characters in an unusual combination. Figure 1.8 shows Monotype's **Italian Old Style,** pressed into service to represent a distinguished waterside resort I dreamed up. I don't know if there really is an Elk Bay anywhere or a resort by that name, but this typeface couldn't do either one of them any harm. The design is beautiful; it's based on William Morris's 1890 **Golden Type** which, in turn, is based on the work of fifteenth-century Venetian printer Nicolas Jenson. (See Chapter 4.)

But we can do better. The logo in Figure 1.8 doesn't really "hang together"; it simply consists of three words

Elk Bay Resort

1.8 Monotype's Italian Old Style used to create an acceptable resort logo.

placed in close juxtaposition to each other. Figure 1.9 demonstrates an improvement. Here we've used the **ITC Bookman** typeface family. Many computer users have been familiar with **Bookman** for years because it has been one of the standard families provided with printers using the PostScript language. **ITC Bookman** was designed by Ed Benguiat in 1975. Like **Bookman** families from other sources, it was based on a design by Alexander Phemister that was released as metal type by a Scottish foundry in 1860. However, only a few basic elements of Benguiat's version have been supplied with those printers: **ITC Bookman Light, Light Italic, Demi Bold,** and **Demi Bold Italic.** Figure 1.9 uses **Bold** and **Bold Swash,** two other members of the family. *Swashes* are decorative flourishes, seen here in the letters *E, k, B, y,* and *R.* I obtained the complete family from Image Club, one of the few sources for the full PC or Macintosh sets. The additional family members include **Bold Italic, Bold Swash Italic, Outline, Outline Swash,** and **Contour**—all worth having.

Why is the second logo better? Simply put, the judicious use of swash characters accomplishes three things: It adds elegance, makes the logo appear unique, and imparts a sense of unity because the swash characters are almost intertwined. The logo seems to have been hand-drawn for the resort's exclusive use. This is probably the ultimate compliment that can be paid to a logo constructed from mass-produced typefaces that are available to the general public.

Don't Show Off Everything You Own

Although I'm trying to demonstrate in this chapter that typefaces do matter and that the right design can make all the difference in a printed piece, don't deduce from these stated

1.9 A better logo, using ITC Bookman Bold and Bold Swash.

positions that you should therefore use as many of your typefaces as possible in each document you produce.

Unfortunately, many computer users have paid good money for their type libraries and therefore would like to show off all of their acquisitions every day. With this sad fact in mind, look at Figure 1.10. This is an ad for a make-believe upscale store specializing in women's fashions. The illustration is an attractive clip-art drawing from Metro Creative Graphics, but it certainly plays second fiddle to a hodgepodge of display fonts. The top line is Kingsley-ATF's **News Gothic Bold Condensed,** a 1908 Morris Fuller Benton design available from Bitstream and several other vendors; it has been popular for

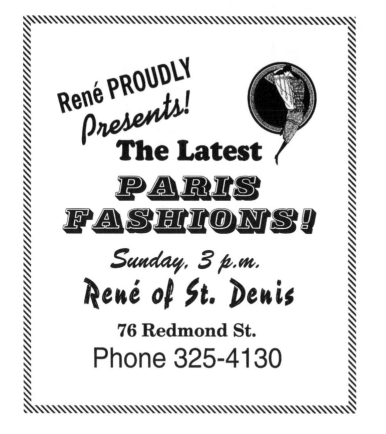

1.10 A fashion ad cluttered by a potpourri of typefaces.

newspaper and advertising work for nearly 90 years. The word "Presents" is in **Kaufmann Bold,** created for ATF in 1936 by Max R. Kaufmann; this is a script face characterized by its connecting letters and *monolineal* construction, meaning that all of its strokes are the same width throughout. **ITC Bookman Bold** reappears on the third line, followed by the Bitstream version of the highly decorative **Profil,** a shadowed *inline* face (meaning that the shape of each letter is traced by contrasting lines drawn inside the character). **Profil** was designed in 1946 by Eugen and Max Lenz. All of these different typefaces are used, and we're only halfway through the ad!

The time and date in this ad are shown in **Brush Script,** designed in 1942 by Robert E. Smith. As the name implies, this typeface imitates brush strokes; it has remained popular and is available through Adobe and many other vendors. I've set the next line (the name of the store making the announcement) in yet another script typeface that mimics brush strokes—**Reporter,** designed in 1938 by C. Winkow. It employs bolder strokes than **Brush Script,** but achieves much the same effect. You can buy **Reporter,** too, from most type vendors.

Hang in there! Only two more to go! The street address is displayed in **New Century Schoolbook.** This very legible family was created by Morris Fuller Benton beginning in 1918, for use in schoolbooks. Its sturdy, conventionally formed characters are still seen in children's textbooks today, so it succeeded admirably in its mission. The original **Century** design goes back to 1894, when it was developed for *Century Magazine.*

Max Miedinger created **Helvetica** for a Swiss foundry in 1957. You see it used for the phone number at the bottom of the ad. Publishers and printers can draft this design into service for headings or body copy. It's readable, attractive, and unobtrusive. Furthermore, Apple selected it years ago as one of the basic faces to be included with the company's PostScript printers. Add all of those factors together and **Helvetica** became incredibly popular—so much so that a reaction has set in. Many professionals avoid its use whenever possible. And, since Microsoft selected Monotype's **Arial** instead of **Helvetica** for use in Windows and other products, we may have seen an end to the Swiss design's days of glory. By the way, the Swiss name for Switzerland is Helvetia, so now you know where **Helvetica** got its name.

Both **New Century Schoolbook** and **Helvetica** are licensed by Linotype-Hell to most companies selling type. I now have to face the reality that you may be one of those readers who thinks the ad shown in Figure 1.10 is perfect in every way—that using a lot of typefaces adds sparkle. I can only respond that you'll think differently after you know a little more about type and how it should be used.

If you *are* a complete neophyte at working with type, don't feel bad about it. We were all beginners at some time; furthermore, I've intended this book for *all* users of typefaces—not merely those who feel they have some degree of sophistication regarding the subject.

A good way for a beginner to stay out of trouble is to follow this simple rule: *Don't use more than two typeface families in a single document.* Furthermore, the two families should not be similar in kind or appearance. For example, don't use two script typefaces together—just one of the errors I deliberately made in Figure 1.10. Don't use two serif typefaces or two sans-serif typefaces at the same time either—unless one is a fancy display face that looks nothing like the other. A *serif* typeface has little nubs, lines, or triangles sticking out from the ends of the main strokes of the characters; examples in this ad are **ITC Bookman, Profil,** and

New Century Schoolbook. A *sans-serif* typeface *doesn't* have those protuberances; in fact, *sans* is a French word meaning "without." Sans-serif examples in the ad are **News Gothic Bold** and **Helvetica.** Chapter 2 goes more deeply into the question of when to use serif or sans-serif.

Figure 1.10 is not the elegant, fashionable ad that an upscale women's store would want. It looks cluttered and a bit garish. We can fix these problems in a jiffy by bringing to bear some restraint and good taste. Look now at Figure 1.11.

Except for the name of the store, this second version of the ad uses a single typeface family: Monotype's **Fournier,** released in 1925. This is a revival of a highly regarded design created by the Paris typefounder Pierre Simon Fournier *le jeune* (meaning "the younger," equivalent to "Junior" today) about 1740. Monotype released the digital version for personal computers in 1993. **Fournier** has all of the dignity and style one might expect from the products of a distinguished eighteenth-century French foundry and includes optional *lowercase* or *Old Style* numerals, which extend above and below the line to add a graceful touch to the otherwise ordinary numbers in a document.

The other typeface in this ad is the ornate **Dorchester Script,** designed by the Monotype staff in 1938 and popular for such uses as calling cards and wedding announcements. Note that I've enlarged the stylish illustration because it does help establish the right mood and therefore deserves more prominence.

So you can select two suitable type designs, combine them in a restrained manner with a sharp illustration, and you end up with a very effective ad. By the way, note the use of *white space*—unused areas around the message, but inside the border. The white space calls attention to the ad and gives it

René proudly presents

The Latest
Paris
Fashions

Sunday, 3 p.m.

René of St. Denis

76 Redmond St.   Phone 325-4130

1.11 Using only two appropriate typefaces improves the ad tremendously.

added prestige. Ad purchasers often cram text into every nook and cranny of the spot they've bought in a publication, in the mistaken belief that, otherwise, they'll be wasting their money. Quite the contrary. The purpose of running an ad is to get people to read and respond to it. An ad doesn't invite readership that's a designer's nightmare, a jumble of words and sales points that fight each other for attention. Usually, you want to keep the message simple and short. If you can make one main point with your potential audience, you've accomplished a lot.

Type Can Be Very Specific

I hope I've convinced the doubters by now that a good choice of type can greatly improve the appearance and effectiveness of the printed word. In Figure 1.12, I want to make an additional point: In fact, there's a *specific* typeface for almost everything!

Letraset's **Shaman,** the top example, is intended to re-create all of the adventure and mystery of **darkest** Africa—and with ornaments to match. England's Phil Grimshaw is the designer of this display face introduced in 1994.

Just under it is a sampling of whimsical drawings from the **Fontoonies No. 1** typeface designed in 1994 by Steve Zafarana of the Galápagos Design Group. If you need to make a statement about toast popping from a toaster, for example, here's a way to do it.

1.12 Special-purpose typefaces that suggest specific subjects.

Quake was designed by Adobe's Fryda Berd, inspired by the 1989 San Francisco earthquake.

The skateboard calisthenics belong to another Adobe typeface, **Rad,** which is the work of John Ritter; in this case, as you can see, each skateboarding scene actually represents a letter of the alphabet.

Bamboo goes all the way back to 1889 and has characters that do indeed look as if they might have been assembled from bamboo stalks. The idea is to generate images in the reader's mind of the Orient. The name of the designer has been lost in the mists of history, but you can order **Bamboo** from Image Club.

Finally, Figure 1.12 shows Adobe's **Toolbox**—the brainchild of Brian Strysko, a typeface with characters composed of tools and other articles you might find around your home or workshop.

All the examples in this figure are either display or novelty faces that you would choose only for some special purpose—because each is so explicit in its message and intended use.

SUMMARY

Words matter and the type conveying words matters too; it can either help achieve the goals the writer has for the text or fight against the ideas, mood, and message.

The amateur can usually avoid disaster by carefully selecting one or two apt designs for a document and staying away from extremes and type that's interesting but hard to read—unless only a few large characters are involved. No one wants to spend extra time trying to decipher the words buried in a paragraph of overly designed type. If you simply don't know what kind of type would be fitting for your message, settle for a neutral, workhorse typeface—one that gets the job done without calling attention to itself.

It may be comforting to know that professionals can make mistakes too. Some of them seem to have forgotten long ago that the primary purpose of words is to communicate. We've all seen artistically designed printed pages that are nearly impossible to read because the designers have used intricate typefaces in paragraphs that are too narrow or too wide for easy reading, that are overwhelmed by other predominant design elements, or that melt into busy backgrounds that provide little contrast. Strangely enough, many of these design monstrosities appear in national desktop publishing and design-oriented magazines; the goal seems to be: "Look artistic first. Worry about the message later." Fortunately, it's possible to be both artistic *and* readable.

2

The Kinds of Typefaces

In this chapter, I'll explain the categories into which the experts place typefaces and when you should use each. What's the impact of a paragraph of script compared to other alternatives? Which is easier to comprehend—a long passage of text in a sans-serif face or the same text in a similar face that has serifs? And what is a typeface anyway? Let me answer that last question first.

IS IT A FONT, TYPEFACE, OR FAMILY?

Some of you may have been mystified all through that first chapter. You might have thought, "Why is this guy talking about typefaces constantly and never mentioning the word *fonts*. They're all fonts, aren't they?" Well, yes and no. The type that finally ends up on a page is always a font—because, technically, a *font* is a typeface in a specific size. However, the two words are not synonyms. A *typeface* consists of all sizes of a particular type design that display the same attributes—like bold or bold with italics.

Here's a more detailed explanation. In the publishing and printing industries, a *typeface family* consists of a group of typefaces with similar design characteristics, intended for use with each other. For example, you might say you're "using only **Times Roman**" in a particular document. This statement would normally be taken to mean that you may have included large bold headings and subheadings on each page, along with regular text in smaller sizes and some words designated for special emphasis appearing in italics—but all of the type would consist of typefaces in the **Times Roman** family. A *typeface* is a single member of a family, such as **Times Roman Bold Italic.** A *font* is one size of a particular typeface, such as 18-point **Times Roman Bold Italic;** 18-point **Times Roman Bold** (without the italic attribute) and 24-point **Times Roman Bold Italic** would be different fonts.

The term font goes back to the days of metal type that was set one character at a time. If you were a printer and bought a font from a foundry, you might buy, say, 10-point **Bodoni Regular.** You would receive a quantity of individual characters—many more of the letter *e* than of *z,* for example, because *e* occurs much more frequently than *z* in both English and European languages. If you wanted to set a single word in italics, you'd have to buy an additional **Bodoni Italic** font in the 10-point size. If you wanted to make your text slightly larger by using 12-point type, you'd have to buy still more fonts. Fortunately, in today's computerized printing world, you can generate any size font you want from a single typeface. (Incidentally, the word *point* is a printing measurement standard equivalent to approximately $1/72$ of an inch.)

Figure 2.1 illustrates these definitions. This figure features the **Ehrhardt** typeface family released in 1937 and 1938 by Monotype and digitized by the company in 1992 for use on personal computers. **Ehrhardt** is a version of **Janson,** a design I've described more fully later in the chapter. Note that the family includes the following typefaces: **Regular, Italic, Semi Bold,** and **Semi Bold Italic.** *Semi* is of Latin origin and means "half"—indicating, in this case, that the typefaces are not as bold as the bold members of most families. Other terms often applied to typeface names to indicate a degree of boldness (or the *weight* of the typeface) are Light, Book, Medium, Demi (which means "half" in French), Heavy, Extra, Ultra, and Black.

Another member of the **Ehrhardt** family shown in Figure 2.1 is an *expert set* that provides additional characters for

a typeface family

Ehrhardt Regular

Ehrhardt Italic

Ehrhardt Semi Bold

Ehrhardt Semi Bold Italic

EHRHARDT SMALL CAPITALS &
LOWERCASE FIGURES: 1234567890

a typeface

Ehrhardt 10 pt. Regular

Ehrhardt 12 pt. Regular

Ehrhardt 14 pt. Regular

Ehrhardt 18 pt. Regular

Ehrhardt 24 pt. Regular

a font

Ehrhardt 10 pt. Regular

a different font

Ehrhardt 12 pt. Regular

2.1 A typeface family contrasted with its components.

special purposes. This particular set consists mainly of small capital letters and lowercase (or Old Style) figures for use with the **Regular** typeface. (Of course, Monotype provides matching expert sets for the **Italic, Semi Bold,** and **Semi Bold Italic** typefaces in the family, too.) Small capitals are often used when you want to display a word in all capital letters without overwhelming the other words on a line and without changing the point size you're using.

You encountered lowercase figures briefly in the remake of the fashion ad in Chapter 1. These alternative numerals are smaller than regular numerals; they are not only attractive from a design standpoint, but—like small capitals—also useful when you don't want to draw too much attention to the characters by making them full-size. For example, setting historical dates in lowercase figures can keep them from detracting from the names of the events or persons that the dates concern. On the other hand, you'll want to use regular numerals in columns of figures to be totaled, so that the numbers will line up properly under one another.

Returning to Figure 2.1, just below the members of the **Ehrhardt** family you can see typical fonts belonging to the **Ehrhardt Regular** typeface. Of course, you could include many other sizes not shown, such as **Ehrhardt Regular** 48 point. Hopefully, this figure will clear up any confusion you may have had about the terms illustrated.

THE ORIGINS OF UPPERCASE AND LOWERCASE

In addition to font, typeface, and typeface family, you should be familiar with other terms used to categorize type. I've used two additional words already in this chapter: *capital* and *lowercase.* Nearly everyone knows that capital letters are the large characters that look like THIS. Lowercase letters are all of the others, except for the small capitals I mentioned previously, which are usually slightly larger than lowercase characters. Capital letters are also called *uppercase.* But where did these terms *uppercase* and *lowercase* come from?

The terms originated from the wooden cases used to hold all of the characters in a font in the days when type was set by hand. Within these cases, the bins created to hold individual characters varied in size and location according to how often each character was used. Therefore, in type cases for English-language fonts, the bin for the small e was the largest; the compositor (or typesetter—the person setting the type) would need a larger supply of this letter than any other because e is the most used character in the language. For easy access, this bin was located in the *lower* case of the wooden unit, the part nearest the compositor when he had the case propped up at an angle in front of him, ready for use. Other so-called lowercase characters were arranged in smaller, adjoining bins, sized according to how many copies of each letter were needed. On the other hand, capital letters were not used nearly so often; all capital letters were located in bins of equal size in the *upper* case. Figure 2.2 shows you a compositor in action, selecting a metal character from the lower case, with the upper case also clearly visible. The illustration is clip art from Dubl-Click Software's Wet Paint collection.

2.2 A compositor setting type one character at a time from a wooden type case.

PROPORTIONAL VERSUS NONPROPORTIONAL

As explained briefly in Chapter 1, every typeface is either proportional or nonproportional. I'll go into a little more detail here. A *proportional* typeface consists of characters that take up only as much space as they need within a word or a line of type. For example, a lowercase *i* requires little space while a lowercase *m* is considerably wider. Nearly all typefaces you see in books and magazines are proportional in nature. There are two advantages: You can include more characters in a given amount of space if they can vary in width, and text is easier to read because the letters making up each word have no large spaces between them and therefore make the word appear more as a cohesive unit within a sentence.

Nonproportional typefaces are also sometimes referred to as *fixed-pitch* or *monospaced*. In a *nonproportional* typeface, each character occupies exactly the same amount of space, regardless of its actual width. Originally, all typewriters used nonproportional typefaces—a necessity because of the way the machines were constructed. Each character was fastened to one of many equally spaced shafts; press the key representing a character and your action would propel the letter forward on its shaft so it would hit an inked ribbon that, in turn, would make an impression on a piece of paper. So that you can create documents that look as if they've been typed on a standard typewriter, designers have created numerous computer typefaces that are monospaced—often adapted from fonts that were originally produced strictly for typewriter use.

Figure 2.3 illustrates the difference between proportional and nonproportional typefaces. In that figure, the word *proportional* is displayed in a popular typeface of German origin called **Neuzeit Grotesk.** The word *nonproportional* appears in **Monaco,** one of the standard typefaces supplied with all Macintosh computers. Note how much more line space **Monaco** requires for its characters than is needed by **Neuzeit Grotesk.** Also, note how the last four letters in *nonproportional* almost seem to constitute a different word because there is so much space between the *i* and the *o* that follows it.

proportional
nonproportional

2.3 A proportional typeface requires less space for each word than its nonproportional equivalent.

By the way, here's an exception to the way proportional typefaces are designed. The basic numbers included in most designs are *not* proportional. If they were, they'd never line up in a statistical table. On the other hand, alternate typefaces within a family—such as a so-called expert set—and some primary text designs of an elegant or casual nature may use lowercase figures that are proportional because the designer never intended these numbers to be used for mathematical purposes.

ASSIGNING TYPEFACES TO CONVENIENT GROUPS

Beyond the categorization you can achieve by determining that typefaces are or are not proportional—or include only capitals or both capital and lowercase characters—you can identify them as members of other handy groups that help people visualize to some extent the probable characteristics of a typeface they've never seen. For example, text typefaces (those suitable for the body copy of books and articles) are divided into two basic classifications—serif and sans-serif, as mentioned in Chapter 1.

Serif versus Sans-Serif

In a serif typeface, the serifs themselves help define characters so they can more easily be distinguished from others of a similar shape or design. Therefore, most experts consider serif typefaces more readable than their sans-serif alternatives. Nevertheless, many book and magazine designers do use sans-serif typefaces for large bodies of text, partially on the theory that the absence of serifs makes these typefaces look more streamlined or contemporary. However, many serif typefaces used today have been designed with subtle variations from tradition that make them appear definitely up-to-date without attracting too much attention to themselves or becoming hard to read.

Figure 2.4 shows the letter H in the two basic typefaces Microsoft has adopted for Windows applications: **Times New Roman** and **Arial. Times New Roman** is a serif design drawn in 1931 at Monotype by Victor Lardent under the supervision of consultant Stanley Morison; the mission was to create a newspaper type family to be used by the *Times* of London. The design was a big success, as evidenced by the fact that it and other versions of **Times** are still widely used today. **Arial** is of more recent origin; Robin Nicholas and Patricia Saunders created it for Monotype in 1982 as a replacement for **Helvetica.**

But getting back to the time-honored argument as to readability, you can conduct your own test right now. By looking at Figure 2.5, you can decide for yourself whether

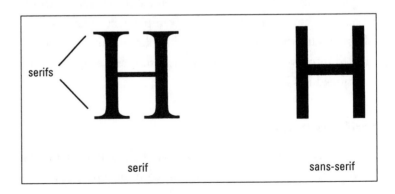

2.4 A serif typeface compared with a sans-serif.

sans-serif or serif is easier to read. I've written a highly technical paragraph describing a statistical procedure, then printed it here in both formats for your consideration. Otl Aicher designed the typeface family I've used—an unusual 1989 release named **Rotis** that was commissioned by Agfa. The unusual part is that **Rotis** consists of four subfamilies: **Sans, Semi Sans, Semi Serif,** and **Serif.** The characters in each group have the same proportions and shapes, as well as the same height and selection of weights. (*Weight* is the relative darkness of the characters, which, as you might expect, is determined mainly by the thickness of the strokes. The weights of the **Rotis** family range from Light to Extra

You can use the correlation statistical procedure to determine whether or not the values in two data sets are interrelated—whether large values in one data set change in relation to large values in the other data set (positive correlation), whether small values in one data set change in relation to large values in the other data set (negative correlation), or whether values in the two data sets are unrelated (with a correlation near zero). The population correlation calculation returns the covariance of the two data sets divided by the product of their standard deviations.

Rotis Sans Serif

Rotis Serif

You can use the correlation statistical procedure to determine whether or not the values in two data sets are interrelated—whether large values in one data set change in relation to large values in the other data set (positive correlation), whether small values in one data set change in relation to large values in the other data set (negative correlation), or whether values in the two data sets are unrelated (with a correlation near zero). The population correlation calculation returns the covariance of the two data sets divided by the product of their standard deviations.

2.5 Compare the same paragraph for readability in matching serif and sans-serif versions.

Bold.) So the design of **Rotis Sans Serif** is exactly the same as **Rotis Serif.** The letters are interchangeable, except that one subfamily does not have serifs and the other does. This fact makes judging readability rather scientific: The only variable in the paragraphs shown here is the absence or presence of serifs; even the line endings are the same. I think you'll pick the **Rotis Serif** paragraph as far easier to understand.

As you might have surmised, the other **Rotis** two subfamilies—**Semi Sans** and **Semi Serif**—represent in-between steps in the transition between sans-serif and serif. **Semi Sans** has only a slight hint of serifs provided by a slight widening of stroke endings; **Semi Serif** has nub serifs except that the feet of characters still have no serifs at all. In Figure 2.5 the headings are printed in **Rotis Semi Serif.**

More Categories—Display, Novelty, Script, and Blackletter

Frequently, professional printers will use a legible serif typeface for their text work and a simple, contrasting sans-serif design for those large titles and headings; the combination is practical and not likely to invite negative comments. However, there are other alternatives for titles and headings. Aside from serif and sans-serif, a third typeface category is customarily called *display* or *decorative* and incorporates typefaces that may or may not have serifs, but are unsuitable for a large body of text. They are unsuitable for this purpose because they were principally designed for use in large sizes and are usually too ornate, detailed, or spectacular to be effective for text use in small sizes. They're great if you have to read only a few words in a big point size, but deadly if you have to struggle on, page after page, trying to interpret small characters that contain too many flourishes or unfamiliar contours.

A fourth category—closely related to the third—can be termed *novelty.* Here you can group typefaces for display use containing letters of the alphabet that resemble something else. The purpose is often humor. For example, the letters may be formed of paper clips, children's blocks, or people in outlandish positions. In most instances, these typefaces must be used in very large sizes so that the reader can identify the components from which the letters have been created.

A fifth category—very popular for headings and small paragraphs of text—is *script,* typefaces that resemble handwriting.

Finally, there's *blackletter*—the overall-name for typefaces in the general category the public often calls Old English— those ornate, usually heavy designs used in church bulletins and in the nameplates at the top of the front page of the *New York Times,* the *Los Angeles Times,* and other newspapers. You encountered one member of this type group—**Goudy Text**— in Chapter 1.

I've illustrated all of these broad categories in Figure 2.6. (You'll learn about several other categories later in the book.) The serif example is **Janson Text**—a family based on designs created about 1690 by the Hungarian Nicholas Kis but wrongly credited to a Dutch printer named Anton Janson. Linotype-Hell released this beautiful digitized version in 1985, which includes some additions and revisions by the legendary modern designer Hermann Zapf; however, the company's initial Janson release was as metal type in 1937, supervised by C. H. Griffith. To complicate the name question, the **Ehrhardt** family, which you encountered in Figure 2.1, is Monotype's version of the same design, developed in 1936 by Sol Hess in collaboration with Bruce Rogers and named for the Ehrhardt Foundry in Leipzig, where some original Kis type was discovered. In any event,

Janson versions have been used extensively since the 1930s in the production of fine books.

The sans-serif example, **Neuzeit Grotesk**—also seen in the proportional/nonproportional figure earlier in the chapter—was designed by C. W. Pischiner in 1928 and inspired by **Futura,** a ground-breaking geometric design that had been released the previous year. *Neuzeit* is German for "new times." Linotype-Hell introduced this current version in

Serif

Janson Text

Sans-Serif or Lineal

Neuzeit Grotesk

Display or Decorative

Letraset Jazz

Novelty

MYTHOS

Script

Monotype Script

Blackletter

Fette Fraktur

2.6 Examples of major typeface categories.

1959. You can find out much more about sans-serif typefaces in Chapter 9, which is devoted to that subject.

Letraset Jazz is a display face in the Art Deco manner, the work of British designer Alan Meeks. Note that the characters in this 1992 release contain an inner design that resembles a piano keyboard.

Mythos, a novelty typeface released by Adobe, consists of letters formed from drawings of mythological creatures. Min Wang and Jim Wasco of the Adobe staff created this one in 1993.

Monotype Script was released in 1931. Bold and very readable, it's still popular today. Monotype's F. H. Steltzer developed the design.

Completing the figure, **Fette Fraktur** is a blackletter design dating back to 1875. *Fette* means "bold" in German. Until World War II, **Fraktur** typefaces were the standard in the German newspapers, believe it or not, and **Fette Fraktur** was used for headlines. Don't try this trick at home! Today nobody recommends setting the sports section in a **Fraktur.**

In reviewing the varied designs in Figure 2.6, even someone completely unfamiliar with typefaces can readily see that switching one of these typefaces with another would drastically change the impression made on a reader by the text involved. The type you use does matter!

SELECTING TEXT FACES TO MATCH THE SUBJECT

People unfamiliar with typefaces will often say something like, "Well, I can see the difference between those fancy display designs, but aren't the text faces all pretty much the same? I mean, this is pretty routine stuff, isn't it?" One way to respond to this observation would be simply to print a paragraph in several different typefaces and let the results answer the question. That's what I'll do now.

Figure 2.7 exhibits three versions of a paragraph that discusses the early days of professional football. First we see the words presented in the Bitstream version of **Kabel,** a 1927 German design by Rudolf Koch, named in commemoration of the laying of the first trans-Atlantic telephone cable. This artistic sans-serif reminds us of the Roaring Twenties or the menu of an exclusive restaurant with Art Deco decor. **Kabel** certainly doesn't remind us of the rugged teams of the National Football League.

The second typeface is Monotype's **Perpetua.** This is a serif design. The family was created by Eric Gill—a famous British sculptor and designer—between 1925 and 1932. Its classical lines are not very appropriate for the subject matter either, unless the paragraph should be part of a feature article that strictly concerned football in the early 1930s, with the emphasis on nostalgia and that period in U.S. history. The reason is that **Perpetua,** like **Kabel,** reflects the flavor of an era gone by. If this article continued to bring the NFL through the years to the present day, either one of these typefaces would be inappropriate.

The third typeface is a contemporary sans-serif—**Poppl-Laudatio,** available through Adobe and designed by Friedrich Poppl in 1982. Although it doesn't lead us into nostalgia, its large characters and rather bold strokes are not ideal for sports copy nor for any extended text use. This design looks great in ads or in a *pull-quote,* which is a short sample from the text of an article, displayed in larger type to draw the reader into the main text.

The New York Giants were big in the early years of the NFL. They lost the championship by only two points in 1933: the score was Chicago 23, New York 21. The following year New York came roaring back, to turn the tables on the Bears and defeat the Windy City team 30 to 13.

Kabel—sans-serif

The New York Giants were big in the early years of the NFL. They lost the championship by only two points in 1933: the score was Chicago 23, New York 21. The following year New York came roaring back, to turn the tables on the Bears and defeat the Windy City team 30 to 13.

Perpetua—serif

The New York Giants were big in the early years of the NFL. They lost the championship by only two points in 1933: the score was Chicago 23, New York 21. The following year New York came roaring back, to turn the tables on the Bears and defeat the Windy City team 30 to 13.

Poppl-Laudatio—serif

2.7 The same paragraph shown in three different text typefaces.

Now let's consider three other type selection possibilities for the same paragraph. The first sample in Figure 2.8 is a 1953 script face—**Mistral.** It's available through Adobe and several other vendors and is based on the personal handwriting of French typographer Roger Excoffon. This design is easy to decipher compared to many script faces, but is entirely unsuitable for a sports-related discussion or general text work because it would make the reader work too hard. Like **Poppl-Laudatio,** you could use it for a brief advertising statement or a pull-quote.

Tekton is much easier to read than **Mistral.** It's a script typeface designed by David Siegel in 1989 and based on the

The New York Giants were big in the early years of the NFL. They lost the championship by only two points in 1933: the score was Chicago 23, New York 21. The following year New York came roaring back, to turn the tables on the Bears and defeat the Windy City team 30 to 13.

Mistral—script

The New York Giants were big in the early years of the NFL. They lost the championship by only two points in 1933: the score was Chicago 23, New York 21. The following year New York came roaring back, to turn the tables on the Bears and defeat the Windy City team 30 to 13.

Tekton—script

The New York Giants were big in the early years of the NFL. They lost the championship by only two points in 1933: the score was Chicago 23, New York 21. The following year New York came roaring back, to turn the tables on the Bears and defeat the Windy City team 30 to 13.

Oranda—serif

2.8 Three additional typefaces applied to the same paragraph.

personal lettering style of architect Frank Ching. However, reading the casual, irregularly-shaped characters becomes a chore and an irritant if there's a lot of text involved—despite the fact that Ching has published books on architectural subjects that he hand-lettered in this style. **Tekton** is one of Adobe's most popular typefaces, but it's best for short blurbs—not game scores or other statistics.

The final example in Figure 2.8 is printed in **Oranda**. This Bitstream typeface is by the prolific Dutch designer Gerard Unger. It's sturdy, contemporary, and highly readable, but doesn't draw undue attention to itself. This would be a good choice for the subject matter.

You can repeat this exercise with your own selection of typefaces for text, whenever you're uncertain about which to use. Your eye will probably tell you what's right and what's wrong.

USING GOOD JUDGMENT WITH THOSE DISPLAY FACES

As far as display typefaces are concerned, it's not enough that you know which is attractive or reminiscent of the subject at hand. You need to exercise good taste as well. Figure 2.9 gives you some examples. The first one is the headline for a news story: *Western Star Murders Wife.* On the left, the headline is reproduced in Adobe's attractive **Rosewood** typeface. Someone might say, "Wow! What could be more appropriate! A western typeface for a story about a western movie star!" However, using this typeface under such circumstances would be in the worst of taste. We're not talking about the star making a personal appearance or reflecting on his great career. We're talking about murder. The typeface on the right

WESTERN STAR MURDERS WIFE

WESTERN STAR MURDERS WIFE

Japanese Businessman Elected to City Council

Japanese Businessman Elected to City Council

ELECTRONIC TOOLS HELP COMPANIES TO COMPETE

2.9 The type for a headline should be fitting for its subject.

matches the subject better; it's **ITC Machine,** obtained from Image Club.

Another word about those typefaces: **Rosewood** was designed by Kim Buker Chansler, Carl Crossgrove, and Carol Twombly in 1994; it's based on an 1874 design by William Page. This design comes with a matching Fill version. You can apply a color to the Fill version and overlay the Regular version seen in the figure, to obtain a striking two-color heading. **ITC Machine** was designed by Tom Carnase and Ronne Bonder in 1970; it's a geometric display face that looks good both in headlines and industrial uses.

Let's move on to the second case with the headline *Japanese Businessman Elected to City Council.* On the left, the typeface is **Japanet,** designed in 1893 by a Chicago foundry for the *Chicago Herald* and originally called **Wedge Gothic.** I obtained the digitized version you see in a Brendel CD-ROM collection. The **Japanet** design would certainly look "oriental" to most occidentals and would therefore seem to be aptly named. In fact, I suspect that the *Herald* commissioned this typeface for use in the many articles the newspaper intended to run about the huge area of innovative Japanese exhibits at the World's Columbian Exposition; this fair was held in Chicago for six months during 1893 and was attended by more than 27 million visitors. The problem with using the **Japanet** typeface in our sample is that this use would seem to overemphasize the Japanese businessman's origins and could certainly seem intended to expose him to ridicule as a racist act. The headline isn't about the food at a favorite Japanese restaurant or a picturesque exhibit at a world's fair. It's a straight business news story and should be reported with customary news-related typefaces, such as the ever-popular **Times Roman Bold,** seen to the right of the **Japanet** version.

Now the bottom example is another situation entirely. This is apparently the heading for a feature article on computerization in the business world. The typeface is **Digital,** created by Image Club in 1994 to mimic an electronic LCD display. Its use is perfect for the subject.

For our final example of display type selection, consider Figure 2.10. Whether the top typeface is appropriate for a baseball game would probably depend upon how you feel about the game. If baseball is a religion to you, Image Club's **Daily Tribune** typeface would be ideal. However, in most instances, the bottom example would be more fitting; it's Letraset's **Bendigo,** a bold, informal script face with characters that look like they were created with a brush. British designer Phil Grimshaw created this excellent display

2.10 Baseball—a religion or a game?

design in 1993. Chapter 12 is devoted entirely to display and novelty typefaces.

CONSIDERING THE TYPEFACE FORMAT

Another way to categorize typefaces is by the software format in which they appear. All computer typefaces used to be *bitmaps;* they consisted of little dot patterns in rigid sizes. If you wanted 10-point **Times Roman,** you needed a specific bitmap file for it and another file for 12-point **Times Roman** or any other size. To have access to italics to go with those fonts, you were forced to purchase an entire group of additional bitmap files—again, one for each size. It was almost as awkward as using metal type. Furthermore, the resolution was fixed. If you had a font designed at 300 dots per inch (dpi) and printed it out on a printer offering a higher resolution, the font wasn't going to appear any sharper; it was still the same 300 dpi image.

With the advent of Adobe's PostScript printer language, that situation changed. It changed yet again when the TrueType format was introduced by Apple and Microsoft. Adobe's Multiple Master technology came next. Now we have QuickDraw GX, an Apple environment that alters the ground rules once more. I'll finish out this chapter by explaining briefly how these various formats will affect your work with type today—and possibly tomorrow.

The Bitmap Isn't Dead

First of all, you'll still need bitmap fonts if you're working with type on a PC that's running under the MS-DOS operating system without Windows. You can buy those fonts on floppy disks from a few vendors who still offer them.

Adobe doesn't sell bitmaps, but provides a utility called Font Foundry in its PostScript type packages; this utility lets you create bitmaps from the PostScript files in the packages. To install those bitmaps for use by a program you're running under MS-DOS, consult the manual for the particular program. If you're using a current Macintosh computer with PostScript typefaces, you'll need bitmaps because the operating system uses them to create the screen image of the fonts you select.

PostScript: The Professional Standard

The PostScript language created quite a sensation when it was introduced because it lets you print sharp images in any size from its files, limited only by the resolution of the printer. For MS-DOS computers, there are four kinds of PostScript typeface files. Files with the extension .PFB are called *outline* files; they're actually tiny programs that will draw characters in the proper designs and proportions according to mathematical descriptions, in whatever size the user specifies. The .PFM files work with the outline files, providing data they need, such as the typeface name, character width information, and a table of *kerning pairs*—a list of characters that should be spaced close to each other when used together, along with the spacing instructions for each pair. Most desktop publishing programs and some word processing software can read these kerning tables and adjust character-combination spacing automatically in your documents. The third PostScript file category is .AFM—the kerning table and spacing information in a text format (AFM stands for Adobe Font Metrics). Finally, an .INF file is used to create fonts for MS-DOS applications. For example, the DOS versions of Microsoft Word and WordPerfect use .INF files for this purpose. Adobe Type Foundry requires the use of all four file categories, as do a few other programs that create or modify typefaces.

If you simply want to install typefaces for use by standard Windows programs, you'll need only the .PFB and .PFM files. You can install them through the Windows version of Adobe Type Manager (see Chapter 13). ATM will store the .PFB files in a *psfonts* directory and the .PFM files in a subdirectory within that called *pfm*. With the help of ATM, Windows will then generate the needed screen fonts on a temporary basis from the .PFB outline files when you start using a typeface and employ those same files to form the characters for printing.

The Macintosh uses three PostScript typeface file formats. The bitmap screen version of a design is stored in a *font suitcase,* a special folder that can contain several members of a type family. The accompanying printer outline file is called a *PostScript font.* And an AFM text file (the Adobe Font Metrics format) is provided for the few applications that need it—mainly typeface design programs. You can install Mac typefaces by merely dragging the files into your closed System folder. Beginning with version 7.1 of the Mac operating system, the system automatically places those files in a special subfolder called Fonts within the System folder.

Using either a PC or Macintosh, you won't want hundreds of unused typefaces clogging up and slowing down your operating system. Therefore, people who need a lot of typefaces employ special utilities that let you organize your typefaces into sets, store them outside the operating system, and activate only those you want to use for a specific job. Read about these utilities in Chapter 13. Most of these type management utilities can also handle all the remaining typeface categories I'll discuss here: TrueType, Multiple

Master, and QuickDraw GX, letting you store these wherever you like.

Before I discuss the remaining categories, let me stress that PostScript is the standard used in the professional world. You can create a PostScript file on a personal computer, save it, and take it to a *service bureau,* a facility that specializes in transforming such files into a form that can be used by major printing and publishing organizations the world over. The typical service bureau has thousands of PostScript typefaces, so they'll normally have exactly the faces you used.

Incidentally, you may hear the terms *Type 1* and *Type 3* used in reference to PC and Mac typefaces. Originally, only Adobe had the specifications to create PostScript typefaces with certain refinements; the versions with these refinements were called Type 1, while the faces created by other companies were called Type 3. Eventually, Adobe shared their Type 1 secrets with the remainder of the industry and nearly all PostScript typefaces now are in the Type 1 format.

TrueType: Apple and Microsoft Got Together

The TrueType format requires only one file for each typeface: a printer outline that is also used to create the screen image in any size specified. TrueType, developed by Apple and Microsoft, is being heavily promoted by Microsoft; that company uses the format exclusively for the typefaces they've provided for Windows 95 and its successors (except for a couple of bitmapped serif and sans-serif faces supplied to provide compatibility for older software). Under Windows, you can use the Install New Font command on the Windows Explorer's File menu to install any TrueType file into a special Fonts folder within the Windows folder. As an alternative, you can open the folder containing the typeface to be installed and drag the icon representing it into the Fonts folder.

You install Macintosh TrueType files as you would PostScript—drag the typefaces into your closed System folder. Again, remember that you can use special utilities to avoid storing these files with the operating system.

Multiple Master Typefaces— Seeing Double and Triple

Using Adobe's Multiple Master typeface technology, digital foundries create typefaces that can be easily manipulated by the user to create new versions. For example, you may be able to make the characters in a particular design wider, bolder, or with smaller serifs. Professionals use Multiple Master files to fit type exactly into a restricted space without changing the point size. See this technology in action in Chapter 14.

QuickDraw GX

QuickDraw GX almost sounds like the name of a gun-toting hero in a Western movie. However, it's really a new Apple-developed technology that lets you use typeface files that contain hundreds of characters and rely on menu options to insert special characters exactly where you want them in your documents—completely automatically. For example, if you want the available *ligatures* used (two or more characters combined into a single symbol), you choose that option. (Read Chapter 3 to see the use of ligatures illustrated.) You could specify that proportional numbers be used instead of the usual monospaced variety or that the first word in a line begin with a fancy swash character. You could also vary the height and width of characters—whatever options the designer of the typeface chooses to provide.

Several of the major vendors are offering GX typefaces now for the Macintosh, but there are very few applications as yet that will let you use them. A notable exception is Ready,Set,Go!, the desktop publishing program from Manhattan Graphics; this company has been shipping a capable GX version for a long time. Another company, Lari Software, publishes LightningDraw GX, an innovative drawing program with 3D capabilities that was written specifically to run under QuickDraw GX. To use GX type, you must also use the System 7.5 version of the Mac operating system (or a later version), and you must have a driver for your printer that supports the technology, too.

SUMMARY

In this chapter I've shown you that good judgment is essential in selecting among categories of typefaces and then the individual designs in order to get your job completed in a form that's readable, attractive, and printed with type appropriate to the subject matter.

In choosing between formats like PostScript and TrueType, you can exercise good judgment, too. If the job's going to a professional printer, try to use PostScript type only. On the other hand, if you're creating a company newsletter to be run off internally and you have a large assortment of TrueType families that were included with your Windows applications, you may be wiser to use what you have rather than investing in PostScript typefaces that will look no better to most of your fellow employees.

As far as Multiple Masters and GX are concerned, they can be a godsend to professionals who have the time and dedication to make all of their documents typographical delights. However, in the frantic pace of the mainstream

business world—with making a profit always an essential—
you may not be able to afford the luxury of making several
alternate versions of a typeface or experimenting with swashes
until your page has just the right amount of swirls and
curlicues, neither too many nor too few.

Above all, note that I started this summary by
mentioning first that your work must be *readable*. The
primary purpose of writing and printing is to communicate.
Always select your typefaces with that thought in mind.

3

The Anatomy of Characters

In order to recognize specific typefaces when you see them, you should be familiar with characteristics that make letters look different from one another and know the correct names for those characteristics.

Why do you need to identify typefaces at a glance? As I indicated in the Introduction, it's more than being able to show off your superior knowledge to friends or fellow workers. There are better reasons. First of all, you may have to revise and reprint documents that were produced by someone who's no longer around. This situation happens all the time in the business world and, of course, requires that you be able to duplicate the exact typefaces used so that the reprinted document will look the same as the original. The document could be a restaurant menu that needs new prices or a widget brochure with a paragraph that must be changed to reflect added features in the latest model.

Another good reason for knowing the anatomy of characters is that you may come across a typeface you admire and want to add to your own library. If you can't figure out what the face is, you won't have much luck.

A third reason, which comes into play as you become a bit more sophisticated about the subject, is that knowing what makes up characters helps you determine *why* you like or dislike a typeface—why the design works or it doesn't. This

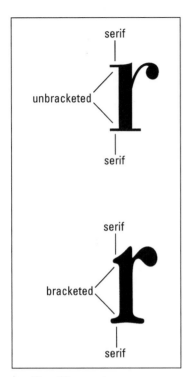

3.1 The difference between bracketed and unbracketed characters.

knowledge can be key to selecting a replacement for a faulted design or, perhaps, appreciating to the fullest a typeface you really admire.

In this chapter I'll try to get you up to speed by identifying those bumps and lines and loops that make one design look different from another.

BRACKETED VERSUS UNBRACKETED SERIFS

In the first two chapters, I both explained and demonstrated what serifs are. But, as you might imagine, there's more to the story. Some serifs are *unbracketed;* others are *bracketed.* Bracketed serifs often resemble nubs rather than lines; you can imagine that those brackets provide added support for delicate lines, just as you might use a metal bracket in your kitchen to attach a shelf to the wall. Figure 3.1 shows you the difference between these two kinds of serifs. The top example is the lowercase *r* in the Bauer **Bodoni Roman** typeface, which has no brackets. The bottom example is the same letter as it appears in **ITC Garamond Book,** which does use brackets. Therefore, if you were evaluating a typeface whose name you didn't know and noticed that its serifs were not bracketed, you would know positively that it was not **ITC Garamond.** However, you'd need to examine more clues to determine whether it was **Bodoni,** since there are many typefaces that incorporate unbracketed serifs as part of their design.

STRESS AS A DESIGN CHARACTERISTIC

Another distinguishing feature in typefaces is the *stress* of a character—the degree of incline (or the axis) formed by the relationship between the thick and thin portions of rounded letterforms such as the *bowl* (the enclosed round or oval area) of a letter like O or Q. The two main categories are *vertical stress*—wherein the axis is vertical, with no slant at all—and *inclined stress*—wherein the axis is tilted either slightly or more dramatically. Figure 3.2 shows typical examples, using the lowercase *o* from four different typefaces. At the top you'll find two examples of vertical stress—**Clarendon Extra Bold** and **New Century Schoolbook Roman.** Underneath, the **Extra Bold** example is **Albertus,** which features a strong inclined stress, accompanied by Monotype's **Plantin,** in which the *o* is slanted more subtly.

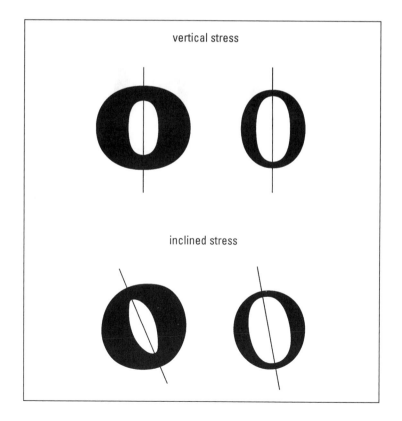

3.2 Examples of vertical and inclined stress. The lines have been added to emphasize the angles involved.

TYPEFACES WIN THEIR SPURS

Sometimes type designers add a small *spur* at the bottom of a character to give it a distinctive appearance. These spurs often resemble the bony projections that appear on the legs of some birds or the spurs a cowboy wears over his boots to assist in controlling a horse. However, occasionally, a typeface spur is merely a short line that projects at an angle from a main stroke. Figure 3.3 shows three examples of spurs. The first two are characters from Monotype's **Centaur Regular** typeface; the example on the right is the capital *G* in the Bitstream version of **Schadow Roman.**

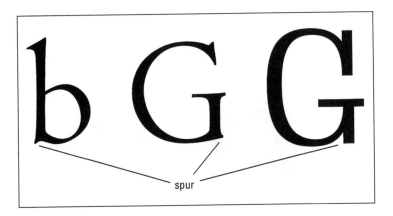

3.3 Examples of spurs on typeface characters.

EVER HEAR OF A TWO-STORY G WITH AN EAR?

The size or shape of an *ear* will affect the overall appearance of a typeface. What is an ear? Just one of the terms used to describe parts of a lowercase *g* and labeled in Figure 3.4. Specifically, an *ear* is a small projecting stroke attached to the right side of the top of the bowl. (I defined bowl a few paragraphs earlier.) The *counter* is the enclosed white space inside the bowl. The *link* is a line that connects the bowl and

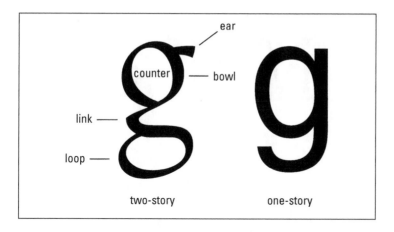

3.4 Labeled components of the lowercase g.

loop of the *g* and is occasionally omitted entirely in some typeface designs. Designers often refer to a lowercase *g* with a complete lower loop as *two-story,* obtaining the term by comparing the appearance of the character to a two-story house. Therefore, the character on the right is a one-story *g.*

Incidentally, the typefaces in this figure are **Centaur Regular** again on the left and **Helvetica Regular** on the right.

OTHER FEATURES THAT HELP DEFINE TYPE DESIGNS

Additional factors that affect the appearance of a typeface include the relative height of characters and the size and shape of some letter components I haven't identified yet. Figure 3.5 explains a few of these terms. For example, printing professionals usually determine the height of a typical lowercase character by measuring the height of a lowercase *x;* this measurement is therefore called the *x-height.* Characters like the lowercase *d* have a stroke that extends above the x-height and are called *ascenders.* Characters like the lowercase *p* and *q* have a stroke that extends below the

3.5 Some type components labeled.

baseline (the imaginary line on which most characters rest) and are called *descenders.* The upper diagonal stroke of the letter *k* is called an *arm,* the lower diagonal stroke is called a *leg,* and the vertical stroke is called the *stem.* The enclosed empty space within a lowercase *e* is called the *eye.* Short horizontal strokes are often *crossbars.* A capital *M* whose legs are not vertical (in other words, they're spread out at the feet) is said to be *splayed.*

In this figure, the top typeface is the Bitstream version of **Schadow** again, which features capital letters that are the same height as lowercase ascenders. The bottom typeface is

Monotype's **Plantin,** which displays the same characteristic. Note, however, that the middle typeface—Letraset's **Figural**—contains capital letters shorter than its lowercase ascenders. This feature lets **Figural**'s regular capitals almost substitute for small capitals where inconspicuous characters are desired; however, the **Figural** family does include small caps, which are considerably smaller and therefore even more inconspicuous.

Notice another design characteristic: In the top typeface, the lowercase *o* has vertical stress. The middle typeface features a slight inclined stress. The bottom typeface has a strong inclined stress. These differences do affect the impression made by the designs. Incidentally, Moltke is not a meaningless combination of letters put together to illustrate type characteristics. History offers two Danish statesmen and two German generals with the last name Moltke.

Figure 3.6 shows you how a difference in x-height can change the entire look of a typeface. The figure features Rudolf Koch's **Kabel** typeface, which you just encountered in Chapter 2. However, observe the great difference in appearance between the type on the first line and that on the second line. The shapes of the characters are the same. The difference is caused by the fact that Koch's original design—seen on the top line—has a small x-height. The **Kabel** on the bottom line—a version created for International Typeface Corporation and named **ITC Kabel**—has a huge x-height that completely alters the effect achieved. Incidentally, this company was founded by designers connected with the advertising industry who were concerned about the readability of ads in magazines and newspapers and who felt that a large x-height was a major factor contributing to that readability. Most typefaces released by ITC reflect this firm's preference for a large x-height.

This is Kabel.
This is Kabel too.

3.6 Two versions of Kabel—one with a small x-height (top), the other with a large x-height.

USING SPECIAL CHARACTERS

Even if the x-height is the same in two versions of a typeface, they can appear quite different from one another for many other reasons, such as slight variations in the shaping or width of the characters. However, the availability and use of special characters can make changes that are really dramatic. Some designers will squeeze a few special characters into the main file of a typeface. For example, if the face is an ornate design suited for the discussion of the fine arts, the designer may discard the math symbols normally included with standard typefaces and insert special characters in their place. You can access these characters (which don't appear on your keyboard) by pressing specified key combinations or by using typeface utilities that will display the characters and let you select them with a mouse click. (See Chapter 13 for demonstrations of some of these utilities.)

More often, designers adhere to the conventions and include those math symbols in the character positions in which they're expected—even if they feel a typeface is unsuited for the printing of math-related text. Then they create an auxiliary typeface to contain the extra characters. In their simplest form, standard typefaces are often accompanied by a file offering small capitals in place of the usual lowercase characters and Old Style or lowercase figures in place of the standard full-sized numerals. But many designers go further. They'll create extra files containing decorative alternate letters, unusual ligatures, and matching ornaments. These files may be called *expert sets* (the term used by Adobe and Monotype), *typographer sets* (the term used by Bitstream), or some similar name. In most cases, to use a character from these extra files, the computer user must change typefaces through the Font menu in the middle of a word, type the character in the auxiliary typeface, then switch back to the first typeface again. The procedure is awkward, but the results can be very attractive.

Figure 3.7 provides an example of special characters being used to change the appearance of a typeface. Here—in Monotype's **Centaur**—you see at the top the name Moltke displayed in the family's **Regular** typeface. Under this, you can find the same word in **Centaur Italic** (originally named **Arrighi** and created by a different designer than the **Regular Centaur**). Italic typefaces like this are usually modeled after *chancery cursive* lettering—elegant handwriting developed by scribes working in fifteenth-century churches and courts. Finally, below the other two samples, you have the same italic typeface enhanced by the addition of special swash characters, inserted from a special swash typeface included as a companion to the **Centaur** expert set. You see swashes here in the letters *M, k,* and *e.*

Incidentally, **Centaur** is considered by many authorities one of the most exquisite of twentieth-century designs.

Figure 3.8 is a more elaborate example of the use of special characters, flourishes, and typefaces within a family. Here the family is Monotype's **Fournier,** which you encountered briefly in Chapter 1 because I used it in the remake of the fashion ad. In the top half of the figure you can see the text of a title page printed without the use of special characters. The capital letters are tall—the same height as the lowercase ascenders. In the word *Halfhourly,* the tops of the *f* and *h* run into one another—not a desirable situation. The date appears in standard numbers.

However, in the bottom half of the figure, I've displayed the same words using alternate characters and typefaces within the family. The capital letters are shorter than the ascenders. The *f* and *h* appear as a single character; this

3.7 Centaur Regular compared with Centaur Italic, then Italic with special swash characters.

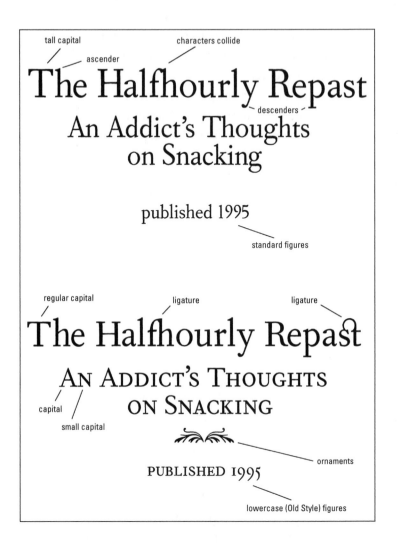

3.8 Standard characters making up a title page (top) are contrasted with the use of special characters applied to the same text (below).

ligature is not usually available, but it avoids that awkward collision between characters seen in the top half of the figure, where the *f* and *h* are separate characters abutting each other. The main reasons to combine and use two or more letters as a single ligature character are either to avoid these collisions or to add a decorative touch. Both uses are demonstrated here.

For the second use, note the ligature that combines the *s* and *t* in the word *Repast.* In the revised version of the title text, small capitals have been combined in the subheading with the regular capitals (not the extra-tall capitals). Below the subheading are two ornaments also provided by Monotype with the typeface family. And, finally, the date appears in lowercase (Old Style) numbers.

Fournier is an unusual family, in that you can choose among small, regular, and extra-tall capital letters.

URW INTRODUCES
NEW CHARACTER CATEGORIES

This is a good place for me to mention that URW now offers not only the standard monospaced figures and Old Style or lowercase figures, but also a third variety. These are intended for use in headings and other display work; they are smaller and narrower than regular figures and are proportionally spaced. Therefore, they look good in headings without being so large and wide that they call undue attention to themselves. URW makes these alternate numbers available with their *DisCaps* sets (short for *Display Capitals*); these character sets also contain a new breed of small capital letters. The letters appear in the lowercase positions in the typeface and are specifically intended to work with the main capital letters for display use. This extra set of small capital letters is larger than normal small caps; when the characters are used, they appear centered from top to bottom on the line, forming a unit with the main capital letters. In other words, DisCaps capitals are positioned above the baseline, not on it.

The left column in Figure 3.9 shows the three categories of figures, with the usual monospaced figures on the first line, normal lowercase figures on the second line, and the new URW DisCaps figures on the third line. In the right column you can see regular text on the first line compared with small caps on the second line and the centered DisCaps capital sets on the third line. The typeface is **Latienne,** designed by Mark Jamra in 1986.

251897164	Regular
251897164	Small Caps
251897164	DisCaps

3.9 URW's three categories of numbers and capital letters.

I've previously discussed and illustrated the use of decorative initial capital letters. Usually, these characters are rather ornate and can be used with many different typefaces. The most common use is as a drop cap—a capital that is dropped into a paragraph of text, as was done with the capital O at the beginning of the revised Tailor's Story in Chapter 1. URW has now released a large number of initial capital sets that are intended for use with *specific* typefaces; usually, they reflect the style and mood of the regular typeface they enhance. Figure 3.10 shows several examples of these typeface-specific initial capitals. Note that I've used them in various ways—as a drop cap, as an initial capital placed to the left of an entire paragraph, and simply as a replacement for the standard capital letter in a line of text.

UNUSUAL LIGATURES AS DESIGN ELEMENTS

The most commonly used ligatures—as I've stated—have been created for "traffic management" reasons—for example,

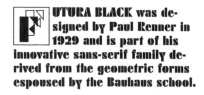

FUTURA BLACK was designed by Paul Renner in 1929 and is part of his innovative sans-serif family derived from the geometric forms espoused by the Bauhaus school.

Ehoe—
Roger Excoffon
1955

AMERICAN UNCIAL was created by Victor Hammer in 1945 but not released for general use until 1953. The design is based on medieval writing of the fourth to ninth centuries.

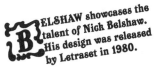

BELSHAW showcases the talent of Nick Belshaw. His design was released by Letraset in 1980.

GALADRIEL IS THE WORK OF PROLIFIC BRITISH DESIGNER ALAN MEEKS. THIS 1974 RELEASE IS A MASTERFUL EVOCATION OF THE ART NOUVEAU STYLE OF DESIGN WHICH BECAME PROMINENT LATE IN THE NINETEENTH CENTURY.

Futura Extra Bold

3.10 URW initial capital letters designed for use with specific typefaces.

to keep the top of a lowercase *f* from running into the period atop a lowercase *i* that follows it. Others, however, exist only because they add an attractive design element or can bring variety to an otherwise dull heading; these you can use much as you would swash characters.

URW provides swash sets for many popular typefaces—as do other major digital type foundries. However, the company is ahead of most competitors when it comes to sets of decorative alternate characters. Figure 3.11 shows an ad heading I concocted for some mythical vendor of merchandise. The heading is targeted toward folks with plenty of money—perhaps the product is a custom-built automobile or a necklace made with jewels from a monarch's

CSTLY BUT

RARE

Avant Garde Gothic
• Alternate Bold Characters

3.11 Alternate ligatures change the appearance of ITC's Avant Garde Gothic.

crown. The heading uses snob appeal: COSTLY BUT RARE. In other words, the rarity justifies the cost. The typeface here is one many computer users have grown sick of, simply because it has been provided for so many years as one of the 35 typefaces sold with PostScript printers. I'm speaking of **Avant Garde**—a very innovative, attractive typeface; it's the design that was used to launch International Typeface Corporation in 1970. Herb Lubalin and Tom Carnese were the designers. The inspiration was a logo they designed for *Avant Garde* magazine. But I doubt if you're sick of the characters you see in COSTLY BUT RARE. In fact, I doubt if you've ever seen most of them. All the letters except the *B* and the *LY* and *RE* combinations are alternate ligatures available for **ITC Avant Garde Gothic Bold** through URW. Although these characters are available to the other ITC licensees, most of these companies have apparently decided that the demand would be too small for them to consider offering them.

By the way, you might think that some of the ligatures in Figure 3.11 are hard to read. You'd be right. This works to the advantage of the heading in COSTLY BUT RARE. A reader will glance at it and sense something odd. This impels a closer look, whereupon it's very easy to decipher the few characters presented. The reader is now hooked and would probably read the rest of the advertising text that would follow. Obviously, you should not use such characters in lengthy lines or paragraphs.

I included **Avant Garde** in its familiar form at the bottom of Figure 3.11 for those of you who are not acquainted with the typeface and who therefore wouldn't know why the characters in the heading are different. **Avant Garde** is typical of ITC faces: The x-height is very large and the characters don't appear at their best unless you use a tight *letterfit*. In other words, the characters should be printed very closely together, as they are in this figure.

Figure 3.12 contains a variation in the use of ligatures. In the **Sophia** typeface shown here, designer Matthew Carter has created individual characters that can be combined to form ligatures. Within the sentence displayed in the figure, these combinations are all "instant" ligatures: *EC, RA, CT,*

SOPHIA INCLUDES TEN
SPECIAL CHARACTERS
THAT JOIN WITH OTHERS
TO FORM LIGATURES:
C E F G H L R T T Z

ALTERNATIVE CHARACTERS:
AA II MM TT 44
EE FF KK RR XX

3.12 The Sophia typeface created by Matthew Carter.

HE, and *FO.* According to Carter, the **Sophia** design "was suggested by hybrid alphabets of capitals, uncials, and Greek letterforms from sixth-century Constantinople." It was released in 1993 and is available from Carter & Cone, a company he cofounded. Incidentally, this famous designer also was a cofounder of Bitstream.

Some clever utilities let you insert special characters without looking up the necessary keystroke combinations in a table. Read all about these programs in Chapter 13.

IT'S TEST TIME: ARE THESE TWO THE SAME?

Now that this chapter has made you an expert at detecting the differences between typefaces, take a break from your studies here and participate in one of those surprise quizzes that students hate so much. Figure 3.13 shows two renditions of a short paragraph of text. Is the typeface in both versions the same? You have 30 seconds to come up with your answer.

Okay, time's up. And, unfortunately, I don't have enough classroom monitors to determine whether you took an extra 15 seconds to complete our quiz. I'll have to rely on the honor system.

The answer is: If your sharp eye found differences between the characters in the two paragraphs, you pass the test. The top specimen is the Font Bureau's **FB Californian,** a loving new digital version of Frederic Goudy's **University of California Old Style and Italic,** a design he created in 1938 for the Press of that school, located on its Berkeley campus. The Font Bureau revival started with a digitization of the roman typeface by Carol Twombly. David Berlow redrew it while adding italics and an expert set. Jane Patterson contributed a boldface. The result was released in 1994; this Font Bureau family is very true to Goudy's original concept.

Plant rows of flowers to make the most of the path of the sun. For example, a north-south orientation should provide both sides of the rows with *equal* amounts of sunlight.

Plant rows of flowers to make the most of the path of the sun. For example, a north-south orientation should provide both sides of the rows with *equal* amounts of sunlight.

3.13 Two typeface samples that appear to be the same design.

The bottom example is **ITC Berkeley Oldstyle,** designed by Tony Stan in 1983. ITC states that it's "based on the original Goudy type design" and that it "carries the flavor and dynamics," but "without being a copy."

Now let's examine the differences. The Font Bureau version has a slightly smaller x-height and is slightly heavier. The hyphen is diagonal rather than horizontal. Crossbars on the lowercase *f* and *t* extend further to the right than in the ITC rendering. The angle of the diagonal crossbar on the lowercase *e* is less pronounced. The italic characters are narrower. A ligature is used for the *st* letter combination in the word *most*. There are other differences, but these are enough to determine that the typefaces are not the same.

Now, admittedly, this was a difficult test, because both typefaces are based on the same original design. I included it to demonstrate that you must compare the separate renderings of each character attribute as well as the overall dimensions and weight of the entire face in order to identify designs correctly. (The flower photo in Figure 3.13 is from the FargoFoto clip-art collection sold by Fargo Electronics.)

In case you're not familiar with the Font Bureau as a type vendor, it might interest you to know that it was founded in 1989 by Roger Black and David Berlow. Berlow is a distinguished and prolific designer who worked for Bitstream for several years, has developed or revised over 200 faces for major publications such as *Newsweek* and *The Chicago Tribune,* and is the author of numerous innovative type designs you'll encounter later in this book. As for the Font Bureau today, it now sells more than 350 typefaces. Some Font Bureau originals are also available from Agfa and Monotype.

Although the Font Bureau has a Boston address, I'll let you in on a little secret. Most of its real work is accomplished out of the company's facility on Martha's Vineyard, where lucky employees can enjoy this quaint island's atmosphere while helping to spread good typography around the globe.

ADDITIONAL TERMS RELATED TO TYPE

At this point, I'll quickly take you through some more terms you should know. You're probably familiar with some of them already, even if you're a relative beginner at computers. If you're a professional user of typefaces, you may think there's nothing in this section for you at all, but I'll be introducing you to some typefaces with which you may not be familiar and giving you some pointers that could help. So stick with it. I want to be sure that everybody knows all this information!

Justification and Related Concerns

Let's start with *justification,* sometimes called *alignment.* These terms refer to how the margins are handled for typefaces within a page or document. If the text is *flush left,* each line starts at the same vertical position—in other words, the left margin is straight. We could also call this *left justification* or *left alignment.* In this configuration, there is no attempt to *end* each line in such a way that the right margin is also straight. If words at the right end of lines end wherever line length puts them, the result is called *ragged right.* In the old days of typewriters, all typewritten text was originally left justification with a ragged right margin.

You can also *center* text. This works quite well for titles and headings, but usually looks a little strange if you use this method of justification for a paragraph of text.

Right justification or *flush right* is the opposite of the first category: You have the text clinging to a straight right margin and the left margin is ragged. This kind of alignment works best when a few words of text are involved—such as a subheading at the beginning of a magazine article.

Full justification or simply *justified* applies to text that features straight margins on both left and right. This method of text alignment is used in most books—and in the text of magazine articles, provided columns are fairly wide. When columns are narrow, full justification can result in awkward spaces and hyphens on nearly every line. The reason, of course, is that words do vary in length. Therefore, the only way a computer can make each line the same length is to cheat. Yes, it can hyphenate long words. But, beyond hyphenation, it must sneak extra spacing between words or even between characters to make every line the same length. If a line is fairly long, no one will notice because the opportunities for cheating are so many. With short lines, wide gaps between words are inevitable. For this reason, many desktop publishing mavens do not use full justification in these situations; ragged right is more attractive than ragged letter-spacing.

Figure 3.14 illustrates the four categories of justification. The typeface family is **Footlight,** created for Monotype in

I never travel without my diary. One should always have something sensational to read in the train. *Left*

Centered

I never travel without my diary. One should always have something sensational to read in the train.

Right I never travel without my diary. One should always have something sensational to read in the train.

Justified

I never travel without my diary. One should always have something sensational to read in the train.

3.14 Examples of text justification.

1985 by the talented Malaysian designer Ong Chong Wah. **Footlight** has a distinctive appearance and calligraphic touches that make it a real delight. The words are a well-known remark by Oscar Wilde.

Tracking and Kerning: Pushing Those Characters Around

Tracking is the overall spacing between characters in a specified selection of text. You can adjust tracking in most desktop publishing programs and with some word processing software. For example, the default setting in PageMaker is No Tracking. However, you can change this setting to any of five other choices. Figure 3.15 demonstrates how the various settings look in print. Here you see the **Rusticana** typeface from Linotype-Hell, combined with a symbol from the related **Rusticana Borders** typeface—both designed by Adrian Frutiger in 1992 and based on ancient Roman inscriptions. (Frutiger is one of those great designers whose work you should know.) The top line shows the word TRACKING with no tracking applied. The succeeding lines show the results of applying the available PageMaker tracking variations, from Very Loose to Very Tight.

Many contemporary typefaces have been designed to look their best with tight tracking—in other words, with the characters close together. Therefore, if you're using a word processor that won't let you adjust tracking, these typefaces will lose some of their effectiveness as attractive design elements. Other typefaces were either created before tracking was possible—in the days of inflexible metal type—or are modern designs that either try to emulate old metal type or for other reasons were simply drawn to look better with loose character spacing.

3.15 A demonstration of tracking options in Adobe PageMaker.

Figure 3.16 presents two very good examples of these points. The top typeface is the **Metropolitaines Poster** display face issued by URW in 1992. It clearly requires tight tracking; if those characters were further apart, they'd look terrible. Contrast this specimen with the second line: The same words are set in URW's **Caslon Antique,** created in 1990 with distressed characters concocted to present the irregular appearance of handset, worn metal type. Here you have the opposite situation. The characters would lose much of that antique effect if they were placed closer together.

This brings us to another type of character spacing—*kerning,* which means adjusting the spacing between individual character combinations so they will look their best and be easy to read. In Chapter 2, I discussed *automatic* kerning briefly—the fact that typefaces contain *kerning tables;* there are lists of *kerning pairs,* characters that look best in that particular design when placed at specified distances apart. These tables can be read and applied by most desktop publishing programs and a few word processors so that most character combinations can be automatically spaced properly. However, you'll always encounter circumstances under which you'll want to fine-tune the kerning manually, adjusting certain character combinations either to achieve correct spacing that the kerning table didn't provide or to alter automatic spacing with which you disagree. Many programs will let you kern character combinations manually, by selecting the characters in question or placing the cursor between them, then making the kerning adjustment

3.16 A typeface that requires tight tracking (top line) contrasted with one that requires loose tracking.

either through special keystroke combinations or through a kerning option in a window or dialog box.

Some typeface files contain a kerning table that presents only a couple of hundred kerning combinations. Others have a kerning table with a thousand combinations or more. If you happen to be working with one of those typefaces offering only limited combinations, you'll encounter many combinations that automatic kerning will ignore.

One of the main reasons for kerning is to avoid awkward gaps between characters. Figure 3.16 shows a good example. At the beginning of the second line, in the word Tour, the capital *T* has a lot of unused space on each side of its stem or main stroke. To make the *T* seem to be more a part of the entire word, you would normally want to kern it with the lowercase *o* that follows, in order to bring the two closer together, with the *o* nestled under the crossbar of the *T*. However, this sort of kerning would destroy the antique appearance of this particular typeface, which generally has the spacing of old metal type, where each character was separately cast in a mold with an alloy consisting primarily of lead. You can't squeeze two pieces of lead closer together!

Figure 3.17 presents a kerning demonstration. The typeface is Adobe **Caslon Regular.** This design—like URW's

unkerned

To Avid Painters

kerned

To Avid Painters

3.17 A kerning demonstration.

Caslon Antique—is based on type created by William Caslon in the early eighteenth century. Carol Twombly is the designer of this 1990 Adobe version; she had no desire to produce a face that would print out as an imitation of weathered individual metal characters. On the contrary, she wanted to retain the beauty of Caslon's work but integrate it into a design that could be used readily in printing today's books, brochures, and magazine articles. Therefore, a tighter letterfit was required than for **Caslon Antique.**

The top line of our example begins with the same *T* plus *o* letter combination that you saw in the previous figure. Here, because of the different nature of the typeface design, the lack of kerning looks awkward. Then, in the following word, there's too much space between the *A* and the *v* that follows. Finally, the third word contains a *P* that is too far away from the *a* that follows. The bottom line shows all three of these kerning problems corrected. Now each word seems to be a unit. There are no awkward-looking spaces between characters.

I hasten to add that you may also want to kern characters so they won't be too close to each other. Always use your judgment. If characters *seem* to be too close together or too far apart, thereby drawing attention to themselves, kerning is probably in order.

Finally, note that, because of Adobe **Caslon**'s roots in antiquity, it still requires looser tracking and kerning than, say, **ITC Avant Garde,** which—as I've stated—was designed for a very tight letterfit.

Figure 3.18 shows the Expert Kerning dialog box in PageMaker, which lets you make delicate manual adjustments to any selected character combination.

Using Quotation Marks and Dashes Correctly

The time-honored way of entering quotation marks on a typewriter is to tap a key on which the apostrophe shares

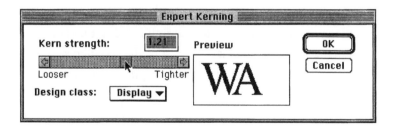

3.18 PageMaker's Expert Kerning dialog box.

space with a double quotation-mark symbol; you hold down the Shift key as you type if you want the quotation-mark symbol to appear. Since only one of these particular character keys appears on the keyboard, the typeface has been designed so that the quotation marks have no curl to them; they're in the form of two parallel vertical lines so they can be used interchangeably either at the beginning or end of a quotation.

However, if you look at the text in any book or magazine, you'll discover that quotation marks in these publications function like parentheses; separate symbols are used to start and end each quotation. Fortunately, you can achieve the same effect in entering text on a personal computer; although *curly* opening and closing quotation marks don't appear on your keyboard, you can press special key combinations to produce them. Some programs will even enter these professional quotation marks for you automatically if an appropriate Preferences option is selected. With this option selected, you simply hold down the Shift key and enter the quotation-mark symbol you see on your keyboard. If a space precedes the symbol, the program converts the character you've typed into an opening quotation mark; otherwise, it produces a closing quotation mark. It will also make an automatic conversion of the "straight up and down" apostrophe to a "curly" apostrophe when you type a phrase such as *Betty's apple.*

Regardless of the method you employ to produce professional opening and closing quotation marks, use them;

your work will look much better. If necessary, consult literature included with your typefaces to determine the correct key combinations for the manual entering of these symbols. Figure 3.19 illustrates the difference in appearance on the printed page.

Also in Figure 3.19, I demonstrate how you substitute on a typewriter for a long dash that you might draw between two words when writing by hand: By tradition, you just type two dashes. However, in printing—and on a personal computer—a long dash symbol is available. It's called an *em dash,* and you should use it for more professional-looking text. Again, it's not shown on your keyboard, but you can produce it by using a special key combination.

Make the Line Lengths Right

No matter which characters you're using—or which typeface—you should pay attention to the length of your lines. Most professionally produced paragraphs of text are

3.19 Correct and incorrect use of quotation marks and dashes.

"Typewriter" quotation marks

"Professional" quotation marks

A dash--on a typewriter

A dash—on a computer

easy to read and have been made so deliberately. The pros know, for example, that if the type is too small and/or if the line of text is too long, the eye will tire trying to read it. Solutions are to use bigger margins, a larger point size, and/or multiple columns.

On the other hand, column width can be too narrow. Very short lines can also tire the eye. If we have to look back and forth too often, fatigue will set in. In addition, very short lines chop up phrases and thoughts so they're more difficult to comprehend as units—not even mentioning the justification problems caused by short lines, which I mentioned earlier in this chapter.

SUMMARY

If you're trying to identify a typeface, you can begin by seeing where it fits within the major classifications and—if the analysis fails at that level—start looking at the fine points of the design. For example, a glance should be enough to tell whether the design is serif or sans-serif. Does it have a large x-height? Are the main strokes of characters all about the same width or do they vary? Does the typeface have vertical or inclined stress?

If the big picture doesn't give you the answer, look closer. If there are serifs, how are they shaped? Is the *g* one-story or two-story? Is there an ear? Any spurs? Is the *a* two-story— with a loop extending upward to the left from the right side of the bowl, as in **Times Roman**—or does this character resemble handwriting, a cursive *a* as in **Times Roman Italic?**

These are only examples. In the chapters that follow, we'll get more specific. I'll show you how to differentiate among Old Style, Transitional, and Modern, as well as several other categories. Along the way, you'll meet a lot of interesting typefaces you might want to use.

What if you think you've positively identified a typeface? You think it looks exactly like **Marvelous Serif,** which you've found in a catalog provided by a major digital type house. However, someone calls a different typeface to your attention, displayed in a catalog from another vendor. This specimen seems to be identical in every aspect to **Marvelous Serif,** except that it's called **Wonderful Serif.** Now you're really confused! There's a simple explanation for this typical incident.

You'll see many typefaces that look like your favorite designs but carry strange names. Here's the reason: If you create or own a typeface, the government lets you protect its name as a registered trademark—provided the name is not already registered to someone else, of course. However, the design itself is not protected. Therefore, some vendors of computer typefaces copy designs and give them new names, to avoid having to pay royalties to the company owning the design. The copy of the design may be of good quality and faithful to the original or it may be really shoddy workmanship. Usually, if you buy from major vendors, all of their type will be of excellent quality.

Sometimes the expense of royalty payments is not the motivation for copying a design. The owner of the trademark may not want to license the design to certain competitors at any price. In those instances, a major vendor may create its own version of a typeface simply because its customers expect to have it available. For example, Bitstream sells a version of **Rockwell** it calls **Geometric Slabserif 712.** In some instances, a company copying a typeface has actually improved on the original design, but certainly not always.

Many type houses issue catalogs that list the standard names for the clones they've created. Others do not. In any case, these multiple names can be confusing for everybody. In this book I use the standard names unless I'm deliberately displaying a variation on a standard design that you may want to purchase under its own name. Okay, let's move on to Chapter 4 and start exploring specific categories.

4

Old Style Typefaces

Before I get into detail regarding Old Style typefaces, I'll give you a quick introduction to this and some of the other serif categories—so you'll know where Old Style fits in.

MAJOR SERIF CATEGORIES

Old Style is certainly one of the most popular serif divisions. Some people write the name as *Oldstyle* or *oldstyle;* I'll use those alternate forms only when they're part of the official name of a typeface. The principal Old Style characteristics appeared first in type of the fifteenth through seventeenth centuries, although designs with these features are still created today. Old Style letters have little contrast between thick and thin strokes, bracketed serifs, and inclined axis stress (remember that I explained these terms in Chapter 3).

Within the Old Style grouping, you'll find two principal subclassifications. One is *Garalde,* a name that was created by combining the names of two noted people: Garamond and Aldus. Claude Garamond and Aldus Manutius were prominent sixteenth-century printers who introduced type designs that are still popular. Some refer to this type classification as *Aldine,* in honor of Aldus Manutius alone.

Garalde typefaces have a lowercase *e* with a horizontal crossbar. Its characters exhibit slightly more stroke contrast than *Venetian*—also called *Humanist*—which is the other major subclassification in the Old Style category.

The Venetian type models originated in fifteenth-century Italy, feature a diagonal crossbar on the lowercase *e,* and usually display a strong inclined axis stress. Some people simplify these perplexing, multiple Old Style classifications. They pay no attention to any names for these designs except Venetian and Old Style: If it isn't Venetian, it's Old Style! Many typefaces include Old Style, Venetian, or Italian as part of their names—in reference to the nature of the designs.

As Figure 4.1 shows, **Adobe Garamond** and **Palatino** are examples in the Garalde subgroup. **Goudy Italien** and **ITC Weidemann** are both Venetian in design. All four of these type families were designed in the twentieth century. **Adobe Garamond** was drawn in 1989 by Robert Slimbach, based on

Old Style	Slab Serif (Egyptian, Mechanistic)
Garalde	Slab Serif
Adobe Garamond	ITC Lubalin Graph
Palatino	**Rockwell**
Venetian (Humanist)	Clarendon
Goudy Italien	**Clarendon**
ITC Weidemann	ITC Cheltenham Condensed
	Typewriter
Transitional	Courier
Adobe Caslon	Prestige 12 Pitch
Times Roman	
	Incised (Glyphic, Lapidary)
Modern (Didone)	AUREA INLINE
Bauer Bodoni	TRAJAN
Linotype Didot	

4.1 Examples in the major serif type categories.

the types of Claude Garamond. **Palatino** was created in 1950 by Hermann Zapf; the design name is owned by Linotype-Hell. **Goudy Italien** is a little-known Frederic Goudy design that's hard to find in digital form; I obtained it on a Brendel CD-ROM. **Weidemann** is a Kurt Weidemann design released by ITC in 1983.

A large number of current typeface designs fall into the Transitional category, simply because Transitional is defined as a group that combines elements of both the Old Style and Modern (or Didone) groups. Therefore, when a contemporary designer creates a new serif typeface, selecting characteristics he likes from existing models, he's likely to end up with a result that falls within the Transitional definition. Its typical characteristics include a vertical or slightly inclined axis stress, a lowercase *e* with a horizontal crossbar, more contrast between thick and thin strokes than is seen in Old Style faces, and thin, bracketed serifs. Examples shown in Figure 4.1 are **Adobe Caslon,** which I discussed in Chapter 3, and **Times Roman,** a version of Monotype's **Times New Roman,** mentioned in Chapter 2.

Just to confuse matters, some experts don't consider **Caslon** typefaces Transitional at all. They've adopted an additional Old Style classification they call Dutch-English, into which they place both **Caslon** and **Janson,** the Nicholas Kis design you encountered in Chapter 2.

More possible confusion: When I start discussing the history of Venetian typefaces, I'll be introducing you to types designed by Nicolas Jenson. Please note that the names Jenson and Janson are not the same, and each represents a different variety of serif typeface.

The first typefaces in the category called Modern originated in the eighteenth century, which is hardly "modern" from today's perspective. That's why some experts concocted a new name for the category: *Didone*. This word was formed from the last names of Firmin Didot and Giambattista Bodoni, two eighteenth-century designers whose typefaces feature vertical axis stress, a strong contrast between thick and thin strokes, a lowercase *e* with a horizontal crossbar, and unbracketed serifs. Examples shown in Figure 4.1 are **Bauer Bodoni** and **Linotype Didot. Bauer Bodoni** was designed in 1926 by Heinrich Jost and Louis Höll and is believed by many to be one of the most authentic of Bodoni typefaces. **Linotype Didot** was designed by Adrian Frutiger in 1992, based on Firmin Didot's original designs.

Because the thin strokes of many Modern (Didone) typefaces are so narrow that they're mere hairlines, you should avoid these designs in small point sizes if you're using a printer with poor resolution (less than 300 dots per inch) or if you're creating newspaper ads—since delicate design features are not reproduced well by the combination of high-speed presses and inexpensive paper used in the newspaper industry.

The emerging popularity of advertising and the poor reproduction quality of early nineteenth-century flyers and handbills led British job printers of the era to adopt yet another typeface category, *Slab Serif.* It features characters in which all of the lines and curves are relatively heavy and of the same width, so none of them will disappear when printed on cheap, porous paper. Furthermore, these bold, plain characters stand out and are easy to read from a distance on billboards and posters. Serifs in the Slab Serif style are square-cut, unbracketed, and are typically the same weight as the lines defining the character. Axis stress is vertical.

Slab Serif typefaces have also been called *Mechanistic,* implying that their design is based on mechanical principles. Some of the first examples were called *Antiques,* but most were soon called *Egyptians.* In both instances, the names resulted from the popularity of Egyptian artifacts after Napoleon's expedition to that country in 1798 and 1799, which resulted in humiliating defeats for the celebrated French general at the hands of the British. Some said the name Egyptian was applied to these typefaces because their rigid design reminded the English of Egyptian art and the pyramids; others said that Napoleon himself had used similar lettering on signs that he wanted to be visible by telescope for many miles across the deserts.

Figure 4.1 shows two typefaces in the general Slab Serif category: **ITC Lubalin Graph** and **Rockwell.** Herb Lubalin created **Lubalin Graph** in 1974, as a seriffed companion to his renowned sans-serif **Avant Garde** family. **Rockwell** was released by Monotype in 1934—the product of staff designers—and is a reworking of a 1910 typeface called **Litho Antique,** designed by William Schraubstädter. Both **Lubalin Graph** and **Rockwell** are appropriate for either display or text usage; however, **Rockwell** is considerably heavier and therefore makes a more forceful statement.

The Slab Serif category has two subgroups: *Clarendon* and *Typewriter.* Clarendons differ from the general category in that they have bracketed serifs and slight variations in line and curve widths. The Clarendon designs appeared starting about 1840. Some sources say they were named in honor of the Clarendon Press at Oxford University; others insist they were named for the Earl of Clarendon, who was active in Egyptian affairs on behalf of the British government. In Figure 4.1, the samples in the Clarendon style are the version of **Clarendon** created by the Bitstream staff and **ITC Cheltenham Condensed,** which you previously encountered as part of a special-effect figure in Chapter 1. Cheltenham types differ from the other Clarendons in that they have short *stub serifs.*

The other Slab Serif subgroup is Typewriter. As you might imagine, these typefaces were either originally designed for use on typewriters or to appear as if the text they produce was created on a typewriter. The lines and curves are nearly of equal width. The lines in the serifs are also the same width and are unbracketed. Usually, the characters are monospaced. The first Typewriter example in Figure 4.1 is **Courier,** designed for typewriter use in 1956 by Howard Kettler of IBM and later redrawn by Adrian Frutiger for the IBM Selectric series. The second example is **Prestige Elite,** designed by Howard Kettler in 1953, also for typewriter use.

Some typefaces have been created for computer or general printing use to impart the flavor of a typewriter font without the monospacing restriction; therefore, the characters are proportional. **ITC American Typewriter** is an example in this category. You can see it in Chapter 7, which is devoted to the Slab Serifs.

The final serif category exhibited here is *Incised.* These typefaces are designed to look as if they've been cut into metal or wood or chiseled in stone rather than drawn or painted. The designs that resemble letters carved in stone are also called *Glyphic* or *Lapidary.* Since many of these imitate the inscriptions on the monuments of ancient Rome, they may include capital letters only. The first example in Figure 4.1 is **Aurea Inline,** an Image Club original released in 1992 and available only from that source. The other example is **Trajan,** designed in 1989 by Adobe's Carol Twombly. Both do consist of capitals only and are intended for display work. Chapter 8 discusses the Incised category, though a few incised typefaces that are sans-serif are covered in Chapter 9 along with the other designs in the sans-serif classification.

Most of the typefaces shown in Figure 4.1 are available from any of several vendors. As I've indicated, **Goudy Italien** and **Aurea Inline** are exceptions.

THE VENETIANS

Now let's take a closer look at Venetian typefaces. Figure 4.2 shows two designs in the Venetian category, to demonstrate both its general characteristics and individual variations. The text sample is from an 1875 poem by Henry Austin Dobson, *The Paradox of Time.* Note that both typefaces feature a diagonal crossbar on the *e* (although the angle differs), little contrast between thick and thin strokes, and inclined stress. However, the stress is more extreme in the top example—**Monotype Italian Old Style**—which is also heavier. The question marks are quite different and the period in the top

4.2 A comparison of two typefaces in the Venetian category.

example is diamond-shaped rather than round. The bottom example—**Schneidler**—features a *splayed M* (feet spread apart), with concave serifs on the feet and no serifs at all at the apexes of its strokes.

As you'll soon see, other Venetian families have similar differences but still fit into the general category because of their major characteristics. **Monotype Italian Old Style** was released in 1911, inspired by the success of William Morris's 1892 **Golden Type,** which I'll discuss shortly. **Schneidler** is the work of F. H. Ernst Schneidler and was released in 1936; versions are available today from Adobe, Bitstream, and other vendors. I used the Bitstream version in this figure.

How did the Venetian type category get its name? Well, its origins really were in Venice, Italy, hundreds of years ago. Gutenberg invented movable type in Germany about 1440; in 1465 the first printers arrived in Italy. Five years later a French printer and designer, Nicolas Jenson, set up shop in Venice, which—because of its strategic location for world trade—quickly became the center of this fledgling industry. The typefaces Jenson created became popular in his adopted country, in part, because they were based on the familiar handwriting of Italian Renaissance scholars rather than on German gothic models. Figure 4.3 contains three additional Venetian typeface specimens, the first of which is the Digital Typeface Corporation's (DTC) 1991 release of **Jenson Oldstyle,** a modern version of a Nicolas Jenson design.

The second example in this figure is Monotype's **Centaur,** which you saw displayed several times in Chapter 3. This design, released in 1929, is definitely within the Venetian boundaries, as is **ITC Berkeley Oldstyle,** which I compared in Chapter 3 with Goudy's **Californian.** However, these Venetians, unlike **Jenson Oldstyle,** are lighter in weight, in line with modern text conventions. Here **Berkeley**'s large

The gingham dog went "Bow-wow-wow!"
And the calico cat replied "Mee-ow!"
The air was littered, an hour or so,
With bits of gingham and calico.

Eugene Field

Jenson Oldstyle

The gingham dog went "Bow-wow-wow!"
And the calico cat replied "Mee-ow!"
The air was littered, an hour or so,
With bits of gingham and calico.

Eugene Field

Centaur

The gingham dog went "Bow-wow-wow!"
And the calico cat replied "Mee-ow!"
The air was littered, an hour or so,
With bits of gingham and calico.

Eugene Field

ITC Berkeley Oldstyle

4.3 Three additional Venetian designs.

x-height becomes particularly noticeable. (A footnote to this discussion: The original fifteenth-century Venetians had no accompanying italics because they hadn't been invented yet! Later in the chapter I'll tell you when the first italics appeared.)

Figure 4.4 traces the historical development of typefaces based specifically on the Jenson design. The first two examples are different versions of **Jenson Oldstyle** or **Old Style.** (Esselte Letraset claims the name **Jenson Old Style** as a trademark.) The second of these is a condensed face and it's

He gave Quincy *five* ⁓ Tom nothing.
Jenson Oldstyle—Digital Typeface Corporation

He gave Quincy *five* -- Tom nothing.
Jenson Old Style Bold Condensed—Linotype-Hell

He gave Quincy *five* ⁓ Tom nothing.
ITC Golden Type—URW

He gave Quincy *five* -- Tom nothing.
Italian Old Style—Monotype

4.4 Four typefaces vary greatly, although based on the same Jenson design.

bold—the only configuration offered by Linotype-Hell; so you'll have to ignore those factors in comparing it to the others. Nevertheless, you should be able to see design differences immediately. The third specimen is **ITC Golden Type,** a revision of the Jenson revival introduced by William Morris under the name **Golden Type** in 1892; the Morris version was acclaimed by the industry at that time and precipitated a renewed interest in Venetian types. The fourth line shows **Italian Old Style** again, which was created to give Monotype customers a typeface with the major characteristics of **Golden Type,** which had already been copied by other foundries.

Now let's compare these four typefaces that all sprang from the same Jenson design. The DTC version has a *g* with a flatter loop than any of the others, but the *g* is different in each. The *e* is also different in each, and the crossbar is at a different angle. The first three examples do not have an italic; instead, that sort of emphasis is provided by a matching *oblique* face. (See the word *five* in each.) An oblique contains a slanted version of the same identical characters used in the regular face and is usually found in sans-serif type families. On the other hand, an italic—although usually slanted to the right like an oblique—is normally a different design altogether, resembling fine handwriting, with characters that are shaped differently than those in the regular face it accompanies.

The first and third examples contain a diagonal hyphen; the hyphens are horizontal in the other two faces. Each of the designs has a *Q* with a different tail. Each version of the *y* is different; the Monotype design even sports a *y* with a tail ending in a thicker, diagonal terminal stroke. The letter combination *fi* in each is a ligature and each of the ligatures is different. The relative height of the *t* varies. There are more differences, but these will suffice to illustrate again that you must look closely at the design of each character if you want to make a positive identification of a typeface.

Before we finish with the Venetians and move on to the remainder of the Old Style classification, consider Figure 4.5. Here I've taken the Tailor's Story material used in Chapter 1 and substituted **ITC Golden Type** for the other typefaces you saw in Figure 1.2. As you can see, both the appearance and effect of the page change dramatically. I think you'll find **Golden Type** even more appropriate for a fairy tale than **Goudy Text** and **Dante**. This design reminds you of the days of castles and kings because its genesis dates back to that era.

The Tailor's Story

 NCE UPON A TIME, in a land far away, there lived a poor man who earned his living as a tailor. He sewed magnificent garments for the king and his friends, but he received very little money.

However, one day those circumstances were to change. He met an elf in the forest who promised to make him a rich man. All he had to do in return, the elf said, was to sew a suit of clothes with cloth spun from moonbeams.

"Where will I find such a cloth?" asked the tailor, worried.

The elf nodded his head wisely. "You will know it when you see it."

4.5 The Tailor's Story acquires a new look through the use of ITC Golden Type.

THE OTHER OLD STYLE DESIGNS

Once you leave the Venetian or Humanist designs, you enter a gray area of hotly disputed Old Style classifications. As I stated a few pages back, the simplest way to consider the Old Style designs that emerged after the Venetian craze was past is to lump them all together: If the face isn't Venetian, it's a member of the main Old Style category—period. That category has three major characteristics: (1) a horizontal crossbar on the *e*, (2) a stroke contrast more pronounced than in the Venetians, and (3) usually a vertical stress. As in the Venetians, you'll encounter variations and exceptions. Figure 4.6 shows the **Granjon** design, which meets all of the basic requirements to be considered Old Style rather than Venetian. However, just below it, you can see **Garth Graphic Condensed,** which has a slightly inclined stress, a splayed *M,* and foot serifs that are slightly concave. Nevertheless, they're both Old Style members. **Granjon** was designed for Linotype in 1928 by George Jones and was named for Robert Granjon, a sixteenth-century French printer and designer. **Garth Graphic Condensed** is part of the Agfa family, a John Matt design modified by Renee LeWinter and Constance Blanchard and released in 1979.

As mentioned earlier, some experts break down the Old Style classification further by adding a Dutch-English group. For their own internal organizational purposes, Bitstream gurus use the names Venetian, Aldine, and Dutch and add four additional groups, which I'll discuss later in the chapter.

In any event, the Venetian designs originated in Venice and—for the most part—were replaced after a few years by a different breed that also originated in Venice, based on the designs that Francesco Griffo created for Aldus Manutius. Aldus was a major publisher and printer in that city during the late fifteenth and early sixteenth centuries. Griffo started producing typefaces with capital letters inspired by the characters chiseled in stone on the ancient Roman monuments. He adjusted the shapes of the accompanying lowercase characters so they would fit comfortably into this rather formal mold. This concept was a definite departure from the Venetian designs which, as I've stated, had been influenced by the handwriting of Italian scholars.

In 1495, Aldus published a book written by 25-year-old Pietro Bembo, later to become a cardinal in the Catholic church. It was an account of a visit he made to Mount Etna. The Griffo typeface used for the book became tremendously successful and was subsequently called **Bembo,** after its author. As is the case with other Griffo designs, **Bembo**

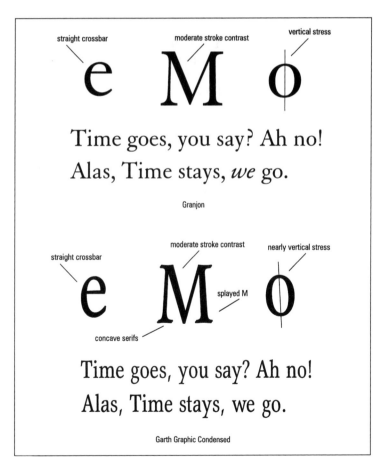

4.6 A comparison of two typefaces in the Old Style category.

featured capital letters slightly shorter than the lowercase ascenders, a departure from the Jenson designs. Monotype revived **Bembo** in 1929 and it became tremendously popular. However, the Monotype version features a larger x-height and a lighter weight than the original. In Figure 4.7, you can see the digital version of this design that precipitated the revolt against the Venetian faces and started a new era of type following classical conventions. I wrote the text for this figure to give you more background on Griffo and also to explain briefly the process by which these metal typefaces were produced.

DEATH IN VENICE
THE END OF VENETIAN TYPEFACES

FRANCESCO GRIFFO arrived in Venice from Padua about 1480. He was originally a goldsmith but became a skilled punchcutter, a master of the most creative step in the mechanical production of metal typefaces of the era. His designs were very influential in replacing the early Venetian type styles with others based more on the capital letters of classic Roman inscriptions. These typefaces were soon grouped by his contemporaries into a classification later called Old Face. By 1495 they were replacing the earlier Venetian concept. In fact, because the Griffo designs were given such prominence in the books printed by the renowned Venetian publisher Aldus Manutius, they were copied throughout Europe and adopted as a standard by the French court. Today this type category is referred to as Old Style or Garalde or Aldine.

The making of metal type consisted of only a few major steps. First the punch was cut for each individual letter. A punch was a bar of steel about three inches long, on the end of which the character was cut. The steel was then hardened, and the punch was driven into the matrix, a bar of soft iron or copper. This action created an indented image of the letter. The matrix was then inserted into an adjustable mold. Molten metal was poured into the mold to cast the piece of type in the shape the punchcutter had created.

Because of this sequence, books dealing with the history of typefaces often contain sentences such as, "The design was cut by Griffo under the supervision of Aldus." In many cases, the word cut used in this way implies that the punchcutter created the actual design. Frequently, this was true. In other cases, a designer drew the characters on paper, and the punchcutter merely reproduced these designs in metal. However, regardless of who was responsible for the design, punchcutting was an art requiring considerable skill.

4.7 The Monotype version of Griffo's Bembo typeface.

Prior to the **Bembo** restoration, Monotype revived another Griffo design in 1923. This was **Poliphilus,** which Griffo introduced in 1499. The name is derived from *Hypnerotomachia Poliphili,* a book by Francesco Colonna in which the design was first used. In re-releasing **Poliphilus,** Monotype copied the actual printed characters from that era. Therefore, this revival is much more authentic than the **Bembo** release and gives you a better idea of Griffo's work. Figure 4.8 shows the Death in Venice page again, reprinted in **Poliphilus.**

DEATH IN VENICE
THE END OF VENETIAN TYPEFACES

FRANCESCO GRIFFO arrived in Venice from Padua about 1480. He was originally a goldsmith but became a skilled punchcutter, a master of the most creative step in the mechanical production of metal typefaces of the era. His designs were very influential in replacing the early Venetian type styles with others based more on the capital letters of classic Roman inscriptions. These typefaces were soon grouped by his contemporaries into a classification later called Old Face. By 1495 they were replacing the earlier Venetian concept. In fact, because the Griffo designs were given such prominence in the books printed by the renowned Venetian publisher Aldus Manutius, they were copied throughout Europe and adopted as a standard by the French court. Today this type category is referred to as Old Style or Garalde or Aldine.

The making of metal type consisted of only a few major steps. First the punch was cut for each individual letter. A punch was a bar of steel about three inches long, on the end of which the character was cut. The steel was then hardened, and the punch was driven into the matrix, a bar of soft iron or copper. This action created an indented image of the letter. The matrix was then inserted into an adjustable mold. Molten metal was poured into the mold to cast the piece of type in the shape the punchcutter had created.

Because of this sequence, books dealing with the history of typefaces often contain sentences such as, "The design was cut by Griffo under the supervision of Aldus." In many cases, the word cut used in this way implies that the punchcutter created the actual design. Frequently, this was true. In other cases, a designer drew the characters on paper, and the punchcutter merely reproduced these designs in metal. However, regardless of who was responsible for the design, punchcutting was an art requiring considerable skill.

4.8 The Monotype version of Poliphilus.

Ironically, Griffo created the first italics, yet both the **Bembo** and **Poliphilus** revivals released by Monotype are accompanied by italics inspired by the typefaces of other designers. For **Bembo,** Monotype based the italic on a design by a talented Venetian printer named Giovantonio Tagliente. The **Poliphilus** italic—called **Blado**—is derived from a font designed by Ludovico degli Arrighi about 1526; however, Monotype gave it the name of a Roman typographer, Antonio Blado, who merely acquired the font after Arrighi's death. In the late 1920s, American Frederic Warde created an italic he named **Arrighi,** in tribute to the sixteenth-century designer, whose work had inspired it. Bruce Rogers soon persuaded his friend Warde to let Monotype use this beautiful face as the italic for the company's 1929 release of Rogers' **Centaur.**

There is some justification for assigning italics to Griffo designs that were created by others. Griffo designed his italic typefaces to be used independently. It wasn't until the 1540s in France that the custom originated of designing and using roman and italic typefaces together as a family.

Now let's look at other Old Style designs—some of them drawn in recent years, others a century ago. The first specimen in Figure 4.9 is **Plantin,** designed by F. H. Pierpont for Monotype and released in 1913. It was named for a sixteenth-century Dutch printer, although not based directly on his work. It's a solid face with moderate contrast, inclined stress, and a splayed *M*—very readable even under difficult conditions. The Autologic version is called **Platinum;** the Bitstream version is **Aldine 721.**

The next specimen is not elegant, doesn't have a small x-height, and isn't very graceful. However, it certainly is noticeable. It's **ITC Gorilla,** a 1970 Tom Carnese/Ronne Bonder adaptation of **Post Oldstyle Roman No. 1,** designed

> Minds are like parachutes; they function only when they're open. Plantin
>
> **Minds are like parachutes; they function only when they're open.** ITC Gorilla
>
> Minds are like parachutes; they function only when they're open. Century Oldstyle
>
> Minds are like parachutes; they function only when they're open. ITC Beguiat Book Condensed

4.9 Four Old Style examples.

in 1900 by artist E. J. Kitson for the *Saturday Evening Post* magazine and based on the lettering of Guernsey Moore. Obviously, **Gorilla** is intended for display purposes. And, despite its bloated proportions, its characteristics definitely place it in the Old Style category. I obtained **Gorilla** from the Bitstream library.

Third, we have **Century Oldstyle,** designed by Morris Fuller Benton in 1906 for American Type Founders Company (ATF). This face is one of the many designs with the Century name released by ATF, all springing from an 1894 assignment to create a typeface for use in *Century* magazine. The original Century was created by Linn Boyd Benton, an ATF executive who was Morris' father and whose principal interest was in the mechanical side of the business.

However, **Century Oldstyle** is really not related stylistically to the other Century typefaces at all; it's a renovation of an 1860 Old Style design by Alexander Phemister and was given the Century name purely to increase its marketability. **Century Oldstyle** has a large x-height, is slightly condensed, and is still popular today. You'll find the digital version in most computer type libraries. Experts place the real Century designs in other type categories.

ITC Benguiat completes Figure 4.9. We see the **Book Condensed** face here. The busy Ed Benguiat created this decorative text family for ITC in 1977. It has an Art Nouveau flavor of the 1890s, particularly in the capital letters. Note that the lowercase *e* has a diagonal crossbar, like the Venetian models. Nevertheless, the other qualities of the design mark it as an Old Style. It's available from most type vendors.

SEEING HOW SOME OLD STYLE CHOICES AFFECT AN AD

At this point, let's apply some Old Style typefaces to an ad and discover how different designs impact on the effectiveness of the ad.

Figure 4.10 shows an ad layout featuring artwork consisting of clip art from the Metro ImageBase library. The style is Art Deco, reminding us of the 1920s. The word *sodas* is actually part of the drawing. In order to select type to go with the other elements of this layout, it's important not to choose a style similar to that in the cartoon. Most readers develop a sense of uneasiness when they find two "almost the same" type designs in the same ad. Something is wrong that they can't quite articulate. Something doesn't match. So, since we can't match the hand-lettered word *sodas*, we don't want to use any of the many typefaces that are in the Art Deco tradition. However, we do need to play off the message in the headline below the cartoon: nostalgia. Therefore, an Old Style typeface family would be fine, so long as we pick something light and airy rather than ponderous and overbearing. In this figure, I've used **Bitstream Carmina Bold** and **Medium,** designed for the company by Gudrun Zapf-von Hesse in 1986. This family has a pen-drawn flavor and, in fact, is assigned by Bitstream executives to their own Old Style subgroup they call Calligraphic.

How does it look? Well, for my taste, it *is* light and airy, but I think it appears too modern.

4.10 An ad using the Bitstream Carmina type family.

In Figure 4.11 you can consider a different approach. The type family is **Phaistos,** drawn by David Berlow of the Font Bureau with the help of Just van Rossum in 1990 and 1991. Since **Phaistos** is a reworking of a 1922 design by Rudolf Koch, perhaps it will have the antique flavor we want. The original Koch design was called **Locarno**—and sometimes **Koch Antique.** It featured tapered vertical strokes and small serifs—two features the Font Bureau has retained—although in a diminished form. However, Koch used a tiny x-height, with long lowercase ascenders. Berlow and van Rossum have greatly increased the x-height in order to give the design a more contemporary flavor. To me, the result is very attractive, but not antique.

4.11 The same ad with the type design changed to Phaistos.

Maybe we should look at Koch's original design. Figure 4.12 shows the Koch family as resurrected by Bitstream. Right away you can see how much more suitable the **Phaistos** version is for today's uses. **Locarno** produces an ad that's hard to read. The body copy is in the very light **Locarno Roman** typeface—so pale that it almost disappears on the page. Furthermore, the tiny x-height makes the words so small that they simply don't attract attention. Incidentally, the Locarno design falls into a special subset of Old Style typefaces that Bitstream calls *Kuenstler,* after the German word for artist. These designs originated in Germany early in the twentieth century, when a group of German artists started drawing typefaces that mixed Old Style foundations

4.12 The ad redone using the original Locarno typeface on which Phaistos is based.

with blackletter traditions. (Read about blackletter designs in Chapter 11.) Kuenstler typefaces are easily identified: They typically feature unusual proportions, small serifs, intricate detailing, and curves broken to interrupt the expected flow of the characters.

Perhaps we can save the day by increasing the font size of **Locarno** and using the Heavy and Bold family members rather than Roman and Bold. Figure 4.13 demonstrates how these changes work out. Although the message is easier to read, the use of the Heavy version in the heading and in the name of the shop diminishes the ad's lighthearted quality. The type family begins to reveal its Teutonic origins. And, unfortunately, Bitstream offers only the three weights:

4.13 Using Heavy and Bold weights rather than Roman and Bold makes Locarno easier to read, but a bit ponderous.

Roman, Bold, and Heavy. So we'd better continue our search for a typeface that will be just right.

Now consider **Codex,** shown in a Bitstream version in Figure 4.14. This typeface was designed by Georg Trump and released in 1955. Although it's a roman, it has many calligraphic characteristics that make it seem to belong to an earlier era. Yet it's lively and easy to read. I think **Codex** is a good choice for this ad. What do you think?

The various versions you've seen of this ad demonstrate the process you can go through in order to select a typeface that will produce exactly the effect you want. Remember that even the greatest type design will not be appropriate for every print job that comes up. Don't hesitate to reject a face that

4.14 Codex gives an antique quality to the ad, but is still easy to read.

doesn't meet your current requirements. You can always use it later in another project.

Here's a layout tip: Usually, advertising art directors will try to limit a design to as few separate visual elements as possible. This strategy makes the ad seem to "hang together," instead of seeming to be composed of several independent graphic units. I arranged all versions of this soda fountain ad so that they contain, basically, only two design elements. The heading is close enough to the drawing to be considered by the reader as related to it. And the name and location of the shop are close enough to the small paragraph of text to be perceived as an extension of that unit. In any layout, you should try to relate objects to each other when you can. The amateur will usually do the opposite; he will space objects evenly on the page whenever possible.

THE BITSTREAM OLD STYLE CLASSIFICATIONS

Bitstream has been kind enough to share the company's internal classification system with me and to let me share it with you. It's of interest because it illustrates how professionals detect patterns and categories in type design that most of us would not be able to discern.

Figure 4.15 shows all of the Bitstream groupings for Old Style typefaces. The text in the examples is the title of a book by Charles Schulz, creator of the Peanuts comic strip; I happen to own a warm puppy and agree with the sentiment in that title.

Bitstream defines the company's Venetian group in approximately the same terms I've used, so I won't discuss it further. The Venetian type specimen in Figure 4.15 is the same **Goudy Italien** I showed you earlier in the chapter. It's the only typeface in the figure that is not available from

Venetian

Happiness Is a Warm Puppy

Goudy Italien

Aldine

Happiness Is a Warm Puppy

Sabon

Dutch

Happiness Is a Warm Puppy

Kis

Revival

Happiness Is a Warm Puppy

ITC Italia

Calligraphic

Happiness Is a Warm Puppy

Raleigh

Lapidary

Happiness Is a Warm Puppy

Bitstream Arrus

Kuenstler

Happiness Is a Warm Puppy

Belwe

4.15 The Bitstream classifications for Old Style typefaces.

Bitstream, either under its standard name or one Bitstream has assigned from its classification system.

As you might expect from its name, Bitstream says the Aldine category consists of the early Old Styles that were produced in the tradition established by Aldus when his books gave wide distribution to the typefaces cut for him by

Griffo. These relatively formal designs—inspired by those Roman monument inscriptions—were used as models for typefaces created by later designers, notably, the French printer and punchcutter Claude Garamond. **Sabon,** shown in Figure 4.15, is one of many faces derived from Garamond's work. **Sabon** was designed in 1964 by Jan Tschichold and is specifically based on a page printed by Konrad Berner. Berner was married to the widow of another printer, Jacques Sabon, who had introduced Garamond's fonts to Frankfurt in the sixteenth century, then cut variations of his own. The **Sabon** design is part of the Linotype-Hell library.

In the low countries—the region currently comprising Belgium, the Netherlands, and Luxembourg—Old Style designs became slightly heavier and acquired a larger x-height during the seventeenth and eighteenth centuries. Therefore, Bitstream breaks these typefaces away from the Aldine classification and calls them Dutch. The Dutch example in Figure 4.15 is **Kis,** the Bitstream version of **Janson** that uses the name of the actual designer. Other well-known families that Bitstream places in the Dutch category include **Times Roman, Caslon,** and **Ehrhardt,** even though the first two were designed in England.

The next category is Revival. Bitstream defines this group as consisting of those typefaces that—for nostalgic purposes—return to Old Style principles without copying specific Old Style designs. In other words, the types still have the look of their nineteenth- and twentieth-century origins. The example in Figure 4.15 is **ITC Italia.** This popular typeface is listed as a Venetian by Adobe and is available in most libraries. It was designed by Colin Brignall in 1974; the talented Brignall joined Letraset in 1964, was appointed type director in 1980, and has designed many well-known typefaces, and supervised the development of countless more.

The Calligraphic category includes typefaces that have hand-drawn characteristics but also the discipline of the Old Style romans. Therefore, they're called Calligraphic Old Style designs rather than scripts. **Raleigh** is the example here, based on **Cartier,** a design created by Carl Dair for the 1967 Montreal World's Fair. It was renamed **Raleigh** after his death. Revisions and added weights were completed by David Anderson, Adrian Williams, and Robert Norton. The result was released in 1977. It's available through Linotype-Hell and most other vendors, in addition to Bitstream. Others assigned to the category include the famous **Palatino** designed by Hermann Zapf in 1950 and **Carmina,** which I used in one of the soda fountain ad examples.

Lapidary typefaces are those that are based on the Aldine tradition but exhibit a stronger influence from the Roman stone-cut inscriptions. The example is **Arrus,** designed by Richard Lipton for Bitstream and released in 1991. Another in the category is **Perpetua,** a notable family drawn by Eric Gill between 1925 and 1932 for Monotype. Gill was a stonecutter before he started designing typefaces.

I explained Kuenstler as a category earlier in the chapter, in reference to Koch's **Locarno.** The example in Figure 4.15 is **Belwe,** designed by Georg Belwe in 1926. Note the blackletter influence represented by the decorative flags on the *W* and *y.* **Belwe** is licensed by Letraset to other vendors.

Bitstream also places **Schneidler** in the Kuenstler group, although I showed it in Figure 4.2 as a Venetian. Adobe and Agfa call **Schneidler** a Venetian. Completely confusing matters, a standard reference work, *Encyclopedia of Type Faces* classifies it as a "Glyphic," defined as "chiseled rather than calligraphic in form"—in other words, the same as Lapidary! So here we have experts placing the same typeface in three different categories, illustrating just how much disagreement there is on how these designs should be organized. Nevertheless, the classifications are useful. They'll bring to your attention significant features of typefaces that do set them apart from each other.

MAKING IMAGES WITH TYPE

Old Style typefaces are well-suited to projects where you want to create patterns with type. These faces are usually sturdy, with strokes of nearly equal weight that make characters easy to decipher even when they're displayed in weird shapes or unexpected angles. And, other than a certain antique quality, most don't relay any specific message of their own—only the message formed by the words. They're neutral in mood and style. I'll present two examples.

Figure 4.16 brings back **Bitstream Arrus** for an encore. Here, as you can see, I've bent the lines of type to produce a human eye—complete with pupil. The humor, of course, comes from the reproducing of the last line in boldface, imitating the look of an eye to which has been added an over-generous amount of eyeliner.

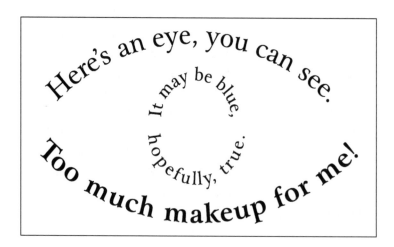

4.16 Bitstream Arrus is used to create a word picture.

Finally, Figure 4.17 illustrates the use of type to create a kind of poetry. The positioning and choices in type reinforce the words used. The type family is **Janson Text,** the Linotype version of the **Kis** design, which I explained in Chapter 2. The drawing is from Dynamic Graphics.

SUMMARY

Most Old Style typefaces are appropriate for a variety of work, although a few—like **ITC Golden Type**—strongly suggest bygone days rather than space travel. They hold up well under difficult printing conditions, with the exception of very light family members and some Kuenstlers with a small x-height. You'll encounter many other type categories later in the book, but few as serviceable.

4.17 The Janson text family put to poetic uses.

5

Transitional Typefaces

Someone once said that a camel is a horse designed by a committee. As an extension of this thought, it's hard to imagine a successful typeface designed by a committee. Nevertheless, in 1693 in France, a committee was appointed by the Académie des Sciences to create a typeface that would be an improvement on the Old Style models that had by then been used for nearly 200 years. The result of this investigation was a typeface that appeared in 1700, but became the property of the French national printing office and couldn't be used by other printers. The design received its share of criticism anyway, but some of its principles were adopted by Pierre Simon Fournier *le jeune* in typefaces he offered for sale in 1742. Shortly thereafter, in England about 1750, John Baskerville set up shop as a printer and introduced a type that really headed Europe away from the Old Style traditions.

There were two main changes: Inclined stress was practically abandoned—a result of the increasing formal discipline being placed on type—and stroke contrast was increased, made possible by improvements in the printing process itself. Printers could use narrow strokes without fearing that they might disappear by the time they were imprinted on paper. By 1780 this trend would result in elegant types with great stroke contrast; some of the strokes became mere hairlines, resulting in yet another style, to be called Modern. I cover Modern in Chapter 6. In the meantime, all of the typefaces that paved the way from Old Style to Modern have come to be called Transitional. The name is also applied to designs created in our own time that seem to have the Transitional characteristics. Actually, many current types qualify as Transitional because the designers have felt free to adopt qualities they happen to like from both models in order to produce something different.

EXAMINING TRANSITIONAL CHARACTERISTICS

Figure 5.1 shows the principal features of two Transitionals: **Berthold Baskerville** and **Bulmer.** As the figure demonstrates, the straight crossbar is still in style and more stroke width variation is permitted—in addition to the characteristics mentioned previously.

This Berthold version of **Baskerville** was developed into a family by the foundry's staff between 1961 and 1972. Yet another version, **Berthold Baskerville Book**—released from 1980 to 1983 and designed by Günter Gerhard Lange—was a lighter interpretation with greater contrast, suitable for fine book printing with the presses and papers currently available.

Bulmer was resurrected by Morris Fuller Benton in 1928 for ATF; it's based on a typeface cut by William Martin for William Bulmer of the Shakespeare Press about 1790. The Shakespeare Press was an English firm dedicated to the printing of the works of William Shakespeare. Martin had been a pupil of Baskerville, but was also an admirer of Bodoni. Both influences are evident in Bulmer.

Figure 5.2 shows three more Transitionals with other characteristics: **Fournier, Photina,** and **Adobe Caslon Italic.** Bear in mind, however, that although Adobe classifies **Caslon**

5.1 A comparison of two typefaces in the Transitional category.

types as Transitional, others place them in a Dutch or Dutch-English group within the Old Style classification.

I gave the background on **Fournier** in Chapter 1 when I used the Monotype version in the remake of a fashion ad, so I won't repeat names and dates here. However, I am showing you the design again for two reasons: to exhibit it here in the chapter dedicated to the category in which it belongs and to let you see its attractive *ct* and *st* ligatures.

The next typeface is **Photina**, released in 1991. It doesn't have those ligatures, but it does have a large x-height.

Act well today, so tomorrow
you can remember glories past.

Fournier

Act well today, so tomorrow
you can remember glories
past.

Photina

*Act well today, so tomorrow
you can remember glories past.*

Adobe Caslon Italic

5.2 Three additional Transitional designs.

It is the result of a Monotype assignment received by José Mendoza y Almeida to create an up-to-date seriffed family with character weights and widths that could easily be used in combination with Adrian Frutiger's **Univers** sans-serif family. Mendoza had worked in the Paris studio of Roger Excoffon, who designed type for the advertising industry.

Finally, note all of the special characters in Carol Twombly's **Adobe Caslon Italic**. Not only do you find the *ct* and *st* ligatures, but also a fancy swash *A* and even two versions of the lowercase *w*—both seen on the first line. I gave the history of this family in Chapter 3.

TWO STANDARD TRANSITIONALS THAT ARE STILL POPULAR

Figure 5.3 introduces **Scotch Roman,** originally cut by a Glasgow foundry in 1813. It may have been designed by Richard Austin. Monotype released its version in 1908, shown here. **Scotch Roman** has been very popular, partially because it steered a middle course between the traditional Old Styles and some of the more extreme Modern faces. It's rugged, yet stylish.

Caledonia is the Latin name for Scotland; William Dwiggins designed the **Caledonia** typeface for Linotype in 1938, planning to blend the features of **Scotch Roman** and **Bulmer.** He ended up with a design that differed considerably from its models and improved on some of their elements. In Figure 5.4 you see the Bitstream version. In the late 1980s Linotype issued **New Caledonia,** a digital reworking that eliminated some of the design restrictions that had been imposed by the metal version. The illustration in the figure is from Dynamic Graphics.

Justification

There was a young lady from Wales
Who often ate puppy-dog tails.
She ate them, you see,
When going to sea,
Much better than munching on whales!

5.3 Monotype's Scotch Roman is the typeface used for this limerick.

A bicycle waits while its owner contemplates the wonders of autumn.

5.4 Caledonia combines features of Scotch Roman and Bulmer.

TWO LATE TWENTIETH-CENTURY TRANSITIONALS

Friedrich Poppl was an award-winning German calligrapher before he entered into an agreement with Berthold to create typefaces. The 1974 release seen in Figure 5.5—**Poppl-Pontifex**—was his first text family. It's charming and friendly and falls into the Transitional classification. The illustration is from the Dubl-Click Wet Paint library.

Matthew Carter drew **ITC Charter** at Bitstream in 1986. It was designed specifically as a digital family that would work well even on low-resolution printers. In Figure 5.6 **Charter** is used with another Dubl-Click clip-art selection. This library contains many renderings of objects from previous eras.

Oz-mosis

The Wizard of Oz was released by MGM in 1939, fated to become a classic. However, the path to immortality was not easy. First of all, the studio had wanted Shirley Temple to play Dorothy and Edna May Oliver as the Wicked Witch; neither choice became possible. Buddy Ebsen was signed as the Tin Woodman, but the metal paint makeup made him sick, and he was replaced by Jack Haley.

5.5 Poppl-Pontifex adds life to the Wizard of Oz.

When I was a boy, we had a wind-up phonograph (they called it a Victrola), with records by the Two Black Crows (a vaudeville comedy team), Paul Whiteman and his orchestra, Enrico Caruso, and Sir Harry Lauder. I liked the Two Black Crows the best, but my mother preferred Sir Harry's *Roamin' in the Gloamin'* sung in his broad Scottish accent. She would sit in her rocking chair and listen, rocking slowly with her eyes closed and a slight smile on her face. I always figured she was remembering some event from her youth, but she never told me what it was.

5.6 Bitstream Charter is a workhorse that performs well even under adverse conditions.

MORE LINOTYPE STANDARDS

William Dwiggins recommended designer Rudolph Rudzicka (sometimes spelled Rudolf Ruzicka) for a job at Linotype. The company hired him for what turned out to be a 40-year relationship. His initial assignment was to create a new type family. It was called **Fairfield,** and its first member was released in 1940. For the 1991 conversion of the family to the electronic medium, Alex Kaczun added additional weights, small caps, swash caps, and lowercase figures. He also created *caption* typefaces for the family, which in design are halfway between the roman and italic members. The idea was that these alternate faces could be used for picture captions, providing a unique appearance but retaining a family resemblance to the others. Figure 5.7 shows some members of the family. The text is the title of a poem by Mallarmé.

Electra was designed by Dwiggins in 1935. After its introduction, he continued to add to the family. For example, he designed an italic for **Electra** that was really a slanted roman; in 1944 he added an alternate italic, **Electra Cursive,** that was more conventional. This second italic is the only one included in Linotype's digital release of the design. **Electra** includes specific Display typefaces, to be used for headings

A Throw of the Dice Will
Never Abolish Chance.

Fairfield Light

*A Throw of the Dice Will
Never Abolish Chance.*

Fairfield Light Caption

*A Throw of the Dice Will
Never Abolish Chance.*

Fairfield Light Italic

A THROW OF THE DICE WILL
NEVER ABOLISH CHANCE.

Fairfield Medium Small Caps

**A Throw of the Dice Will
Never Abolish Chance.**

Fairfield Bold

***A Throw of the Dice Will
Never Abolish Chance.***

Fairfield Swash Heavy Italic

5.7 Members of Linotype's Fairfield family.

and other large-point-size purposes. Figure 5.8 shows Display, Regular, and Cursive fonts. Note that the heading features more condensed characters than the text roman below it. You can also see lowercase figures. The Cursive appears in the caption below the illustration, which is available in color on a PhotoDisc CD-ROM.

Galeazzo Sforza, Duke of Milan

Galeazzo Maria Sforza became Duke of Milan in 1466, upon the death of his father. Apparently, Galeazzo was a capable ruler.

From a panel portrait in the Uffizi, Florence.

He instituted many agricultural improvements, including the construction of canals. He also promoted the manufacture of wool and silk. In addition, he was interested in the arts and served as a patron to artists, poets, and musicians. However, his popular reputation was that of a cruel, vain, and dissolute ruler.

He was assassinated on December 26, 1476 by three local citizens who hoped his death would end the Sforza family's régime. There was no popular uprising, and he was mourned by his subjects.

5.8 Italian history provides a showcase for the Electra type family.

SUMMARY

I could have shown you many, many other Transitional typefaces in this chapter because—as I stated at the beginning—almost any design that combines elements of Old Style and Modern can be welcomed into the category. These faces are versatile, provide few printing problems, and have graced the pages of books and magazines for decades.

Next we'll examine the Moderns and you can see once and for all what the Transitionals were leading up to.

6

Modern Typefaces

Firmin Didot is credited with cutting the first Modern typeface in Paris about 1784. About three years later, Giambattista Bodoni—inspired by Didot's example—started creating Modern typefaces in Italy. The Didot family had a print shop in the Louvre from which they published a series of fine books that were praised and highly regarded all over Europe. Nevertheless, today we find the Bodoni name attached to many faces in the Modern category and Didot is hardly mentioned. The only Didot typefaces widely available for personal computers today are found in a revival created for Linotype-Hell in 1992, which you'll see shortly.

At least the Didot influence survives in the name *Didone*—the word coined in Europe in the 1950s by combining the Didot and Bodoni names and promoted as a replacement for Modern by some who consider that word confusing. However, Modern is so firmly entrenched in the history and lore of typefaces that it's still preferred by most as the name of the category.

Figure 6.1 shows typical Modern features, using two Bodoni versions as examples. The first is **Berthold Bodoni,** produced by the Berthold staff in 1930; Berthold has started referring to this version as **Berthold Bodoni Antiqua** since introducing another Bodoni in 1983. The second sample in the figure is **Bauer Bodoni,** released in 1926 and considered

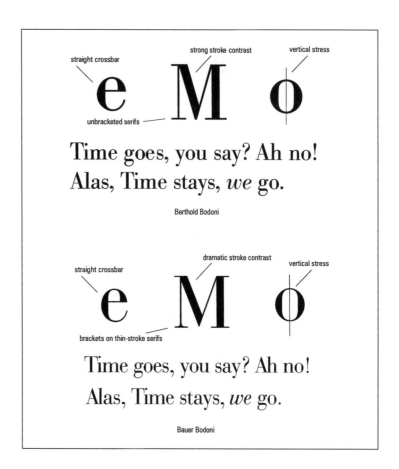

6.1 A comparison of two typefaces in the Modern category.

by many to be a close approximation of the original Bodoni fonts.

Note that both typefaces displayed in Figure 6.1 feature a horizontal crossbar on the lowercase *e,* vertical stress, noticeable stroke contrast, and marked variations in the width of curved lines. However, the **Berthold** version has foot serifs that are unbracketed, while the **Bauer** font contains small bracketed foot serifs on the thin strokes of capital letters. The stroke contrast is more pronounced on the **Bauer** font. Bodoni's own fonts featured the heavier stroke contrast and bracketed serifs, indications of the more authentic nature of the **Bauer** version.

THE DIDOT REVIVAL

At the time Firmin Didot cut his first Modern fonts, copperplate engraving had become very popular. Its influence could be seen in the fine lines he used in his characters—often mere hairlines rather than the slightly thicker variety favored by Bodoni. Another attribute that set Didot's types apart from those of Bodoni was his consistent use of unbracketed serifs.

When Linotype commissioned Adrian Frutiger to create a type family in the Didot tradition, this master designer used as his model a document that had been set in the original Didot alphabet. Of course, he had to make some design adjustments to accommodate today's technology.

Frutiger followed Didot's lead by producing a Headline member of the family, slightly heavier with narrower letters, for use in titles. Throughout the history of type, thoughtful designers have created separate versions of a design for text and heading purposes. Usually, for maximum readability, text fonts contain wider characters with a looser letterfit than are found in those fonts intended for display use. When letters are large, they can be narrower and closer together without adversely affecting the reader's comprehension of the material.

Linotype Didot contains no italics for display faces because Frutiger found that Didot used italics only in his text fonts. Incidentally, Bodoni didn't use boldface italics, so you'll see that they're missing from some of the Bodoni versions displayed later in the chapter.

Figure 6.2 shows **Linotype Didot** at work—in a notice directed to the guests of an imaginary hotel. This family is a

Dining

The hotel's noted West Bank Room is open for your dining enjoyment each evening between 7 and 9 p.m., under the supervision of our justly renowned chef François. Reservations required. Black tie optional.

The Management

6.2 A hotel notice using Linotype Didot Heading, Regular, Italic, and lowercase figures.

good choice when you want a touch of elegance. The decorative frame is from Metro.

At this point I'll give you a first peek at a document that I've used to display all the Modern typefaces discussed in this chapter. Seeing the same words rendered in different ways will provide some dramatic evidence of how even the so-called Bodonis vary from each other. This layout uses an antique map of Italy as a background for the title and for a brief quotation from Bodoni himself about his philosophy and work. The map is available on a PhotoDisc CD-ROM; for this project, I grayed out the image in Photoshop so it would be suitable for the overprinting of headings. In Figure 6.3, **Linotype Didot** is the type family used, even though the text gives background only on his rival, Bodoni.

6.3 The Linotype Didot type family is featured in this document about Bodoni.

> # Bodoni and the Duke of Parma
>
> "Beauty is founded on harmony, subordinate to the critique of reason."
>
> For 45 years Giambattista Bodoni served as the director of a royal printing office for the Duke of Parma. This appointment offered him the time and luxury of undertaking almost any kind of printing project that appealed to him, with no necessity to turn a profit. He established his own foundry and cut new typefaces that differed sharply from the Fournier and Didot designs with which he began this career. His work was widely praised and copied. However, the scholarly content of his books was in doubt because of sloppy proofreading. His personal interest was in the appearance of a page, not its content.

THE POPULAR VERSIONS OF BODONI

This section of the chapter will show you each of the Bodoni revival families that are generally available today for use on personal computers.

The Benton Bodoni

About 1907, Morris Fuller Benton began the design of a Bodoni family for ATF. Members of the family appeared over a period of several years, were received enthusiastically, and—perhaps the greatest compliment—were immediately copied by other foundries. Benton started a revival of Bodoni and other Modern designs that has continued to this day.

A *revival,* you say? Had Modern typefaces fallen out of favor by the beginning of the twentieth century? As a matter of fact, they had—starting in the early nineteenth century. By a few years after Bodoni's death in 1813, slab serif and sans-serif designs were becoming the latest fad. You'll read about those categories in Chapters 7 and 9, respectively.

Benton supposedly consulted with Italian sources in designing his Bodoni. However, it's not as authentic as other versions. For example, serifs are unbracketed—in the manner of Didot. Nevertheless, it's Benton's Bodoni that most people think of when they discuss the category; it remains the favorite of most printers. Figure 6.4 shows our sample document rendered with the **Benton Bodoni** family. In particular, the heading—shown in an extra bold family member called **Poster**— is the essence of Bodoni to many present-day typesetters. Note that the family has been provided with a **Bold Italic,** seen in the quotation.

6.4 The Benton Bodoni family, created for ATF early in the twentieth century.

Other variations available in the **Benton Bodoni** family include two other display type choices: **Bold Condensed** and **Poster Compressed,** which has extremely narrow letters. You can purchase this design—usually called simply "Bodoni"— from most digital sources.

Berthold Bodoni

The original **Berthold Bodoni** was chosen as the official IBM corporate typeface. It avoids extremes, looks distinguished, and holds up well under most printing conditions. The family has several condensed members and includes small caps and lowercase figures in an Expert Collection that includes ligatures such as *ff* and *ffi.* If you look closely, you can pick out these special ligatures in the Berthold sample displayed in Figure 6.5.

Bodoni and the Duke of Parma

"Beauty is founded on harmony, subordinate to the critique of reason."

For 45 years Giambattista Bodoni served as the director of a royal printing office for the Duke of Parma. This appointment offered him the time and luxury of undertaking almost any kind of printing project that appealed to him, with no necessity to turn a profit. He established his own foundry and cut new typefaces that differed sharply from the Fournier and Didot designs with which he began this career. His work was widely praised and copied. However, the scholarly content of his books was in doubt because of sloppy proofreading. His personal interest was in the appearance of a page, not its content.

6.5 Berthold Bodoni Antiqua, released in 1930.

Under the name **Berthold Bodoni Antiqua,** this Bodoni family is sold by Adobe and other vendors that carry the Adobe library.

Berthold Bodoni Old Face

In 1983, Berthold released a new Bodoni family with less contrast—in other words, without any extremely narrow strokes that might not reproduce well on printers with poor resolution, including some of the early equipment used with personal computers. At Berthold, Günter Gerhard Lange was in charge of the design team that produced this effort, named **Berthold Bodoni Old Face** in tribute to its use of contrast norms reminiscent of Old Style designs. This family, too, is accompanied by an Expert Collection, with the same extra ligatures that are available for the **Antiqua** types. If you compare the **Old Face** specimen in Figure 6.6 with the **Antiqua** sample in Figure 6.5, the heavier look of the **Old Face** should be immediately apparent.

6.6 Berthold Bodoni Old Face, released in 1983.

Bauer Bodoni

The Bauer version of Bodoni was cut in 1926 by Louis Höll, under the supervision of Heinrich Jost. It's more delicate than the other Bodoni revivals shown here. Its proportions, fine lines, and contrast have attracted supporters for many years who've claimed that it is the most authentic Bodoni available. Here it is again in Figure 6.7.

For 45 years Giambattista Bodoni served as the director of a royal printing office for the Duke of Parma. This appointment offered him the time and luxury of undertaking almost any kind of printing project that appealed to him, with no necessity to turn a profit. He established his own foundry and cut new typefaces that differed sharply from the Fournier and Didot designs with which he began this career. His work was widely praised and copied. However, the scholarly content of his books was in doubt because of sloppy proofreading. His personal interest was in the appearance of a page, not its content.

6.7 Bauer Bodoni, released in 1926.

ITC Bodoni

Bauer has a new rival, **ITC Bodoni,** released in 1994. For this project, ITC engaged Sumner Stone as art director. You'll see several of his other designs throughout this book. He's probably best known for his **ITC Stone** typefaces, which consist of related serif, sans-serif, and informal families, originally created for Adobe. The purpose of the Bodoni assignment was to create a new Bodoni family based on the historic originals. Therefore, ITC sent Stone to Parma to examine Bodoni's actual types and many of the books he printed, which are preserved in a museum there. Stone was accompanied on the trip by Janice Prescott Fishman and Holly Goldsmith, who were to join him in designing members of the new family; Allan Haley, who at the time was

ITC's executive vice president; and Ilene Strizver, ITC director of typeface development. Later, back in the United States, designer Jim Parkinson was added to the team.

The result? Stone was pleased. His group did not try to simplify the geometry of the characters—a failing in earlier Bodoni revivals. The faces are lively rather than coldly formal. Furthermore—within reason—they tried to follow Bodoni's practice of designing slightly different characters to be used in different sizes. Consequently, **ITC Bodoni** is offered in Six, Twelve, and Seventy-Two versions—the numbers referring to the point size for which each was created. Of course, each version will work beautifully when printed in a range of other point sizes somewhat larger or smaller than the referenced size.

You can see **ITC Bodoni** in Figure 6.8. The family includes small caps, lowercase figures, and even swash

Bodoni and the Duke of Parma

"Beauty is founded on harmony, subordinate to the critique of reason."

For 45 years Giambattista Bodoni served as the director of a royal printing office for the Duke of Parma. This appointment offered him the time and luxury of undertaking almost any kind of printing project that appealed to him, with no necessity to turn a profit. He established his own foundry and cut new typefaces that differed sharply from the Fournier and Didot designs with which he began this career. His work was widely praised and copied. However, the scholarly content of his books was in doubt because of sloppy proofreading. His personal interest was in the appearance of a page, not its content.

6.8 ITC Bodoni, released in 1994.

capitals. You can order it directly from ITC if you don't find it available from other vendors

Figure 6.9 shows the **ITC Bodoni Seventy-Two** swash capitals designed by Sumner Stone. Of course, these letters are intended for display use and therefore are provided only with italics in the 72-point format.

Bodoni was born in 1740. His father was the master printer of Saluzzo, Italy, from whom he learned printing and block engraving. He was hired by the Vatican printing house at age 18 and eventually became the Royal Printer to the Duke of Parma. This portrait is from the Manuale Tipografico, the specimen book published by his widow.

6.9 The ITC Bodoni Seventy-Two swash capitals.

OTHER MODERN TYPEFACES

In the remainder of the chapter, I'll discuss other typefaces in the Modern category. Many reveal the debt they owe to Bodoni.

Berthold Walbaum

Berthold Walbaum is the exception to the Bodoni frenzy. It was designed about 1805 by Justus Erich Walbaum, a talented German typefounder and printer. He based this work on Didot's types, using strong contrast and unbracketed serifs. A century later, the Berthold foundry bought Walbaum's original matrices. Günter Gerhard Lange created the Berthold version in 1975, using Walbaum's original 16-point matrices as a model. The digital release includes an Expert Collection containing small caps, lowercase figures, and extra ligatures including *ff* and *ffi*, which I've used in Figure 6.10.

Bodoni and the Duke of Parma

"Beauty is founded on harmony, subordinate to the critique of reason."

For 45 years Giambattista Bodoni served as the director of a royal printing office for the Duke of Parma. This appointment offered him the time and luxury of undertaking almost any kind of printing project that appealed to him, with no necessity to turn a profit. He established his own foundry and cut new typefaces that differed sharply from the Fournier and Didot designs with which he began this career. His work was widely praised and copied. However, the scholarly content of his books was in doubt because of sloppy proofreading. His personal interest was in the appearance of a page, not its content.

6.10 Berthold Walbaum, released in 1975.

Hermann Zapf's Melior

Adobe places **Melior** in the Slab Serif category, which I discuss in the next chapter. However, most authorities consider it a Modern. It was designed by the great Hermann Zapf, who made use of the *superellipse*—a squared-off circle— in the shaping of its characters. Zapf created **Melior** for Linotype. It was originally intended as a newspaper text face and released in 1952. This design, as you can see in Figure 6.11, bears little resemblance to the Bodonis. **Melior** has been widely copied by other foundries.

Bodoni and the Duke of Parma

"Beauty is founded on harmony, subordinate to the critique of reason."

For 45 years Giambattista Bodoni served as the director of a royal printing office for the Duke of Parma. This appointment offered him the time and luxury of undertaking almost any kind of printing project that appealed to him, with no necessity to turn a profit. He established his own foundry and cut new typefaces that differed sharply from the Fournier and Didot designs with which he began this career. His work was widely praised and copied. However, the scholarly content of his books was in doubt because of sloppy proofreading. His personal interest was in the appearance of a page, not its content.

6.11 Linotype's Melior, released in 1952.

ITC Modern No. 216

Ed Benguiat designed **ITC Modern No. 216** to be a contemporary addition to the ranks of Modern typefaces. He achieved his goal admirably. It's available in Light, Medium, Bold, and Heavy weights and was released in 1982. However, with its very large x-height, heavy brackets, exaggerated spurs, and sharply curved lowercase tails, it cannot be called a Didot or a Bodoni. Rather, it has the individualistic ornate touches that often distinguish Benguiat designs. Judge for yourself by studying Figure 6.12. Incidentally, I was curious as to how the family got the mysterious 216 portion of its name. No one seemed to know. Finally, I asked Benguiat himself and found that 216 simply refers to the street address of the design company with which he was affiliated when he drew it.

You won't find **Modern No. 216** available from all foundries that normally sell ITC-licensed typefaces. You can order it from Linotype-Hell.

Bodoni and the Duke of Parma

"Beauty is founded on harmony, subordinate to the critique of reason."

For 45 years Giambattista Bodoni served as the director of a royal printing office for the Duke of Parma. This appointment offered him the time and luxury of undertaking almost any kind of printing project that appealed to him, with no necessity to turn a profit. He established his own foundry and cut new typefaces that differed sharply from the Fournier and Didot designs with which he began this career. His work was widely praised and copied. However, the scholarly content of his books was in doubt because of sloppy proofreading. His personal interest was in the appearance of a page, not its content.

6.12 ITC Modern No. 216, released in 1982.

Torino

Torino—seen in Figure 6.13—is a condensed Modern family created by the Nebiolo foundry in Turin in 1908. It's elegant and distinctive. The entire family is available from Agfa. Bitstream offers its versions of the basic roman and italic variants only.

Zapf Book

More than 20 years after creating **Melior,** Hermann Zapf designed another Modern family using the superellipse; it was developed for ITC and called **ITC Zapf Book.** Released in 1976, it's available from many vendors and includes Light, Medium, Demi, and Heavy weights. **Zapf Book** features less contrast than **Melior,** wider strokes, and a larger x-height—obvious characteristics displayed in Figure 6.14. He drew a third superellipse family around the same time, also for ITC, called **Zapf International.**

Bodoni and the Duke of Parma

"Beauty is founded on harmony, subordinate to the critique of reason."

For 45 years Giambattista Bodoni served as the director of a royal printing office for the Duke of Parma. This appointment offered him the time and luxury of undertaking almost any kind of printing project that appealed to him, with no necessity to turn a profit. He established his own foundry and cut new typefaces that differed sharply from the Fournier and Didot designs with which he began this career. His work was widely praised and copied. However, the scholarly content of his books was in doubt because of sloppy proofreading. His personal interest was in the appearance of a page, not its content.

6.13 Torino, released in 1908.

Bodoni and the Duke of Parma

"Beauty is founded on harmony, subordinate to the critique of reason."

For 45 years Giambattista Bodoni served as the director of a royal printing office for the Duke of Parma. This appointment offered him the time and luxury of undertaking almost any kind of printing project that appealed to him, with no necessity to turn a profit. He established his own foundry and cut new typefaces that differed sharply from the Fournier and Didot designs with which he began this career. His work was widely praised and copied. However, the scholarly content of his books was in doubt because of sloppy proofreading. His personal interest was in the appearance of a page, not its content.

6.14 ITC Zapf Book, released in 1976.

Letraset Charlotte

Figure 6.15 shows **Charlotte,** which Michael Gills designed for Letraset (Esselte Letraset Ltd., the British company that purchased ITC several years ago). Although Gills was influenced by Fournier's designs, **Charlotte** is a Modern family featuring vertical stress and unbracketed serifs. The family members are Book, Book Italic, Medium, Bold, and Small Caps; there is no bold italic. Gills also designed **Charlotte Sans,** a matching sans-serif family. Both families were released in 1992 and are available in Letraset's Fontek library. Since these typefaces are not mannered or extreme in any way, they fit unobtrusively into almost any text assignment.

Bodoni and the Duke of Parma

"Beauty is founded on harmony, subordinate to the critique of reason."

For 45 years Giambattista Bodoni served as the director of a royal printing office for the Duke of Parma. This appointment offered him the time and luxury of undertaking almost any kind of printing project that appealed to him, with no necessity to turn a profit. He established his own foundry and cut new typefaces that differed sharply from the Fournier and Didot designs with which he began this career. His work was widely praised and copied. However, the scholarly content of his books was in doubt because of sloppy proofreading. His personal interest was in the appearance of a page, not its content.

6.15 Letraset Charlotte, released in 1992.

ITC Fenice

The talented Italian designer Aldo Novarese is responsible for **Fenice,** which was produced for Berthold in 1977 and

For 45 years Giambattista Bodoni served as the director of a royal printing office for the Duke of Parma. This appointment offered him the time and luxury of undertaking almost any kind of printing project that appealed to him, with no necessity to turn a profit. He established his own foundry and cut new typefaces that differed sharply from the Fournier and Didot designs with which he began this career. His work was widely praised and copied. However, the scholarly content of his books was in doubt because of sloppy proofreading. His personal interest was in the appearance of a page, not its content.

6.16 ITC Fenice, released in 1977.

licensed to ITC in 1980. This family is a dramatic contrast to **Charlotte. Fenice** is easily recognizable and attracts attention to itself because of its large x-height, condensed characters, sharp spurs, and other stylistic traits. Therefore, you might not want to use it for extensive text passages. It's available in Light, Regular, Bold, and Ultra weights, with matching oblique faces rather than italics. Note the **Bold Oblique** used for the quotation below the heading in Figure 6.16; it's simply a slanted version of the family's Bold member.

Ellington

Monotype's **Ellington** was named in tribute to the great jazz composer/musician Duke Ellington. The family was drawn by Michael Harvey, an eminent lettering artist who combined the Modern form with calligraphic touches in this 1990 release. Its letters are condensed but highly readable, as you can verify in Figure 6.17. It has a large x-height and is heavier than most Moderns. The design is offered in Light, Regular, Bold, and Extra Bold weights, with matching italics. There are no small caps or lowercase figures. This is another distinctive Modern that is too recognizable for extensive text use.

In 1995 Monotype released a matching sans-serif family called **Strayhorn,** also designed by Harvey.

Bodoni and the Duke of Parma

"Beauty is founded on harmony, subordinate to the critique of reason."

For 45 years Giambattista Bodoni served as the director of a royal printing office for the Duke of Parma. This appointment offered him the time and luxury of undertaking almost any kind of printing project that appealed to him, with no necessity to turn a profit. He established his own foundry and cut new typefaces that differed sharply from the Fournier and Didot designs with which he began this career. His work was widely praised and copied. However, the scholarly content of his books was in doubt because of sloppy proofreading. His personal interest was in the appearance of a page, not its content.

6.17 Ellington, released in 1990.

Linotype Modern

Figure 6.18 shows **Linotype Modern,** drawn in 1969 by Walter Tracy at Linotype for the *London Daily Telegraph* and intended to provide a Modern family suitable for newspaper work. The design is sturdy with a large x-height. Bitstream offers a version with Roman, Italic, and Bold variations; there is no bold italic. Strangely enough, Linotype itself does not sell a digital version.

For 45 years Giambattista Bodoni served as the director of a royal printing office for the Duke of Parma. This appointment offered him the time and luxury of undertaking almost any kind of printing project that appealed to him, with no necessity to turn a profit. He established his own foundry and cut new typefaces that differed sharply from the Fournier and Didot designs with which he began this career. His work was widely praised and copied. However, the scholarly content of his books was in doubt because of sloppy proofreading. His personal interest was in the appearance of a page, not its content.

6.18 Linotype Modern, released in 1969.

Monotype Modern

In the early years of the twentieth century, the Monotype staff began designing a series of Modern designs that could be used with its Monotype automatic metal typesetting system, which had been in production since 1894. Monotype currently offers digital versions of some of these types in a family that includes these variations: **Condensed, Bold, Extended,** and **Wide**—each with accompanying italics. I've created three figures for the family, in order to demonstrate the tremendous differences in appearance caused by choosing the various text members. In all of these figures, the heading and quotation remain unchanged—being shown in Bold and Bold Italic, respectively, in each version. However, each of the roman text faces appears in a separate figure.

First, look at Figure 6.19. The text face here is **Modern Condensed,** which manages to achieve a certain delicacy,

6.19 Monotype Modern with the Condensed text face.

despite its relatively heavy weight and minimal contrast between thick and thin strokes. Some lowercase characters terminate in decorative hooks, and the x-height is moderate.

The next example (Figure 6.20) shows a text face that you might think would be called **Regular** or **Book** or **Roman**, indicating that it's the primary text offering in the family. It's much wider than the **Condensed** version and looks rather conventional. You could use it almost anywhere. Nevertheless, Monotype calls this face **Extended**—as if it were strictly an alternate choice. Its design characteristics are approximately the same as the **Condensed**.

Finally, in Figure 6.21, we have the same layout with **Monotype Modern Wide** used as the text face. This is a drastically altered vision of the design. Note that the x-height is huge and the lowercase descenders almost nonexistent. This makes for a text face that would be very attractive if used in

Bodoni and the Duke of Parma

"Beauty is founded on harmony, subordinate to the critique of reason."

For 45 years Giambattista Bodoni served as the director of a royal printing office for the Duke of Parma. This appointment offered him the time and luxury of undertaking almost any kind of printing project that appealed to him, with no necessity to turn a profit. He established his own foundry and cut new typefaces that differed sharply from the Fournier and Didot designs with which he began this career. His work was widely praised and copied. However, the scholarly content of his books was in doubt because of sloppy proofreading. His personal interest was in the appearance of a page, not its content.

6.20 Monotype Modern with the Extended text face.

Bodoni and the Duke of Parma

"Beauty is founded on harmony, subordinate to the critique of reason."

For 45 years Giambattista Bodoni served as the director of a royal printing office for the Duke of Parma. This appointment offered him the time and luxury of undertaking almost any kind of printing project that appealed to him, with no necessity to turn a profit. He established his own foundry and cut new typefaces that differed sharply from the Fournier and Didot designs with which he began this career. His work was widely praised and copied. However, the scholarly content of his books was in doubt because of sloppy proofreading. His personal interest was in the appearance of a page, not its content.

6.21 Monotype Modern with the Wide text face.

an advertising blurb of a couple of lines, but that is entirely too radical for easy reading as a main body-copy typeface. In fact, it's inappropriate for this layout.

So, **Monotype Modern** teaches us that typefaces can be vastly different from one another and still belong to the same Modern category—and even the same type family. Also, each member has its uses.

The Century Family

The **Century** family doesn't offer much superficial resemblance to most Moderns because those distinctive hairline strokes have been made wider and decorative touches have been held to a minimum. Other characteristics are a large x-height and bracketed serifs. Some authorities say the Century variations don't even belong in the Modern category, that they should be considered Transitionals—or even Slab Serifs, as a form of modified **Clarendon** (see Chapter 7).

The **Century** story started when the publisher of *Century Magazine* asked Linn Boyd Benton at ATF to create a new typeface for the publication. He accepted the commission and called the face **Century Roman;** it was completed in 1894. However, members of the Typographical Union complained that the design should have had wider characters because of its large x-height. Benton listened and had his son, Morris Fuller Benton, make the changes. The result was **Century Expanded.**

During World War I, a textbook publisher asked ATF to design a typeface with maximum legibility, one that would be appropriate for elementary school children. Morris Benton did some research, then created **Century Schoolbook,** released in 1918. It's still used in textbooks today.

ITC Century Book

Century Handtooled

Century Expanded

Century Bold Condensed

Century Ultra

New Century Schoolbook

Century Schoolbook
Monospace

6.22 Some members of the large Century family.

In 1975, ATF licensed ITC to update and expand the **Century** family. Tony Stan was the designer. Ed Benguiat added **ITC Century Handtooled** based on Stan's work.

You can see many of the **Century** variants in Figure 6.22. They're all available from Adobe and most other type vendors, with the exception of **Century Schoolbook Monospace,** which you can order from Bitstream.

SUMMARY

Finishing up our journey through the Modern revolution that Didot and Bodoni started, we can see that the category went through several stages. First, it became the latest fad, then the standard way of looking at type, then old-fashioned and obsolete, and—at last—back in fashion again. Today many designers are creating Modern designs, and typographers and printers are making generous use of the older ones.

I certainly haven't shown you all of the Modern faces available, any more than I've shown all of the worthy candidates for consideration in the categories previously discussed. There wouldn't be room in a volume of any reasonable size. However, I hope that you've seen enough members of each to get a feel for the classification and to discover some great designs you'd like to use yourself. Now let's explore more categories; hundreds of other typefaces are worthy of your consideration.

7

Slab Serif Typefaces

In Chapter 4, I gave you some background on various serif type categories, including some of the Slab Serif varieties. As you may recall, I explained that bold, heavy types became popular early in the nineteenth century because of the increase in printing related to advertising. The printers wanted designs that would stand out and attract attention; in addition, as a result of the proliferation of flyers, handbills, and posters, they also wanted type that would reproduce well on cheap, porous paper. The early Slab Serifs were called *Antiques. Mechanistic* became another term for the category, since some experts stated that the designs were based on mechanical principles. But most soon acquired the name *Egyptians.* Both the *Antique* and *Egyptian* designations were derived from the English public's fascination with Egyptian artifacts, subsequent to Napoleon's military defeats at the hands of the British during his ill-fated Egyptian campaign. In actuality, these typefaces were neither antique nor Egyptian in origin. They were the latest craze—something very different from the refined Didots and Bodonis that had dominated the publishing field for so many years previously.

As you'll find, there are several classifications within the broad Slab Serif umbrella. However, these types usually feature heavy lines and curves of equal width, with rectangular serifs the same width as the strokes themselves. Most Slab Serifs are

7.1 A comparison of two typefaces in the Slab Serif category.

unbracketed and the faces have vertical stress. Figure 7.1 presents two examples, with differing characteristics.

The top example is Monotype's **Rockwell,** one of the most popular Slab Serif families. The original version was designed by William Schraubstädter in 1910 for the Inland foundry and was called **Litho Antique.** ATF revived it in the 1920s and added more weights. The Monotype version dates from 1934. This family actually fits into a Geometric group within the Slab Serif category—typefaces with rounded letters such as the lowercase *e* and *o* shown in the figure.

The bottom typeface is Bitstream's version of **Clarendon,** designed by Robert Besley in 1838. Clarendon is a Slab Serif category distinguished by the fact that the serifs are bracketed. For many years after the design's introduction in England, the word Clarendon was considered a synonym for bold. Note that this family does have some stroke contrast.

THE IMPACT OF A SLAB SERIF ON A PAGE

In Figure 7.2 I've given you an entire Slab Serif page, to show you how these designs usually create a strong, authoritative document. In addition, if you read the text of the page, you'll

Napoleon Invades Egypt

In February of 1798 France was involved in a sea war with England, and the government had selected Napoleon to command an army assembled to invade the British Isles. However, he insisted that the project could not succeed until France controlled the seas. Instead, he suggested an invasion of Egypt, which would cut off a source of British wealth and also, he said, restrict the enemy's access to India. This alternate strategy was approved.

At first the Egyptian campaign was very successful. Napoleon quickly occupied Malta, Alexandria, and the Nile delta. But the tide turned abruptly on August 1st. Admiral Nelson's British fleet destroyed the entire French naval squadron. Napoleon was now unable to leave the land he'd occupied. So he started to reform the Egyptian government, introducing European methods and technology, while he plotted his next military move.

He didn't have long to wait. Turkey declared war on France, claiming sovereignty over Egypt. In an attempt to forestall a Turkish invasion of Egypt and find a way home, he led his army into Syria early in 1799. The British met him at Acre, fended off a seige, and forced him to retreat back into Egypt. Finally, he managed to escape Egypt by sea in two frigates, leaving his army behind. The Egyptian campaign was over.

The British victories awakened a renewed interest in Egypt and its artifacts, many of which had been stolen and displayed in England.

7.2 A page composed with the Berthold City Slab Serif family.

learn more about Napoleon's Egyptian campaign, which inspired the application of the term Egyptian to these typefaces. The type I've used here is the **City** family, designed for Berthold in 1930 by Georg Trump. It fits into a group called Square Slab Serif, because the design is based on the use of the square rather than the circle. The illustration is a photo from the extensive Corel stock library.

THREE SLAB SERIF DIVISIONS

Figure 7.3 shows you the three main Slab Serif divisions—Egyptian, humanist, and geometric. There aren't many examples available in digital form of the original, pure-bred Egyptians. **Antique No. 3** is one of them. This design dates back to about 1820 and features practically no stroke contrast, large square serifs the same width as the narrower strokes, and no brackets. Early typesetters used to use the face for emphasis and headings, while still relying on their traditional Moderns for setting text. You can buy **Antique No. 3** from Bitstream.

Early in the twentieth century, some designers began modifying the Slab Serif model by basing character proportions on the classic roman letters; typographers often refer to these variations as humanist Slab Serif. Then, after Germany's Bauhaus school and kindred innovators began grounding their art in geometric principles, other designers created Slab Serif geometric faces inspired primarily by the circle. The humanist example in Figure 7.3 is **Egyptienne**, completed in 1960 by the illustrious Adrian Frutiger. The geometric Slab Serif is **Memphis**, designed in 1929 by Emil Rudolf Weiss and soon copied by several foundries under other Egyptian-sounding names including **Alexandria, Cairo,**

Egyptian:

A DOG IS SMARTER than some people. It wags its tail and not its tongue.

Antique No. 3

Humanist Slab Serif:

A DOG IS SMARTER than some people. It wags its tail and not its tongue.

Egyptienne

Geometric Slab Serif:

A DOG IS SMARTER than some people. It wags its tail and not its tongue.

Memphis

7.3 The three principal Slab Serif divisions.

Pyramid, and **Karnak.** Note that **Egyptienne** fluctuates in stroke thickness, while **Memphis** has lines, curves, and serifs of the same width. Both families are available from Linotype-Hell or their licensees.

THE CLARENDONS

As mentioned in connection with Figure 7.1, the Clarendons have bracketed serifs and some stroke contrast. A few gurus don't want them in the Slab Serif classification at all; they call them Modern—or even Transitional. However, I think the Slab Serif connection is pretty strong.

There are even two groups within the Clarendon category: the conventional Clarendons and Clarendon Stub Serif, which—as the name indicates—are Clarendons with extremely short serifs. The standard Clarendon example in Figure 7.4 is **Ionic No. 5,** designed in 1925 as a newspaper text face by Chauncey Griffith at the Mergenthaler Linotype Company. This type family had a profound effect on newspaper typography for years afterward; many subsequent designs borrowed liberally from this model. The Stub Serif is

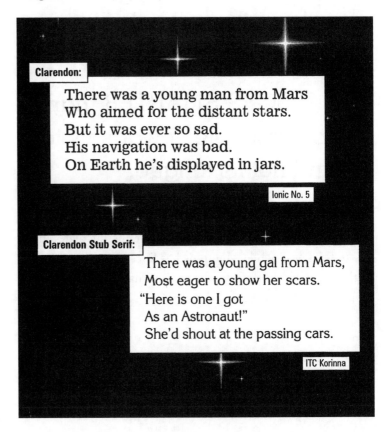

7.4 A Clarendon contrasted with a Clarendon Stub Serif.

ITC **Korinna,** introduced in 1904 at the Berthold foundry as an Art Nouveau design and revived with new weights in 1974 for ITC by Ed Benguiat and Vic Caruso. **Ionic No. 5** is a bit too heavy to use for extended text passages in today's market and **Korinna** is slightly mannered. I'd use the first for brief body-copy segments requiring emphasis and the second for decorative invitations and letterheads or fashion-related ads. Bitstream has the version of **Ionic No. 5** shown here. You can obtain ITC **Korinna** from most vendors.

Figure 7.5 is a reworking of the *Napoleon Invades Egypt* layout; this time I used **Aurora,** a Clarendon designed by Jackson Burke at Mergenthaler in 1960. I wanted to show

NAPOLEON INVADES EGYPT

In February of 1798 France was involved in a sea war with England, and the government had selected Napoleon to command an army assembled to invade the British Isles. However, he insisted that the project could not succeed until France controlled the seas. Instead, he suggested an invasion of Egypt, which would cut off a source of British wealth and also, he said, restrict the enemy's access to India. This alternate strategy was approved.

At first the Egyptian campaign was very successful. Napoleon quickly occupied Malta, Alexandria, and the Nile delta. But the tide turned abruptly on August 1st. Admiral Nelson's British fleet destroyed the entire French naval squadron. Napoleon was now unable to leave the land he'd occupied. So he started to reform the Egyptian government, introducing European methods and technology, while he plotted his next military move.

He didn't have long to wait. Turkey declared war on France, claiming sovereignty over Egypt. In an attempt to forestall a Turkish invasion of Egypt and find a way home, he led his army into Syria early in 1799. The British met him at Acre, fended off a seige, and forced him to retreat back into Egypt. Finally, he managed to escape Egypt by sea in two frigates, leaving his army behind. The Egyptian campaign was over.

The British victories awakened a renewed interest in Egypt and its artifacts, many of which had been stolen and displayed in England.

7.5 The Aurora family demonstrates how a Clarendon can change the layout on Napoleon.

you the difference in impact realized by replacing the Square Serif design with a Clarendon. Also, note that I changed the layout considerably. Now a giant heading seems to be toppling over the photo of the pharaoh, adding some symbolism to the story of the invasion. In addition, I split the body copy into two columns, which increases readability because the eye has a shorter distance to travel on each line. As you can see, **Aurora** is emphatic, but doesn't have the somewhat distracting idiosyncrasies of **City. Aurora** is available from Bitstream.

X-HEIGHT CHANGES CHELTENHAM

Cheltenham is a popular Clarendon Stub Serif drawn by architect Bertram Grosvenor Goodhue in 1896 at the request of Ingalls Kimball, director of the *Cheltenham Press* in New York City. Kimball wanted a stronger face than many of the anemic designs of the period. This design has long ascenders and short descenders because research studies at the time indicated that readers primarily recognize word shapes by scanning the upper half of the line. **Cheltenham** was refined by ATF and released in 1904. It was soon copied widely.

In 1975 Tony Stan undertook to revive **Cheltenham** for ITC. He lengthened the descenders, but his major changes were to increase the x-height tremendously and create a tight letterfit, in the typical ITC tradition. Compare the two versions in Figure 7.6; to the inexperienced eye they look like two entirely different designs. You can obtain the original **Cheltenham** from Bitstream. **ITC Cheltenham** is available everywhere.

There was an old man from Paris
Who did his best to embarrass.
At the fair he told bad jokes,
Plainly discomfited folks,
'Til they threw him off the ferris.

Cheltenham

There was an old man from Paris
Who did his best to embarrass.
At the fair he told bad jokes,
Plainly discomfited folks,
'Til they threw him off the ferris.

ITC Cheltenham

7.6 The original Cheltenham compared with the ITC version.

THE TYPEWRITER SLAB SERIFS

In a special Typewriter category of Slab Serifs you'll find those designs originally created specifically for use on typewriters or to bring back the look of typewriter-produced text as a bit of nostalgia in this computer era.

In Figure 7.7 the first example is **Courier,** introduced in Chapter 4. As you know, the characters are fixed-pitch or monospaced, with each taking up the same amount of horizontal space on a line. The second example is ITC's **American Typewriter,** a lively 1974 joint effort by Joel Kaden and Tony Stan that brings back the atmosphere of typewritten text in a proportional typeface. Note the geometric letterforms

7.7 A genuine typewriter typeface compared with a proportional revival.

in **Courier,** the lack of stroke contrast, and the unbracketed slab serifs. **American Typewriter,** on the other hand, shows some contrast and has bracketed slab serifs that terminate in a ball effect. Both designs are widely available in digital form. Of course, **Courier** is packaged with most computers and printers.

DISPLAY SLAB SERIFS PROVIDE COLOR

Slab Serif designs intended for use as display typefaces can be very helpful in setting the mood for documents with a historical emphasis. Figure 7.8 shows the **Ironmonger** family created by John Downer in 1991 through 1993 and available

7.8 The Ironmonger Slab Serif display family.

through the Font Bureau. Downer used as models the decorative iron lettering mounted as signs on the masonry walls of businesses in old commercial districts.

Adobe has released a series of Slab Serif designs based on wood type of the late nineteenth century. (See Chapter 12, which covers display faces.) Typefaces with this flavor have long been used to represent the Old West. An example is **Playbill,** which I used for the remake of the dude ranch billboard in Chapter 1. Another is **P. T. Barnum,** shown in Chapter 12. Bitstream refers to this entire group as **Circus.**

SUMMARY

Many Slab Serif designs are so distinctive that you must use them with caution; you can't just stick them on any page where you want a fresh typeface. Others—like the Clarendons—can be applied to a wider range of projects. In any case, the typical Slab Serif epitomizes strength, power, and authority. When you want to make a strong statement, a member of this category can be a good choice.

8

Other Serif Typefaces

Type historians and scholars have concocted an impressive list of typeface categories. Often, as you've seen in previous chapters, these experts don't agree with each other. Some even reject most of the standard names in favor of a private lexicon they can claim as their very own. For example, one prominent typographer and author uses these terms, each followed by the word Letter: Renaissance Roman, Renaissance Italic, Mannerist, Baroque, Rococo, Neoclassical, Romantic, Realist, Geometrical Modernist, and Postmodern—all as replacements for the categories I've already explained and discussed in this book.

Some experts even create separate categories for typefaces that are intended to look as if they were generated by a computer or stenciled. I prefer to include such designs in "catch-all" classifications such as Display or Novelty.

However, I hope you agree that some standards are helpful in understanding and using type. I've tried to use the terms and groupings that seem most widely accepted. This chapter puts the spotlight on some smaller serif categories with which you should be familiar.

LATIN AND FLARESERIF FACES

In the nineteenth century a few designers started creating new seriffed typefaces that were not Slab Serifs, nor did they fit into previously popular categories. They had triangular serifs ending in sharp points and soon came to be called *Latins.* By the early twentieth century they were joined by *Flareserifs,* Latins with serifs that flare out subtly from the main strokes to form triangular tips. Latins often feature inclined stress, usually use a horizontal crossbar on the lowercase *e,* and exhibit some stroke contrast.

Figure 8.1 compares a Latin design with a Flareserif. The Latin example is **Méridien,** designed by Adrian Frutiger in 1957 and distributed by Linotype-Hell. As a family, it offers elegance and readability. The Flareserif is **Albertus,** designed

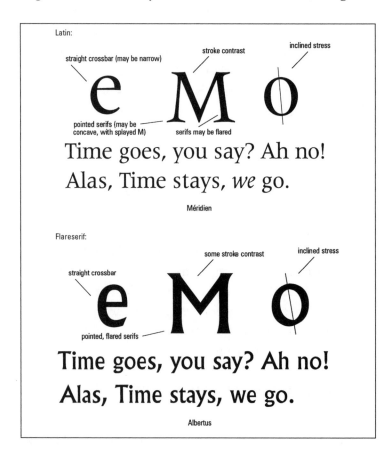

8.1 A comparison of Latin and Flareserif typefaces.

for Monotype by Berthold Wolpe in 1932. The lowercase characters were added in 1940. **Albertus** is primarily a display face and was inspired by Rudolf Koch's 1923 **Neuland** design, which had been copied by Monotype as **Othello.**

Figure 8.2 shows a few more typefaces in these two categories. The ITC releases are sold by almost all type houses that are ITC subscribers. **ITC Novarese** is named for its designer, the noted Aldo Novarese. This stylish family was released in 1979 and licensed by ITC the following year; it

Latin:

Castles in the air are all right
until you try to move into them.

ITC Novarese

Castles in the air are all right
until you try to move into them.

Vendôme

Castles in the air are all right
until you try to move into them.

ITC Barcelona

Flareserif:

Castles in the air are all right
until you try to move into them.

Americana

Castles in the air are all right
until you try to move into them.

ITC Élan

8.2 More Latin and Flareserif examples.

works for both text and display applications. **Vendôme** was designed in 1952 by François Ganeau for Fonderie Olive, a famous French foundry, and is a playful updating of seventeenth-century French types. The crossbar on the lowercase *e* is slightly oblique, and you can see considerable variation in line width. The family has **Condensed** and **Black** members. Unfortunately, this versatile design is not available from many U.S. vendors. I obtained it from Image Club.

ITC Barcelona is another family designed by Ed Benguiat; it was released in 1981. The heavier weights abandon the Latin spiked-serif model for blunted corners, but the family still qualifies as belonging to the Latin classification. **Barcelona** is somewhat ornate, has the usual ITC large x-height, and—as is also customary for ITC releases—was designed for a close letterfit.

Americana is the work of Richard Isbell and, in 1966, was the first Flareserif to become popular in the United States. It features tapered strokes and an enormous x-height. It's suitable for headings and short paragraphs of text and can be purchased from most regular type sources.

ITC Élan is a 1985 release of an Albert Boton design. Strokes flare outward into small, pointed serifs. This is a strong family with minimal stroke variance. It also features a splayed *M* (not seen here) and lowercase bowls that don't quite close. (Note the *a* and the *g*.)

ENGRAVERS' AND INCISED FACES

In the late nineteenth century a variety of typefaces appeared that imitated the most popular designs used by copperplate and steelplate engravers; these types are commonly called *Engravers'* faces. A little later, *Incised* typefaces joined them:

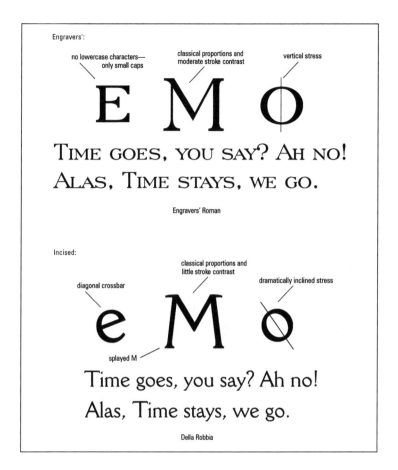

8.3 A comparison of typical Engravers' and Incised typefaces.

These are designs that mimic chiseled rather than etched letters. Figure 8.3 shows an example from each category. As mentioned in Chapter 4, other names used for the Incised category are *Glyphic* and *Lapidary*.

Engravers' Roman has been released under similar names by the major foundries since about 1899. As indicated in the figure, the design has no lowercase characters, only small caps. The characters are of classical proportions and exhibit little contrast. Stress is vertical. The version shown here is available from Bitstream.

Thomas M. Cleland based his **Della Robbia** design on rubbings he made of some fifteenth-century Florentine stone capitals during a trip to Italy. Unlike many Incised typefaces inspired by Roman inscriptions, **Della Robbia** does have lowercase characters. Note the classical proportions, minimal stroke contrast, heavily inclined stress, and the diagonal crossbar on the *e*. The design was named in honor of a fifteenth-century sculptor and released by ATF in 1902. Appropriate for the period in which it was created, it's slightly ornate and has an Art Nouveau flavor. You can buy it from Bitstream.

Figure 8.4 exhibits more examples in both categories. The first is **Bernhard Modern,** designed by Lucian Bernhard and released in 1937 by ATF. Despite its name, it's not a typeface in the Modern category, but rather a modern updating of the 1932 **Bernhard Booklet,** a face inspired by the small x-height Old Style designs used by engravers around the turn of the century. It's available from several of the major vendors. The Bitstream version includes many special characters, unusual ligatures, swash capitals, lowercase figures, small caps, and even ornaments. In Figure 8.4, the initial *Th* combination in the quotation is a ligature, as is the *fl* combination in the word *reflects*. The quotation itself is by the renowned writer Edith Wharton.

ITC Newtext was designed by Ray Baker and released by ITC in 1974. The family is his attempt to squeeze more words into a minimum space—not by narrowing the characters and creating a condensed design, but by widening the characters, using the example of extended copperplate engraving letterforms. The idea is that the letters are easily distinguishable without long ascenders and descenders because they're so wide. Since each line has no strokes that extend much above or below the huge x-height, lines can be

Engravers':

There are two ways of spreading light: to be the candle or the mirror that reflects it.

Bernhard Modern

There are two ways of spreading light: to be the candle or the mirror that reflects it.

ITC Newtext

Incised:

AS EUCLID SAID to King Ptolemy: there is no royal road to geometry.

Perpetua

AS EUCLID SAID TO
KING PTOLEMY:
THERE IS NO ROYAL
ROAD TO GEOMETRY.

Trajan

8.4 More examples of Engravers' and Incised typefaces.

squeezed much closer together. That's where the space-saving comes in. The family is large and available in a variety of weights from several vendors, including Bitstream, Linotype-Hell, and Image Club.

Perpetua can be termed an Old Style design, but it has the chiseled look and proportions of inscriptions on stone monuments. And why not? It was created by Eric Gill, who was a prominent stonecutter before he ever thought of designing typefaces. The family was released by Monotype between 1925 and 1932. The digital version includes an Expert Collection with special ligatures, small caps, and lowercase figures and is available through Adobe and its related vendors as well as from Monotype. This design invokes the spirit of the 1930s. It's attractive and legible, but not well-suited to contemporary subject matter.

Carol Twombly designed the popular **Trajan** for Adobe in 1989, based on classic Roman letterforms. It's available in Regular and Bold weights—no italics or lowercase. It's an excellent display face.

COMING SOON

THESE OLD RUINS
WILL BE REPLACED
BY A BEAUTIFUL NEW

SHOPPING MALL

8.5 Adobe's Charlemagne typeface.

The typeface in Figure 8.5 is **Charlemagne,** inspired by the Roman alphabets used in tenth-century England. The designer is Carol Twombly again. Adobe released it in 1990, also in Regular and Bold weights only. The photo is from the Corel library.

SUMMARY

You'll find specific uses for the four small categories profiled in this chapter—situations where other kinds of typefaces simply won't fill the bill. In addition, many Latins and Flareserifs are versatile enough that you can use them as general workhorses as well. But now let's move on to a huge category: sans-serif. As you might imagine, it has its own divisions for you to learn.

9

Sans-Serif Typefaces

As stated in Chapter 1, the term *sans-serif* simply means "without serifs." (*Sans* is the French word for "without.") Some experts now call sans-serif typefaces Lineales, which means "consisting of lines." We might interpret this definition as meaning, in relation to type, "consisting *solely* of lines"—in other words, no serifs or fancy ornaments.

Ancient Greek inscriptions contain the first sans-serif characters that have come to our attention. Those stone carvings had long been forgotten by 1816 when William Caslon IV published a specimen book in England that showed two short lines of capital letters without serifs. This seed grew. In 1825 a German foundry started selling a series of condensed sans-serif designs complete with lowercase characters. By 1832 three English foundries offered sans-serif types, but the English didn't add lowercase until 1835.

Most of the early sans-serifs were related to the Slab Serif designs that had become so popular: They were merely heavy Slab Serif types without the serifs and were used primarily for display work. Prestigious English printing houses were appalled at these "crude" innovations. Someone soon labeled them "grotesque." The name stuck and is used today with no insult intended. In fact, many designers have included the word grotesque in the names they've given their sans-serifs that fit into the nineteenth-century tradition. In casual speech, grotesque is often abbreviated to "grot." German designers call their types of this sort Grotesk.

In 1837 a Boston foundry responded to the European trend by introducing a series of sans-serifs and calling them "gothic" rather than grotesque. *Gothic* is a term that had been applied for centuries to faces in the blackletter category due to its German origins. (See Chapter 11, which is devoted to the blackletters.) Probably the foundry named its sans-serifs gothics because the bold fonts were heavy and black and were therefore reminiscent of blackletter designs. In any event, the gothic name caught on too; U.S. type designers are still attaching the word to some of their present-day sans-serif creations. By 1850 all the world's typefounders manufactured sans-serifs in endless variations on the grotesque or gothic models.

THE SANS-SERIF CLASSIFICATIONS

Figure 9.1 shows examples of the three principal kinds of sans-serif typefaces: *Grotesque* at the top, then *Humanist,* and finally *Geometric.* The Grotesque example is **Monotype Grotesque.** This is a large family, including condensed and extended faces, that is one of the best examples of the traditional grotesque. It was designed at Monotype under the supervision of F. H. Pierpont, released in 1926, and is actually an updating of a Berthold sans-serif, **Ideal Grotesque.** Note that **Monotype Grotesque** has vertical stress coupled with no stroke contrast. The lowercase *g* is one-story. Usually, a good clue to use in trying to identify any sans-serif typeface is to check the design of this character, since the *g* varies so widely throughout the category.

The second example in the figure is Hermann Zapf's famous 1958 design, **Optima.** Note the tapered, contrasting

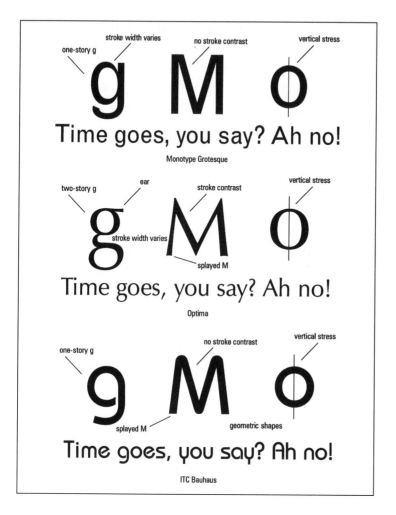

9.1 A comparison of typefaces in three sans-serif classifications.

strokes and the two-story *g*. This typeface belongs to the Humanist sans-serif group—faces that return for their inspiration to the classic Roman letterforms. In fact, its capital letters adhere to the proportions of the inscriptions on the Trajan Column in Rome, completed in 113 A.D.

The third typeface is **ITC Bauhaus,** named for the influential Bauhaus school and created by Ed Benguiat and Vic Caruso in 1975. It's based on the **Universal Alphabet** designed by Herbert Bayer in 1925 while he was a member of the faculty at the Bauhaus in Dessau, Germany. The school's goal was to reduce the elements of art to essentials, basing designs primarily on geometric principles; the slogan: "Less is more." Bayer, in particular, argued for a "*universal*" alphabet that everyone could use, that would have no capital letters because they weren't needed, and that would be constructed of as few arcs and straight lines as possible. You might term it a "mass production" approach to typography. Letters would be created from a pool of a minimum number of components. Any nonessential stroke or detail would be eliminated. He drew the **Universal Alphabet** to illustrate his ideas.

Although Benguiat and Caruso used this alphabet as a starting point, they wisely added harmonious capitals, knowing that capital letters are really very important to the reader in identifying elements of text. They also modified many of the lowercase characters to make them easier to identify. The result is a family that has a unique appearance and is an excellent choice for contemporary headings or short paragraphs of text.

Most Geometric sans-serif typefaces have been based on Bauhaus principles. The successful designers—like Benguiat and Caruso—realize that the Bauhaus staff frequently subordinated practicality and legibility to the rigid artistic code they had contrived. Consequently, tempering Bauhaus principles with common sense has resulted in a number of notable and usable designs.

The introduction of the Geometric and Humanist sans-serifs caused some publication designers to proclaim that the serif typeface was dead. Sans-serif was the wave of the future, denoting progress and the shedding of extraneous detail. However, as I hope I convinced you with the Rotis experiment in Chapter 2, serif typefaces are easier to read *because of the detail they provide.* Furthermore, many new serif faces have been designed in the last few years, with contemporary touches that make text both fresh and readable. In general, I'd use sans-serifs for short blocks of text and for headings—when the message and mood indicate their use. Some of the newer black, poster-type sans designs can be incredibly effective for display work. For example, check out **Berlin Sans,** shown later in the chapter.

CARRYING THE SANS-SERIF STYLE TO EXTREMES

Does the absence of serifs severely restrict the artistic capabilities of a type designer? After all, how much can you accomplish by merely drawing lines and curves? Well, take a look at Figure 9.2. Here you'll see nine different sans-serif lowercase *a* designs. Notice how unusual some of them are. However, if you encountered a couple of the futuristic designs in an actual reading situation, I'm afraid you'd only be able to identify this letter of the alphabet by noting its position in a known word.

To satisfy your curiosity, here are the typefaces represented in Figure 9.2, reading from the top left to the lower right: **Futura 2, Monaco, Helvetica, Digital, Media, Pasadena, Ragtime, Lynz,** and **Tabasco. Futura 2** and **Helvetica** are sold by most major type vendors. **Monaco** is provided with the Macintosh operating system. **Lynz** is an Image Club design. The other typefaces are all available as part of the Serials type collection sold in the United States on a Brendel CD-ROM.

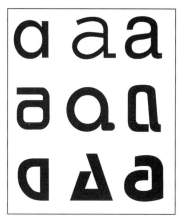

9.2 Nine different lowercase a designs.

Savant Declares Flight By Humans Impossible

Insists New Verne Book Is A Ridiculous Fantasy

Asked after a lecture to comment on the new Jules Verne book From the Earth to the Moon, Professor Hector Blather scoffed at its premise and ridiculed its author.

"My many scientific experiments in this area are well known," Prof. Blather remarked. "As I have stated on many occasions, I have proven beyond the shadow of a doubt that it is absolutely impossible for man to fly, even from one field to the next, let alone to leave this planet. The idea is sheer nonsense."

When he was reminded of other Verne writings that have seemed to predict actual events, Prof. Blather responded sharply: "Pure coincidence. A hundred years from now everyone will realize that the man is an idiot."

9.3 The Bureau Grotesque typeface family.

AN UP-TO-DATE GROTESQUE

Since the Grotesque sans-serifs originated early in the nineteenth century and increased in number tremendously year after year, you might think that we have long had enough entries in this group to provide the perfect choice for any job. Of course, no one ever has enough typefaces, so the answer to that implied question is "no." One of the most popular families of recent origin is **Bureau Grotesque,** released by the Font Bureau in 1989 through 1993. It was designed by David Berlow for use by some major publishing companies and includes many weights. You can see three of its members in the newspaper clipping displayed in Figure 9.3.

Incidentally, you'll find that many sans-serif designs consist of large families. The reason is that, starting late in the nineteenth century, typefounders discovered that they could increase their income significantly by marketing their designs in families. Printers would be encouraged to buy *all* the members of a family in order to be prepared for any occasion; the foundries were particularly successful at selling sans-serifs in this way. Therefore, they created many versions of each design, including condensed and expanded members. The tradition has continued to this day, even though the possible additional income to be achieved is no motivation when digital families are considered. After all, your computer will automatically create any size font you want. In the metal-type era, the poor printer had to buy each and every size he wanted of each variation of the design.

Some type scholars place contemporary sans-serifs such as **Bureau Grotesque** into a separate category, calling them neo-grotesques because they contain modifications to improve their appearance and are therefore not entirely historically accurate. I personally feel that the extra category is not needed; if you followed the reasoning of these scholars to its logical conclusion, you'd have "neo" versions of every type classification.

SEEING HOW SANS-SERIFS WORK

In this section of the chapter, you'll have the opportunity of seeing some standard sans-serifs at work. The subject is an announcement for a mythical university program, which I've reproduced using several different typefaces for the text. In each version, the elements remaining the same are the illustration—which is clip art from the Metro library—and the heading typeface, **Space,** a recent release created by the Bitstream staff.

Franklin Gothic

In Figure 9.4, the text is printed in **Franklin Gothic,** one of the most successful and enduring Grotesques. It's a skillful updating of the nineteenth-century models, with some

The University announces a few openings in our space program operated in conjunction with NASA. Applicants must be graduate students in science, engineering, or mathematics, with an outstanding record of academic achievement and excellent faculty recommendations. For information, see your department head.

9.4 An imaginary university announcement, with the text displayed in the Bitstream version of Franklin Gothic.

Roman touches added. Drawn by Morris Fuller Benton for ATF, it was completed in 1902 but not released until 1905. Ironically, the design was named for Benjamin Franklin, who died 26 years before the first sans-serif appeared. **Franklin Gothic** is available in several weights from various vendors. In this figure you see the Bitstream version, which reproduces closely the rather heavy original Benton release; it's an excellent choice for bold headings and strong text passages.

Move on to Figure 9.5 now and see **Franklin Gothic Book,** a much lighter weight developed in 1979 for ITC by Vic Caruso and licensed to Adobe and most other vendors. ITC has changed the design by making the characters slightly condensed, increasing the x-height, and employing a tighter letterfit. The alterations make **Franklin Gothic** a serviceable text face, but show little resemblance to the previous example. The real point here is—again—that many sans-serifs are available in large families, with members suited for almost any purpose.

9.5 The same announcement using ITC Franklin Gothic Book for the text.

Futura

Futura is the family featured in Figure 9.6. It was designed in Germany by Paul Renner and released by Bauer in 1927, after the foundry eliminated some design idiosyncrasies that had been inspired by the success of the Bauhaus. This is a Geometric that has been a standard for over half a century and is sold by most digital type houses. If you'll compare it with the **ITC Franklin Gothic** example, you can see immediately that, unlike **Franklin, Futura** has long ascenders and descenders and characters that are based on the circle whenever possible. I think it's a bit too elegant and old-fashioned for a space program announcement. It has also been overused for decades. Still, it's an enduring family, with many weights to ensure versatility—although some of the added weights were not designed by Renner.

Neuzeit Grotesk

C. Wilhelm Pischiner drew **Neuzeit Grotesk** for the Stempel foundry in 1928. It was one of the earliest Geometrics to

9.6 The same announcement with Futura as the text face.

have a large x-height. Figure 9.7 shows the Bitstream version of the design. Linotype added additional weights in 1959. The word *Neuzeit* translates from the German as "new times." This family is small, has no obvious oddities, and does not look dated. You can use it effectively both for display and short passages of text, but it's not offered by all vendors.

9.7 The same announcement with Neuzeit Grotesk as the text face.

Britannic

Britannic was designed in England at the Stephenson, Blake & Company foundry about 1901. This unusual condensed sans-serif is actually a Modern without the serifs. You can use it successfully both for headings and brief paragraphs of text. Because of its weight, it conveys a sense of authority, while its Modern ancestry makes it appear at the same time somewhat distinguished. However, it reflects tradition rather than the space age. The version shown in Figure 9.8 is from Digital Typeface Corporation, one of the few sources for this design.

If you were the person at our imaginary university assigned to produce the science program notice, you could use any of the sans-serifs I've applied to the layout without

The University announces a few openings in our space program operated in conjunction with NASA. Applicants must be graduate students in science, engineering, or mathematics, with an outstanding record of academic achievement and excellent faculty recommendations. For information, see your department head.

9.8 The same announcement with Britannic as the text face.

getting fired. But, if you were hoping for a *promotion,* I wouldn't use **Futura** or **Britannic.** Neither one fits in well with the high-tech message and format.

IS LESS REALLY MORE?

Before I discuss more popular sans-serifs with which you should be familiar, let's return to the Bauhaus credo for a moment. As I said earlier, the school's instructors believed in eliminating nonessentials in art and design—getting right down to the basics. Applying the policy to typefaces meant doing away with not only serifs and ornamentation, but also basic strokes of the characters, provided the characters could be identified without those strokes. In 1970 Aldo Novarese designed a set of capital letters based on the Bauhaus principles that I thought you'd enjoy seeing. Now, as we know, the Bauhaus teachers wanted to do away with capitals altogether, so you'll have to look at Novarese's design with that proviso in mind; Novarese did away with the lowercase

9.9 Aldo Novarese's Stop typeface design eliminates nonessential strokes.

characters instead. In any event, Figure 9.9 illustrates just how drastic a design can be when you carry the "Less is more" motto to an extreme. The name of his typeface is **Stop,** and you can obtain it through Linotype-Hell.

As you can see, Novarese felt that an *S* could be recognized without the inclusion of its top curve. *T, P,* and *E* were found to require only a portion of their main stroke. *R, B,* and *H* could do without a main stroke entirely. He modified several characters so he could run a repeating horizontal white streak through a line of text as a design element. In this figure, *T, P, R, E, I,* and *B* contribute to the continuation of the streak. The effect becomes particularly noticeable when two or more of these characters appear next to each other. In this sample, the *IE* and *IP* combinations demonstrate the effect.

The **Stop** typeface is a very creative work. If you use it sparingly in a heading consisting of one or two words, your readers will probably be able to decipher the message rather quickly, simply by relating each character mentally to the others surrounding it in a word. The design is sure to attract attention. However, some readers will be able to identify certain characters only by the process of elimination. For example, that *H* in *BAUHAUS* is not an *E* or an *F,* so it's probably an *H.* Nevertheless, looking at unfamiliar words, readers might never determine just what the *H* might be.

SOME VERY POPULAR SANS-SERIFS

Figure 9.10 shows several sans-serifs that are well known—and used too frequently. First is the **Gill Sans** family, drawn by Eric Gill. This design derived its inspiration—as did several other families—from an alphabet Edward Johnston designed in 1916 to be used in signs for the London Underground Railway. The alphabet is still in use for that purpose today. Johnston was a celebrated calligrapher and teacher, and Gill studied under him. Although **Gill Sans** has geometric elements, its classical proportions and pen-drawn touches identify it as a Humanist. As mentioned previously, Gill was a stonecutter; this experience also registers in the design. The family was released by Monotype beginning in 1928. It's available in a wide range of weights. It appears somewhat dated now, unless your goal in using it is to remind the reader of the 1920s and 30s. Although entire books have been set in **Gill Sans,** it's tiring to read hundreds of pages of this design.

I acquainted you with **Avant Garde** in Chapter 3. This Geometric was not only ITC's first typeface, but it also served as a guidepost for designers wanting to work for the company, since it illustrated perfectly the ITC passion for large x-height and close letterfit. Recent ITC designs have deviated occasionally from that policy, particularly since the company was purchased by Esselte Letraset. In any case, this landmark design has been "done to death" in recent years. If you want your layouts to appear fresh and innovative, you may want to select a different typeface—unless you want to use the extra ligatures shown in Chapter 3.

You encountered **Helvetica** way back in Chapter 1, a family that has been overused much more than **Avant Garde.** One reason is that, for many years, inexpensive PC and Macintosh printers came with **Times Roman** and **Helvetica** built-in, even when they didn't offer the remainder of the basic 35 PostScript typefaces. Another reason is that **Helvetica** doesn't call attention to itself; it has no weird characteristics. Therefore, you can use it again and again with few readers paying much attention to the repetition. It's

INFANT PRODIGIES are often children
with highly imaginative parents.

Gill Sans

INFANT PRODIGIES are often children
with highly imaginative parents.

Avant Garde

INFANT PRODIGIES are often children
with highly imaginative parents.

Helvetica

INFANT PRODIGIES are often children
with highly imaginative parents.

Eurostile

INFANT PRODIGIES are often children
with highly imaginative parents.

Antique Olive

9.10 Other popular sans-serif typefaces.

classified as a Grotesque—or Neo-Grotesque, if you will. Bitstream includes it in a special group they call Swiss, which encompasses types based on the predilection of the Swiss designers of the 1950s for making the white spaces within and around characters an integral part of the design. Every vendor offers some version of **Helvetica,** but I'd substitute something less familiar if you have the option.

Eurostile is another effort by the versatile Aldo Novarese. This 1962 release takes the Geometric form and squares it off. This is a large family, based on a capitals-only design Novarese developed 10 years earlier, called **Microgramma.**

The characters are basically *monolineal*—the strokes and curves are the same width throughout—with a large x-height. This family has been a favorite with publishers and advertising creative directors for so many years that you may want to give it a rest. In any event, it's easily identifiable, so if you use it, do so in moderation. Because of its attention-getting square construction, it's unsuitable for long passages of text. Most vendors can supply this family.

Antique Olive is an unusual typeface that mixes Humanist and Geometric elements with pen-drawn effects. It was designed by Roger Excoffon in 1962 and is an outgrowth of lettering he created as a logo for Air France. The *Antique* in its name comes from the fact that this word is often used in France as a generic term for sans-serifs. *Olive* is the name of the French foundry that released the typeface. The **Antique Olive** family is large and some consider it a good replacement for **Helvetica**. However, it's so individualistic that it fits best into specialized display and advertising blurb situations. It's widely available. To the Bitstream experts, the **Antique Olive** character shapes appear to have been cut out of metal, so they place this family into an Incised class.

Another, more obvious, member of this class is **ITC Eras**, designed by Albert Hollenstein and Albert Boton in Paris in 1968 and expanded into a family for ITC by Boton in 1976. Its capitals were inspired by Greek stone-cut lapidary letters, so I've displayed the design's various members in Figure 9.11 by using events from the life of the Greek hero Ulysses, as chronicled by the poet Homer.

Note that the **Eras** characters tilt slightly to the right and the face gives an angular impression because of the way the lines join. The bowls of some characters don't quite close and varying stroke weights add an interesting irregularity to the design. **Eras** can be used in many ways and would be a good

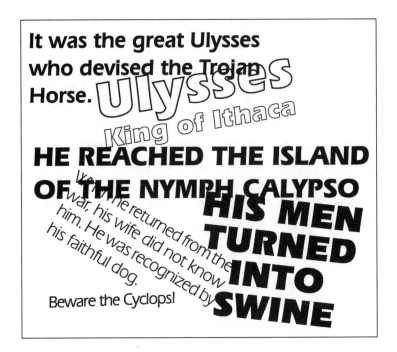

9.11 The ITC Eras type family.

addition to your library. Order it from ITC or most of its licensees.

A FRESH DESIGN YOU MAY WANT TO USE

New typefaces appear constantly, so it's easy to choose a design that won't seem out-of-date and overexposed. However, not all new designs are very creative or interesting. Fortunately, some digital foundries consistently produce outstanding additions to the world library of great typefaces. The Font Bureau is one of these. In Figure 9.12 you can see members of the **Berlin Sans** family. This design was inspired by a little-known alphabet drawn in the 1920s by Lucian Bernhard and is the work of David Berlow, assisted by Matthew Butterick. Although it has Geometric components—particularly in its lowercase—note that lines are irregularly shaped with hand-drawn effects. Strokes are tapered. The family includes four weights, complete with special characters and ornaments. The arrows in the figure provide an example of the ornaments. As for special characters, look at the subheading; it contains the *OO* letter combination as a ligature, as well as an alternate *S* in the word *TWENTIES* that extends below the baseline. The display type at the bottom of the document includes both a standard lowercase *s* and an alternate that extends below the baseline and begins the words *SOCIAL* and *SOMETHING;* also, the *st* and *rt* letter combinations are ligatures. In the body copy, you can find these additional ligatures: *Th, ct, fi, fl,* and *ff.*

Other ligatures not shown in the figure include these combinations: *ck, ffi, ffl, ft, rf,* and *tz.* **Berlin Sans** offers numerous alternate characters, including dual versions of *Q* and *W.*

You may ask, "Why would someone want to use an alternate version of a standard character such as an *s?*" The alternate capital *S* in *TWENTIES* serves to end the line with a little flourish. At the bottom of the document, the lowercase *s* used as the initial letter in two words adds subtle variety to the words. This induced irregularity inserts a definite hint of possible hand-lettering into two otherwise rigid typeset lines—because the other, standard *s* appears either alone or in ligatures elsewhere in the same lines.

The two versions of *s* are obviously related in design, although the alternate version is narrower than its counterpart, has less pronounced curves, and protrudes below the baseline. Therefore, it's okay to use them together. However, the typeface furnishes two versions of other characters that you wouldn't want to mix, because their basic design is not the same. For example, when you use this family, you can choose between a cursive lowercase *a* that

»ART IN BERLIN«
LOOKING AT THE TWENTIES

Going into the 1920s, Berlin was well acquainted with Expressionism and Abstraction as theories of art. These were rapidly joined by Futurism, Cubism, Constructivism, Suprematism, Elementarism, Dadaism, and Surrealism. Another significant influence was the Bauhaus, the prominent German school of art and design that stressed geometric forms and became, to many, almost a religion in itself. The effect of these philosophies could be seen in painting, drawing, sculpture, architecture, furniture design, plastics, the writing of fiction, the theater, and Germany's innovative motion pictures of the era.

From fantasy to social statement
»something for every young artist

9.12 The Font Bureau's Berlin Sans family.

resembles handwriting and a standard roman version. I used the cursive version throughout in Figure 9.12. You wouldn't want to combine these two. Also, the family contains both a one-story *g* and a two-story roman version. (Remember that a two-story *g* has a closed loop at the bottom.) I used the one-story *g* in the document. Using both together would simply look odd. The illustration in the figure is clip art from the Corel library.

Berlin Sans is a versatile family suitable for both display work and short body copy. Although it can evoke the era of the 1920s, its contemporary features make it an excellent choice for many other uses.

MORE SPECIAL CHARACTERS

Figure 9.13 shows **Bitstream Chianti.** This family is a Humanist sans-serif designed by Dennis Pasternak in 1991. It's a graceful and practical design, with no noticeable peculiarities to limit its use. It has a large Typographer Set (as Bitstream calls their expert sets) of extra characters and swash italics, some of which you can see in the figure. In addition, it offers a small caps set, a rare occurrence in sans-serif typefaces.

Let's analyze the figure, starting with the first line. If you ever tire of writing with computers, you might try quill pens; just remember that quill sharpening and dipping constitute quite an art. In any case, a school teaching this art could advertise very effectively using the handy ligatures in **Chianti.** The short words, *Learn Quills* contain four ligatures: *Le, ar, Qu,* and *ll.*

The second line of the figure is composed of **Chianti Italics** and **Swash Italics.** It is very stylish—and appropriate when discussing Bern, the lovely capital of Switzerland. The third line—which might be the name of a travel agency—is in **Chianti Bold** and includes small caps; the ligatures are *ar, la,* and *Co.* The family contains a variety of unusual ligatures, including *gg, HE, TT,* and *TY.*

9.13 Bitstream Chianti samples, showing ligatures and swash characters.

The final example lets you see the design without all the fancy stuff—just text as you'd probably use it most of the time. It holds up extremely well. The subtly tapered curves give it class and individuality without making it appear fussy or pretentious.

PERIOD ATMOSPHERE

If you want to establish a period in history with a typeface, you can do it using sans-serifs almost as well as you can with seriffed designs. Figure 9.14 provides three exhibits to help prove my case. The type in the top example is Ed Benguiat's **ITC Benguiat Gothic,** which he designed in 1979; the character shapes and proportions definitely project an Art Nouveau flavor. Most vendors carry this well-known product, which was created as a companion family to **ITC Benguiat,** shown in Chapter 4.

The Valentino typeface is **Letraset Plaza,** a 1975 design by Alan Meeks. The style is strongly Art Deco. This is a large family with many alternate characters. You can obtain this display version directly from Letraset's Fontek operation. URW stocks the entire family.

The bottom example is **Pilsner,** an innovative sans-serif family designed by Tobias Frere-Jones and released by the Font Bureau in 1995 (also sold by Agfa). The characters consist entirely of wide, straight, tapered lines. Curves are simulated by the joining of multiple strokes to form a series of angles. The family includes a full range of weights, ranging from light to black, but no italics. **Pilsner** has a rugged mechanical quality that calls to mind grimy factories of the early twentieth century. The design looks best if the characters are not too close together—in other words, if the tracking is loose.

Frere-Jones got the idea for the typeface while he was staring at the label on a bottle of beer in Paris, which is why he named it **Pilsner.** Of course, I'm sure he never drank any of the beer. After all, it's not safe to drink and draw.

New York's greatest new hotel opened on October 1, 1907. There were floors of Breche marble and mirrors hung with brocaded old-rose satin.

VALENTINO IN THE SHEIK

New Steam Plant

The new electric lighting station contains fourteen No. 32 dynamos driven by four 800 and three 250 horsepower compound engines. The steam is supplied by eight tubular boilers. Perfected apparatus determines exactly how much coal is consumed.

9.14 Typefaces that suggest periods in history.

SUMMARY

You'll see other sans-serif designs later in the book. Whether you want a strong headline, a delicate paragraph of text, or a legible, space-saving parts catalog, there are hundreds of typefaces in this category from which to choose. Many families have condensed, expanded, and black display members that I didn't show you in this chapter.

Since there are so many faces available, avoid extremes. Remember, the primary purpose of words is communication. If your readers can't decipher the characters or if the design detracts from the message, you haven't communicated much.

10

Script Typefaces

Script typefaces are relatively easy to spot. After all, words printed with them look as if they were written by hand, right? That's true, but gray areas exist. For example, italics are derived from handwriting. Furthermore, in Bitstream's classification system, the company even includes blackletter designs as scripts. However, most typographers consider such examples as belonging to other categories. The reasoning is that, although they were *derived* from handwriting, they have developed into separate classes.

The typefaces recognized as scripts are usually divided into three groups. *Brush script* includes those types that look as if they were lettered with a brush. *Calligraphic* refers to designs that appear to have been drawn with a broad-edged pen. *English roundhand* is a class sometimes called *copperplate scripts* because these designs were printed by means of engraved plates; types in this group have connecting letters and fine detail such as would be produced if the writer used a pointed pen. In the seventeenth and eighteenth centuries, roundhand was the standard method of writing expected of bookkeepers and others involved in commerce in England and was taught to schoolchildren by strict masters as the proper method of putting pen to paper. You can see examples of each group in Figure 10.1.

Brush Script

Letraset Flamme

Calligraphic

Lydian Cursive

English Roundhand or Copperplate

Englische Schreibschrift

10.1 The basic categories of script typefaces.

Letraset Flamme is a flamboyant Alan Meeks design completed in 1993; note that gaps in the letters imitate the streaks that would appear in strokes made by a wide-bristled brush. The design is available from Fontek.

Lydian Cursive was drawn by Warren Chappell in 1940 as an addition to a Lydian sans-serif series he had previously completed for ATF. He chose the name in honor of his wife Lydia. This script mimics drawing with a broad-edged pen held at a 45-degree angle. **Lydian Cursive** is legible and stylish and has remained popular. Bitstream has issued the entire family.

Englische Schreibschrift is a moderately flourished roundhand completed by staff designers at Berthold in 1970. The name translates as "English handwriting." It's well-liked by printers and designers and is available from Digital Typeface Corporation, URW, and Bitstream.

In addition to the three basic script categories, some experts define more. I'll call some of these to your attention as types in those groups are displayed later in the chapter.

MORE ROUNDHAND AND OTHER CONNECTING SCRIPTS

Figure 10.2 shows one of the most recent connecting scripts to be released: **ITC Edwardian Script.** Ed Benguiat is the designer. When I discussed it with him, he stressed that the script is Spencerian—a term often used to describe types in the roundhand tradition—and that it duplicates the effect of writing with a steel-point pen. This means that stroke width is changed by varying the pressure rather than by altering the angle as would be required with a flat-tipped writing instrument. Lines made by the two methods look quite different on paper.

Edwardian Script comes in regular and bold variants, with a full set of alternate capitals. You can buy it directly from ITC. Incidentally, Benguiat has designed over 600 typefaces in a 30-year period, and he's still at it. He also creates corporate identity packages.

Figure 10.3 shows the three variants of Matthew Carter's **Shelley,** which he calls **Andante, Allegro,** and **Volante.** Only the capital letters differ in the three versions; the flourishes become more elaborate in each succeeding rendition. He designed the family for Linotype in 1972. The little poem used in the samples was written by Emily Dickinson around 1884.

ITC Edwardian Script was designed by Ed Benguiat in 1994 and is based on lettering created with a steel-point pen.

10.2 ITC Edwardian Script

The Pedigree of Honey
Does not concern the Bee —
A Clover, any time, to him,
Is Aristocracy.

The Pedigree of Honey
Does not concern the Bee —
A Clover, any time, to him,
Is Aristocracy.

The Pedigree of Honey
Does not concern the Bee —
A Clover, any time, to him,
Is Aristocracy.

10.3 Matthew Carter's Shelley typeface, showing its three variants.

Figure 10.4 illustrates a variety of connecting scripts. The first is **Commercial Script,** designed by Morris Fuller Benton at ATF in 1908. This is a heavy, readable roundhand with minimal flourishes that is still in demand today. Next is **Lucia,** a light roundhand with looped ascenders that was created on an engravers' plate about 1900 and transformed into a machine-set typeface about 1955. The third is **Palace Script,** a standard English roundhand created for the Stephenson Blake foundry in 1923; this design very successfully imitates copperplate engraving through the medium of type. Bitstream offers all these typefaces.

The fourth example is **Künstler Script**—also known as **Künstler Schreibschrift**—designed by Hans Bohn for the Stempel foundry in 1957. This is slightly more elaborate and heavier than **Palace Script** and has looped ascenders. It's available from vendors of the Linotype library, including Adobe.

Flemish Script is a roundhand with looped ascenders and intricate flourishes on the capitals. The staff at Photon

Time is man's angel. —Schiller

Commercial Script

Time is man's angel. —Schiller

Lucia

Time is man's angel. —Schiller

Palace Script

Time is man's angel. —Schiller

Künstler Script

Time is man's angel. —Schiller

Flemish Script

Time is man's angel. —Schiller

Snell Roundhand

Time is man's angel. —Schiller

Gando

Time is man's angel. —Schiller

Linoscript

10.4 More connecting scripts.

originated it about 1960 for their phototypesetters. Bitstream provides it in digital form.

The next example is **Snell Roundhand,** a renowned typeface that Matthew Carter created for Linotype in 1966. It's named for a seventeenth-century writing master, Charles Snell, who wrote a book expressing his theories of penmanship; he wished to eliminate the use of excessive flourishes. This restrained design is available in regular, bold, and black versions.

Gando reflects a mid-eighteenth-century design by Nicholas Gando and was created by Hans Jurg Hunzicker and Matthew Carter for photocomposition at Mergenthaler in 1970. This is an excellent example of the French *Ronde* roundhand, which can be distinguished by its upright, rounded characters and large, looped ascenders. Ronde typefaces have long been used for formal invitations. You can buy **Gando** from Bitstream. Incidentally, the company considers Ronde types to be a separate group in the script category.

At the bottom of Figure 10.4 you can see **Linoscript,** which was copied for Linotype machine use in 1926 from a 1905 ATF design by Morris Fuller Benton that was called **Typo Upright.** This is a Ronde typeface with capital letters that are considerably different from those in **Gando** and more ornate. It's available through Linotype-Hell and its licensees, including Adobe and Agfa. Bitstream has the original **Typo Upright.**

CHANCERY SCRIPTS

Chancery scripts are a group that stems from the writing of Italian scribes in *chanceries,* the administrative offices in fifteenth-century courts and churches. Figure 10.5 shows a

10.5 The Poetica chancery family used in a perfume label.

sample of **Poetica,** a typeface in the chancery tradition that was designed at Adobe in 1992 by Robert Slimbach. The flowered border enclosing the text is a group of decorative corners from the Image Club DigitArt clip-art library. The type family itself includes ornaments, alternate swash characters, and even alternate character sets. Judging from the figure, you might say, "Well, it certainly has intricate swash capitals and fancy characters at the ends of words, and it's very pretty, but you couldn't use it for anything but a perfume label." Not so! It's a big family!

Now look at Figure 10.6. Here we have additional members of the **Poetica** family merely used in a bit of nostalgia. The body copy is easily readable. The heading was created with small caps included in the family. Unless you compare the lowercase letters carefully, you might think that the type design in this figure is entirely different than in the preceding example.

> ENOCH THE FISH MAN
>
> *Among the vaudeville acts you could see around 1910 was Enoch the Fish Man, who sang under water - with the help of a bucket over his head that provided him with air. It seems there's a trick to everything.*

10.6 Another example of Poetica's versatility.

Figure 10.7 may be a shock to you. If you've used PostScript printers for years, you're probably acquainted with **Zapf Chancery** as one of the 35 typefaces built in to many of these printers. And you may have thought of it as a standalone design that could be used on wedding invitations. In fact, when Apple co-founder Steve Jobs was still at that company, he wanted **Zapf Chancery** included in the type group for that very reason; people would need a face they

Self-love is the greatest of all flatterers.

Bold

Self-love is the greatest of all flatterers.

Light

Self-love is the greatest of all flatterers.

Italic

Self-love is the greatest of all flatterers.

Demi-Bold

Self-love is the greatest of all flatterers.

Light Italic

Self-love is the greatest of all flatterers.

Roman

10.7 The ITC Zapf Chancery family.

could use for those formal invitations. However, he selected only **Zapf Chancery Italic;** Figure 10.7 shows the complete family designed by Hermann Zapf in 1979, based on the High Renaissance chancery scripts.

Note that the *fl* combination is a ligature. You can buy the family through almost any vendor who sells ITC typefaces. The text in the samples is from the seventeenth-century writings of François, Duc de La Rochefoucauld.

FORMAL AND DEMI-FORMAL SCRIPTS

Next you can see three examples that Bitstream places in two additional script categories the company has originated. The bottom specimen in Figure 10.8 is **Ondine,** designed by Adrian Frutiger in 1954. Bitstream classifies this as a Formal script which, they explain, is a descendent of the roundhand and Ronde styles I've just described. At the same time, Bitstream calls the other two examples—**Bernhard Tango** and **Liberty**—*Demi*-Formal scripts—designs "less serious in intent" but "still showing real design discipline." Just glancing at these specimens, you might disagree. You might rate **Ondine** as the least formal of the group, assign it to the brush category, and call the others roundhand variants. But such

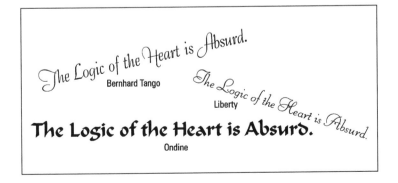

10.8 Three relatively formal script faces.

disagreements occur every day in the world of typefaces and, as I've said, there are usually good points to be made for each of the varying opinions. Perhaps the reason for Bitstream's "Formal" designation for **Ondine** is that this bold design owes a lot to the blackletter tradition, which—as the next chapter reveals—was certainly formal.

Bernhard Tango was designed by Lucian Bernhard and released by ATF in 1934; it's still in use everywhere, is distinguished, and completely legible. **Liberty** was drawn for ATF by Willard T. Sniffin in 1927, based on a type created by Bernhard two years earlier; it's almost upright, with rounded characters and long ascenders that end in hooks. All the typefaces shown in Figure 10.8 are available from Bitstream. The statement used in the type samples is a wise comment gleaned from a letter written in 1774 by Julie de Lespinasse. See! I've been peeking at other people's mail again.

SOME TIRED EXAMPLES

At this point, I can't help showing you a couple of script typefaces that have really been done to death—**Coronet** and **Park Avenue.** Both were designed in the 1930s and definitely reflect that period to many who see them. Therefore, I've coupled them in Figure 10.9 with an illustration from the same era advertising hot dogs and hamburgers for 10 cents. The drawing is from the Metro library. **Coronet** is used in the heading and for the name of the hot dog company. The remainder of the text is in **Park Avenue.** You should never mix two similar typefaces in the same document as I've done here, but forgive me. It's to make a point: Don't use these designs unless you want to satirize the Thirties.

Your Invitation

to our five friendly
stands at the County
Fair -- July 18-24.

The Dog-Gone Good Company

10.9 Coronet (in the heading and company name) and Park Avenue script faces from the 1930s.

Park Avenue is the oldest. It was drawn for ATF by Robert E. Smith in 1933, has a small x-height, and is one of the designs created in an attempt to bring some informality to script faces. Like **Coronet,** it has lowercase letters that don't quite connect with one another. **Coronet** is a 1937 design by Robert Hunter Middleton that has many of the same characteristics. You can buy versions of both from either Agfa or Bitstream. Bitstream gurus put both typefaces into a category they call Ribbon—reserved for scripts intended for use in wedding invitations.

SOME FRESHER ALTERNATIVES

If you're bound and determined to print wedding invitations, I'll give you some alternatives. Figure 10.10 shows you three other typefaces that Bitstream includes in the Ribbon category. These are seen far less often, don't automatically remind people of the 1930s, and are informal but dignified and attractive. They're **Amazone, Murray Hill,** and **Nuptial.**

10.10 From top to bottom: Amazone, Murray Hill, and Nuptial script typefaces.

The illustration is from the Image Club library. The text is a quotation from Cervantes' *Don Quixote*.

Amazone was designed by Leonard H. D. Smit and released by the Amsterdam foundry in 1959. Note that the lowercase characters connect, the x-height is fairly large for a script face, the weight is relatively bold, and the capitals have energetic flourishes. Both the ascenders and descenders are long and looped.

Emil Klumpp designed **Murray Hill** for ATF in 1956, primarily as a refreshing display face for the advertising industry. The name comes from that of a district in Manhattan where many major advertising agencies were located. It was also the name of a telephone exchange in that area, in those days before the phone companies switched to all-number dialing. **Murray Hill** has a rather large x-height, lowercase characters that do not connect, some looped ascenders and descenders, and capitals with small flourishes. The letters are nearly vertical.

Nuptial—as the name might indicate—was designed specifically for use in wedding invitations. It was drawn by the Intertype design staff about 1952, under the supervision of Edwin W. Shaar. This script has indications of serifs, flowing ascenders and descenders, and flourished capitals that combine to give it a charming, slightly archaic quality.

TWO MONOLINES AND A CASUAL

Bitstream defines its Monoline script category as designs that resemble writing, have linked lowercase characters, and "an absolutely even stroke weight." I've included two of these in Figure 10.11: the solid **Monoline Script,** created by the Monotype Type Drawing Office staff in 1933 from drawings by manager F. M. Steltzer, and **Kaufmann,** a lighter effort

10.11 From top to bottom: Monoline, Kaufmann, and Lucida Handwriting typefaces.

drawn for ATF in 1936 by Max R. Kaufmann, who was a lettering artist and art director for *McCalls* magazine. The third typeface is quite different. It's **Lucida Handwriting**, a 1992 casual joining script that's part of the large **Lucida** family created by Charles Bigelow and Kris Holmes. The family members—which include serif, sans-serif, and even blackletter typefaces—share capital heights, x-heights, and stem weights so that the typefaces can be intermingled.

The illustrations in the figure are all from Fontek's DesignFont series—digital typefaces that consist of artwork. With the exception of the bat, drawn by David Sagorski, the drawings are by Tom Lulevitch, whose brilliant evocations were inspired by the sixteenth-century Flemish paintings of Pieter Bruegel and the work of nineteenth-century British illustrator Dick Doyle.

> **Monoline Script** is the top typeface example. This is a very legible, attention-getting script that's appropriate for many uses, except wedding invitations! The poem was written in 1916 by the noted American poet and biographer Carl Sandburg.

> **Kaufmann** is the middle typeface. This joined script closely resembles actual informal handwriting and is therefore harder to read. The poem is a parody of *Twinkle, Twinkle, Little Star* that Lewis Carroll included in his *Alice in Wonderland*.

> **Lucida Handwriting** completes the page. It has a large x-height, rather heavy strokes, and a mannered grace that makes it a good choice for display uses. Its capitals are unusual in that they were designed so they can be used to form words in combination with each other. The poem is nonsense verse by the British artist and writer Edward Lear, author of the beloved *Owl and the Pussy-Cat*.

Monoline Script and **Kaufmann** are widely available. You can obtain **Lucida Handwriting** from Y & Y or through Linotype-Hell.

A NOSTALGIC FACE WITH
1930 TO 1940 OVERTONES

Harlow Solid, seen in Figure 10.12, is a 1979 typeface by Letraset's Colin Brignall. This is a heavy but casual monolineal display script with characteristics reminiscent of the 1930s and 1940s and letters that overlap rather than join. The capitals can be used separately as initials. If it's too black for your needs, you can use the original **Harlow,** released two years earlier, which is the same design in outline form. The illustration is from the Image Club library.

10.12 Letraset's Harlow Solid display face.

FREEHAND SCRIPTS

Bitstream uses a category called Freehand in which to group informal scripts "freely written with little regard to rule." Designers have certainly created plenty of these to enrich your documents, so I've gathered some of them for your approval in Figure 10.13. All are available from Bitstream except for **Repro Script,** a Varityper design available through PrePress Direct; **Brody,** licensed by Kingsley-ATF to Image Club and several other suppliers; and **Lucida Casual,** which you can purchase through Y & Y or Linotype-Hell. The illustration is from the Metro library.

> **Lucida Casual,** the type in the "Channel 7" heading is also shown at the bottom of the figure. This is another member of the Bigelow and Holmes **Lucida** family, completed in 1994. Kris Holmes drew the original design with a fiber-tipped pen, which is reflected in

10.13 Nine casual scripts.

the appearance of the face. It consists of carefully formed, unconnected upright characters with high legibility. You could use it for personal correspondence, memos, menus, and display headings.

Mandate is a connecting script that was designed by Robert H. Middleton in 1934. The general style was used frequently in signs and billboards of the era. Some of the capital letters extend below the baseline, including the *C* shown in the figure.

Jefferson and **Bingham Script** are informal designs seen in the advertising of the late 1950s and early 1960s—often hand-lettered. Their origins are unknown.

Brody was designed by Harold Broderson for ATF and released in 1953. This heavy, upright design provides a crisp, commanding vehicle for display messages.

Impress was created for Autologic about 1975 and provides a casual atmosphere combined with the clarity of typeset lettering.

Repro Script was designed for ATF by Jerry Mullen in 1953. It's almost monolineal in design. The characters are narrow and most of them interconnect. **Repro Script** is very legible but appears a bit dated by modern standards.

Mr. Earl is a poster face designed for Bitstream by Jennifer Maestrae in 1991. She based it on lettering in a "how-to" book of the 1930s. Its narrow, bold characters are reminiscent of that period and can produce unique-looking display copy. The design is named in honor of Earl Bisco, a Bitstream designer diagnosed with cancer.

Oz Handicraft was designed for Bitstream in 1990 by George Ryan and developed from a hand-lettering sample by Oswald Cooper. Cooper was a highly regarded Chicago lettering artist whose innovative typefaces were often best-sellers in the years after 1918—particularly his **Cooper Black,** which you can see in Chapter 12. **Oz Handicraft** has very narrow characters and a large x-height. Although it can project the aura of the 1920s, its stylish look has broader applications. For example, Bitstream itself used this design for the entire back cover of a typeface CD-ROM package for the retail market.

BRUSH SCRIPTS

Figure 10.14 shows several popular brush typefaces at work. The illustration is from the Metro library. **Palette** and **Bison**

10.14 Five popular brush scripts.

can be ordered from Bitstream. **Dom Casual** is available from almost everyone. **Ruling Script 2** and **Sho** are Linotype-Hell designs that can also be purchased through Adobe.

Palette is a flowing brush script with conventionally shaped characters that make it easy to read. Martin Wilke created the design for Berthold in 1950. Some of the capitals extend below the baseline; note the *S* in the figure.

Sho was designed by Karlgeorg Hoefer in 1992. It's composed of wide, black, upright characters with strokes that resemble calligraphy. Several terminate in ball shapes. These unusually shaped letters retain maximum legibility in large point sizes.

Ruling Script 2 was designed in 1992 by German calligrapher Gottfried Pott. It's a light, elegant face. Some characters have unusual shapes. Tiny penstrokes protrude from many, extending serifs or—in the case of the lowercase *l* and *h*—adding a flag to the ascender. Avoid this type if your printer has poor resolution because you'll lose much of the interesting detail.

Bison was designed by Julius Kim in 1935. It's a heavy, slightly inclined brush script, with short ascenders and descenders. Some capitals extend below the baseline. It is both sturdy and readable.

Dom Casual is the best-known brush script. Created for ATF in 1952 by Pete Dom (Peter Dombrezian), this bold, no-nonsense, upright design is a real workhorse. It will attract immediate attention to your display text without making any personal statement. Not very original anymore, it is a practical tool that's good to have around.

SUMMARY

You certainly don't want to use script typefaces for the text of a book—or even a magazine article, with very few exceptions. They simply require too much effort on the part of the reader. Some people like the idea of printing their correspondence in a script face because "it looks more personal." Well, most of your friends and acquaintances would thank you in this instance if you weren't quite so "personal." They'd rather absorb your message in a less painful fashion. A few designs—mainly those that look more like careful hand-lettering than hasty scribbling—can be deciphered fairly easily. But is deciphering what you had in mind?

Turning to other uses—such as headings, blurbs in ads, and invitations—scripts can be the perfect solution. They can look lively or distinguished or even commanding, in the case of some of the blacker, broader models. Just select one that's not trite or illegible or indicative of some period in history you didn't intend to invoke. And you'll usually want to print scripts in a larger size and with more leading than other types. Those loops and curves can be delicate and also take up more space than you might have imagined.

11

Blackletter and Uncial Typefaces

As its title advises you, this chapter deals with blackletter and uncial typefaces. Actually, uncial lettering originated before blackletter; it developed from the medieval handwriting of the scribes of the fourth to ninth centuries. However, by the time printing was invented in the fifteenth century, the blackletter forms had long been predominant. Therefore, it was these that were copied by Gutenberg when he created the first movable type. Today, they're still much more popular than the uncials. Consequently, I'll cover the blackletters first. You can use both kinds in many ways.

THE BLACKLETTER CATEGORIES

During the time of Charlemagne—in the ninth century—uncial lettering gave way to a round, open cursive hand called Carolingian minuscule. However, by the twelfth century, university scribes in northern Europe had different needs. They wanted to save time and space wherever possible in producing the many pages of their textbooks, so they began combining some letter combinations into a single character—the equivalent of modern ligatures—drawing very narrow characters and replacing tapered stroke endings with stubs and, finally, with diamonds. Soon the end result was what we now call blackletter.

Prior to the fifteenth century, few people could read and write. One of the main reasons was that few could obtain access to the books and manuscripts that existed; they were expensive, ornate products created laboriously by hand, the work of those scribes laboring in universities, government offices, and monasteries. Of course, when Gutenberg successfully experimented with reusable metal characters that could be printed in different combinations by means of a machine adapted from wine presses of the period, his goal was to reproduce the style of lettering in fashion among the scribes and monks. Today, most experts divide these so-called blackletter typefaces into four groups. The oldest is referred to as Textura, Text, or *Gotisch*—the style that most closely resembles the type in the *Gutenberg Bible.* In Figure 11.1, the

Textura, Text or Gotisch

Old English Text

Rotunda or Rundgotisch

Weiß Rundgotisch

Bastarda or Schwabacher

Alte Schwabacher

Fraktur

Fette Fraktur

11.1 Examples in the blackletter type categories.

category is represented by **Old English Text,** which is a Monotype copy of **Engravers' Old English,** designed by Morris Fuller Benton for ATF in 1901.

Incidentally, the word *Textura* is Italian and originated from the woven appearance of the blackletter pages. Note that the lowercase characters don't have curves; instead, the letters end at both head and foot in oblique rectangles.

The German word *Gotisch* means Gothic. The scribes of southern Italy originally described the Textura typefaces using this term, which was intended to be derogatory. The Italians thought the style incorporating those heavy, black characters looked absolutely barbaric. In calling the typefaces Gothic, they were referring to the Goths, the Germanic barbarians who invaded the Roman Empire in the early centuries of the Christian era.

An adaptation of Textura that originated in Italy is *Rotunda*—called *Rundgotisch* in Germany. This second category features rounded characters that don't terminate in rectangles. The example in Figure 11.1 is **Weiss Rundgotisch,** designed in 1936 by Emil Rudolf Weiss. Note that the word *Weiss* in the figure ends in a ligature; this character is a German convention that represents a double *s*. The next word, *Rundgotisch,* contains a single "long *s*" (an *s* resembling a lowercase *f*). Later in the chapter, I'll explain the rules for using both characters.

As the fifteenth century drew to a close and printed works became more prevalent, printers wanted to add more type styles to the rather formal Textura and Rotunda designs. Consequently, they began to copy casual, handwritten lettering with slightly wider characters, flourishes on both capital and lowercase components, a lowercase cursive letter *a*, and almond-shaped counters. In Germany the style came to be called **Schwabacher,** after the Bavarian town of Schwabach

—although no one remembers why. Because the style was unconventional, in France and England it was called **Bastarda.** Both terms are still used today. As an example, Figure 11.1 shows **Alte Schwabacher,** a traditional Schwabacher that has been a longtime favorite. (*Alte* means "Old" in German.) I obtained both **Weiss Rundgotisch** and **Alte Schwabacher** from the URW library.

Finally, a fourth blackletter style is **Fraktur,** a result of the influence of the baroque art and architecture of the Renaissance. **Fraktur** typefaces are slightly condensed and usually feature many characters with elaborate flourishes, a lowercase cursive *a,* forked tops on lowercase ascenders, and a lowercase *g* with an open, curved tail. By the middle of the nineteenth century, Fraktur was dominant in Germany, both for headings and the text of books and newspapers, although its use in the rest of the world for the most part had long been relegated to headings alone. Even in 1930, nearly 60 percent of new German books were set in **Fraktur.**

Then Hitler came into power. Initially, he saw **Fraktur** as a German cultural triumph that ranked far above the typeface formats used in other nations. Soon he decreed that it was the *only* proper typeface style for the printing of the German language.

However, by 1940, by which time he had dreams of conquering the entire world, he realized that roman type styles—which were certainly easier to read—prevailed everywhere outside Germany. Therefore, he reversed himself. He declared that **Fraktur** was a "Schwabacher-Jewish type" and had the country convert to roman lettering, which has predominated there ever since.

The **Fraktur** shown in 11.1 is a classic: **Fette Fraktur,** first issued by the C. E. Weber foundry in 1875. You saw it first in Chapter 2, where I told you that *Fette* means *bold.* This version is from Linotype-Hell.

Later in the chapter you'll see other blackletter typefaces that might interest you for titles and headings with real character.

Blackletter Category Variations

Figure 11.2 is interesting. Here you see the same blackletters I used as examples in the first figure, except that each is now coupled with a second specimen from its group. The purpose

11.2 Typical variations within blackletter groups.

is to give you an idea of the variations you'll find within the groups. The German words used in the figure, *Das Holz,* mean *wood* or *the wood,* in the sense of *a piece of wood.*

The new Textura example is Linotype's **Linotext,** designed by Morris Fuller Benton for ATF in 1901 and originally called **Wedding Text.** Note that the *H* and *z* are very different from those in **Old English Text.** Also, the **Linotext** letters are not as condensed as most Texturas and the x-height is smaller. However, in both instances, the *o* is in the shape of a hexagon and the *l* has a split top ending in a thorn-like decoration—both typical Textura features.

San Marco is the added blackletter in the Rotunda category. It's a relatively recent design, created for Linotype in 1990 by Karlgeorg Hoefer. Both **Weiss Rundgotisch** and **San Marco** display class characteristics such as rounded letters and enormous contrast between thick and thin strokes.

I've chosen **Duc de Berry** as the second Bastarda example. Gottfried Pott is the artist; he drew it for Linotype in 1990. Both specimens have a freehand flavor, a relatively small x-height, a cursive *a,* a *d* whose ascender terminates in a flourish, and an *o* that is pointed at top and bottom— standard details for the class. Note that the *H* and *l* differ greatly between the designs.

Wittenberger Fraktur was issued by Monotype in 1906. It's based on an earlier release from a German foundry which, in turn, was based on type that was popular with printers in Wittenberg in the sixteenth century. It's available in Normal and Semibold weights; the Normal is shown here. As you can see, **Wittenberger Fraktur** is similar in design to **Fette Fraktur,** when you ignore the difference in weight between the two specimens. Both have an *o* that is flat on the left side and a split *l,* expected in Fraktur designs. The word *Fraktur* means "broken."

Using the Lowercase S and Other Special Ligatures

As previously mentioned, the German language has special rules for using the various forms of the lowercase *s* in blackletter typefaces. Figure 11.3 illustrates those forms, as well as examples of their correct use. Immediately, you may say, "I never saw letter variations like that. Where do I find them?" The answer is that some digital foundries will

die Strasse—the street

das Wasser—the water

der Staatsmann —the statesman

ist—is   sind—are

aussagen—to give evidence

11.3 The use of the letter s in blackletter typefaces.

eliminate unneeded characters or symbols from their blackletter typefaces and, in their place, will substitute the extra German *s* forms. However, many vendors, including Adobe, provide two versions of each blackletter design. One version has the standard, English-type *s* you would expect. The other version is labeled *Dfr* and includes the extra German characters. The typeface in Figure 11.3 is **Wilhelm Klingspor Gotisch** from Linotype-Hell. It was designed by Rudolf Koch in 1924 and is justly renowned for its beauty and legibility.

As the figure shows you, German blackletter typefaces have three *s* variations. The first is the *long s*. I've displayed the letter *f* to the right of it so you can see the difference; the *f* has a crossbar. There are rules as to when you use the long *s* and when you use another variation—shown on the right in the second line: the *round s*.

The *double s* symbol is used in some situations where you find the combination *ss*. Unfortunately for non-Germans, you must learn that not all *ss* combinations take that symbol. There are rules in this situation, too.

First, let's deal with that double *s*. You never, ever show the combination as *ss,* as you would in English. You represent it by two long *s* characters together when the letter combination is located between two vowels and the first vowel is a short sound. Otherwise, you use the double *s* symbol. Note *die Strasse* in the figure. The *ss* combination is between two vowels, but the *a* is a long sound; therefore, you use the double *s* character. Now look at *das Wasser* just below it; the *a* in *Wasser* is short, so you use the long *s* twice.

The rule regarding a single *s* is that you use the round *s* character at the end of a stem-syllable or at the end of a word. So, in *der Staatsmann,* the *s* at the end of the stem-syllable *Staats* must be a round *s*. On the other hand, in *ist,* the *s* is not at the end of a syllable or a word; consequently, you show the *s* as a single long *s*.

Finally, at the bottom of Figure 11.3, *aussagen* shows both single *s* symbols used together. The round *s* is used first, at the end of the syllable *aus*. Then, the long *s* starts the remainder of the word, *sagen*.

In German and in Dfr fonts, you use a ligature for the double long *s*; you can see it in *Wasser* in the figure. Other ligatures are *ch, ck, ff, ft, si,* and *ts*.

Obviously, if you're not reproducing words and sentences in the German language, you can ignore all of these rules and select the non-Dfr version of a blackletter typeface. Then print the words as you normally would in English or any language other than German, without those special characters. You may be using the type as the heading for a church newsletter or for a wedding invitation. Either way, just use the rules and characters of your usual language.

Using Blackletter Type in Paragraphs

Many blackletter typefaces are so intricate that they're hard to read if employed for more than a few words. Others—mainly the recent designs in the category—have been created with extended use in mind. You can choose some of these with confidence for a paragraph or two, knowing that your readers will easily identify the letters and words.

Figure 11.4 reproduces a long sentence in four different blackletter styles. The first is **Lucida Blackletter,** another typeface in the **Lucida** series by Charles Bigelow and Kris Holmes, available from Y & Y and Linotype-Hell. This modern blackletter interpretation was completed in 1992.

The second example is **American Text,** available from Bitstream. It's a condensed blackletter designed by Morris

Justice is blind, so they say, but seldom is it too blind to distinguish between the defendant who has a roll of bills and the one who is dead broke.

Lucida Blackletter

Justice is blind, so they say, but seldom is it too blind to distinguish between the defendant who has a roll of bills and the one who is dead broke.

American Text

Justice is blind, so they say, but seldom is it too blind to distinguish between the defendant who has a roll of bills and the one who is dead broke.

San Marco

Justice is blind, so they say, but seldom is it too blind to distinguish between the defendant who has a roll of bills and the one who is dead broke.

Blackmoor

11.4 Four blackletter typefaces used as text.

Fuller Benton in 1932. It's very readable, since many ornamental touches of the category have been eliminated or softened. It's composed entirely of straight lines, giving it a striking angular quality.

The third typeface is **San Marco,** which I described in connection with Figure 11.2 but displayed there in only two words.

Letraset's **Blackmoor** is the bottom example, available from Fontek and Letraset licensees. This David Quay design was completed in 1983. You may not be able to tell from the reduced-size reproduction in this book, but the typeface has a *distressed* quality, meaning that the characters have been deliberately drawn with rough edges, to simulate the wear that would show on type in an antique document.

Now, if I had to rate these four typefaces for readability, I'd give the prize to **American Text,** with **Blackmoor, San Marco,** and **Lucida Blackletter** finishing second, third, and fourth. Unusually shaped characters and flourishes are pretty, but they do slow down comprehension. However, these would all be good choices for short passages of text.

Alternate Capitals

Figure 11.5 shows a particularly versatile blackletter. This is **Goudy Text,** designed by Frederic Goudy in 1928 for Monotype. The versatility comes from the two sets of capital letters Goudy designed for the face. On the top you see the conventional capitals for a Textura design. However, the bottom line shows the alternate Lombardic capitals he devised—also shown in Chapter 1 in the heading for the remake of the Tailor's Story document. When you use the Lombardic capitals, the words immediately become easier to read for those not familiar with blackletter characters.

11.5 The two variants of Goudy Text.

Furthermore, as I stated in Chapter 1, any formal or religious connotation to the typeface is diminished. It's now appropriate for fairy tales or a travel brochure about the old cities of Europe.

UNCIAL TYPEFACES

As mentioned at the beginning of the chapter, scribes were writing uncial hands starting in the fourth century—hundreds of years before the blackletter forms appeared. However, since there were no printing presses in those days, there were no uncial printing types. By the time the first typefaces were developed in the fifteenth century, based on the Textura blackletters then popular, uncials had long been considered archaic. In fact, it wasn't until the nineteenth century that a few printers cut uncial types—and then only for those interested in antiquities. In the early twentieth century this situation changed. Several prominent designers started experimenting with uncials. Publishers began to use them to give a medieval flavor to titles and documents. Finally, we have several in digital form from which to choose.

The original uncial writing had no capital letters. Nevertheless, some type designers have added capitals to their creations for clarity and utility and to make their uncials more like conventional typefaces and therefore more acceptable in the marketplace. Figure 11.6 shows six different specimens— half with capitals and half without. The sentence displayed in the samples is a quotation from the writings of St. Jerome, who died in 420 A.D.

The first example is **American Uncial,** designed by Victor Hammer, an Austrian who moved to the United

The face is the mirror
of the mind, and eyes   American Uncial
without speaking
confess the secrets of
the heart.

the face is the mirror
of the mind, and eyes
without speaking
confess the secrets of
the heart.   Frances Uncial

the face is the mirror of the mind,
and eyes without speaking confess
the secrets of the heart.
                    Libra

The face is the mirror
of the mind, and eyes
without speaking   Kells
confess the secrets of
the heart.

The face is the
mirror of the mind,
and eyes without
speaking confess
the secrets of the
heart.   Omnia

The face is the mirror of the mind, and eyes
without speaking confess the secrets of the
heart.   Meath

11.6 Six uncial typefaces.

States in 1939 because of the Nazi menace. He had been hired to teach art and lettering at Wells College in upstate New York. While there, in 1943, he created **American Uncial,** but no foundry offered it for sale until 20 years later because executives doubted that there would be a market for an uncial. He had been designing typefaces since 1921—always uncials.

American Uncial is bold, with a large x-height, strokes that widen at the tops, and a lowercase cursive *a*. Hammer created a set of capitals for it based on roman origins. The design eventually achieved recognition and popularity. In its digital form, you can purchase it from Image Club. Unfortunately, it's not available from Adobe, Agfa, Bitstream, Linotype, or Monotype.

Frances Uncial is a new addition to the class, released in 1995 by Letraset. Note that, although the typeface contains no capital letters, some of the characters resemble typical roman seriffed capitals in their shape. The *a* is two-storied rather than cursive. **Frances Uncial** was designed by Michael Gills and can be ordered from Fontek.

Libra is the work of S. H. De Roos, completed for a Dutch foundry in 1938. It was widely used in Europe and migrated successfully to the United States after World War II. This is strictly a lowercase or *minuscule* uncial, with a two-story *a*. Bitstream has a digital version.

Both **Kells** and **Meath** are light in weight, were developed for Casady & Greene, and released in 1992. **Kells** was named in honor of the *Book of Kells*, a famous ninth-century copy of the Gospels in Latin, which was written in an uncial hand and illuminated in an Irish monastery near Kells. Kells is located in County Meath, which gives you the origin of the other typeface name. The two typefaces have different sets of capital letters but share the lowercase alphabet, with the exception of *a*, which is two-story in the Kells design and cursive in Meath.

Omnia was designed in 1990 by Karlgeorg Hoefer for Linotype. This is a bold design with no capitals and a two-story *a*.

Analyzing these alternatives, I'd pick **American Uncial** as the face with the most character. It really has an archaic quality.

SUMMARY

Well, you've seen some interesting blackletters and uncials—
but how would you use them? You might say, "Frankly, I'm
not the editor of a church newsletter, and I don't do wedding
invitations." In that case, I'll give you some other suggestions:
gothic novels, European travel brochures, historical articles or
books (particularly about Germany), horror movies or stories,
merit certificates and awards, diplomas, new year's
resolutions, lists of do's and don'ts, ski competitions, wise
sayings, graduation invitations, legal articles and documents,
government-related information, and fairy tales. (Now why
did I place those last two items next to each other? Must have
been something subconscious.) Uncials are also appropriate
for Irish legends and celebrations.

12

Display and Novelty Typefaces

You'll find plenty of gray areas when you try to define display and novelty typefaces, simply because most of these designs are derived from other categories or may even be members of those categories. For example, **Helvetica** is a certified sans-serif that is used for text every day, yet it also works very well for display purposes. Any of the **Bodoni** families belong in the Modern category, but make excellent headings and titles too. However, many display faces are too intricate, black, or irregular to be useful for text. And some novelty designs are so wild that no one would consider assigning them more than a word or two—in a very large point size. You'll encounter all varieties in this chapter. I hope to familiarize you with some and warn you against others.

FROM CHAOS TO COMPLETE DISCIPLINE

To be impressed by the extremes of this category, you don't have to go any further than to compare Figure 12.1 with Figure 12.2. Let's talk about Figure 12.1 first. Against a brick wall from the large Image Club DigitArt library, you see four examples of typefaces that imitate graffiti with startling realism. These designs are all the work of Jeremy Dean of House Industries. Starting at the upper left and continuing clockwise, they are **Crackhouse**—completed in 1993—and **Condemdhouse, Burnthouse,** and **HouseArrest**—all completed in 1995.

Several other designers have attempted to represent graffiti in typefaces, but usually the results are unimpressive. In most cases, the characters are too regular—betraying the designer's formal training in lettering—and give no hint of the medium supposedly involved in the vandalism. In these House Industries offerings, you can see chipped paint, paint blotches, and even different crude versions of the same letter. You can increase the effect of authentic casual scrawling by

12.1 Four typefaces by Jeremy Dean that imitate graffiti.

rotating some characters slightly, not placing characters over cracks or holes in the background you're using, and changing the color of some messages if more than one appears in your image.

Figure 12.2 shows **Rubino Serif** and **Rubino Serif Solid,** two unusual typefaces designed for Image Club by Noel Rubin in 1994. He says he got the idea for them from studying the work of Renaissance artist Albrecht Dürer who created paintings, copperplate engravings, and woodcuts based on strict mathematical principles. The **Rubino** designs are typefaces created in the Dürer manner—with the notable exception that the mathematical guidelines used in their creation are still showing. You can use them to make headings for design- or architecture-related documents of all kinds. The body copy underneath the Rubino examples was set in **Poppl-Laudatio,** a graceful sans-serif type drawn by calligrapher Friedrich Poppl and released in 1982; it's available through Adobe.

Well, you'll have to admit that the first two figures in this chapter do offer a study in contrast.

CREATE

Type designers creating decorative or display faces are often able to use their imagination freely.

12.2 The Rubino typefaces show how they were constructed.

SOME TIRED DISPLAY FACES

Typefaces that are overused get into that group for one of only two reasons: either there's nothing else available or they're great designs. Certainly, in these days of thousands of typefaces being offered to the public at very low prices, the first reason is hardly valid—unless you're referring to a particular individual or organization that simply doesn't have the money to buy more. So all the faces in Figure 12.3 are worthy accomplishments. If you're creating documents for people who don't read much, you can probably use them very successfully. However, others may think documents in which they appear are somewhat dull and uninteresting, without knowing why.

Here's some background on these attractive offenders.

Broadway is an Art Deco design created by Morris Fuller Benton in 1927, with capital letters only. The following year Monotype copied the design, engaging Sol Hess to add a lowercase. Note that this is a sans-

12.3 Some overused display typefaces.

serif with extreme contrast between thick and thin strokes and a very large x-height. The design is so recognizable that you'd want to use it sparingly, even if it weren't so well known. It's available from Bitstream and Image Club, among others.

P. T. Barnum, a nineteenth-century display face originally called **French Clarendon,** can be obtained from Bitstream and Image Club. The horizontal strokes are wider than the vertical ones, typical of the Slab Serif types used on circus posters. That's why ATF called it **P. T. Barnum**—after the famed showman and circus impresario—when it was re-released in 1933. There are many other circus or Old West designs available today, so you might want to pick a more recent entry in this group.

Helvetica, previously discussed, is included here simply because I want to make the point that it's been selected for display use again and again. The same comment applies to **Avant Garde.**

Revue was designed by Colin Brignall for Letraset in 1969. It features heavy, curved letterforms and is very effective in headings. Nearly every vendor offers it.

Peignot mixes modified small caps and lowercase characters in the creation of its lowercase, combined with more conventional capital letters. This Art Deco sans-serif was designed by A. M. Cassandre in 1937 for a French foundry and is often used to generate a "French" atmosphere. It is sold by vendors of the Linotype-Hell library.

University Roman was introduced by Letraset in 1972. Mike Daines and Phillip Kelly were responsible for this Art Nouveau design. The digital version includes

It's a very odd thing—
As odd as can be—
That whatever Miss T. eats
Turns into Miss T.

—**Walter de la Mare**

12.4 ITC Souvenir—an attractive display typeface.

swash alternative characters that can help break up its too-familiar appearance. Letraset offers regular and bold weights, plus an italic designed by Freda Sack. It is sold by Fontek and several Letraset licensees.

Figure 12.4 shows **ITC Souvenir,** based on a 1914 Morris Fuller Benton design which, in turn, was based on some older models. The ITC version was created in 1970 by the ever-present Ed Benguiat. Here's another type with an Art Nouveau flair. It was very much overused for a few years, but the world seems to have forgotten it recently, so you might be safe in selecting it. This is a large family that even includes an outline member. However, it's a bit too busy for extended text use.

ALTERING DESIGNS TO FRESHEN THEM UP

Sometimes you can change the alignment of characters in a tired display face so that it will appear different to your readers. **Davida** is a heavy, decorated set of capitals with an Art Nouveau style. It was designed by Louis Minott in 1965 and has been used extensively ever since. Among the vendors who offer it are Bitstream and Image Club. You can see it in its usual form on the first line of Figure 12.5. The second line shows the typeface with the same characters shoved close together to make a single unit, which might be a logo for a clothing company called Madridwear.

Figure 12.6 takes this idea a step further. Here you have Image Club's 1991 typeface that bears the company name— **Image Club**—a sans-serif consisting of individual letters mounted on white panels with a drop shadow. In the second line, I overlapped the characters to change the effect.

In the next chapter, I'll tell you about several programs you can use to create special effects with type. You can distort characters in many ways. Figure 12.7 shows the famous **Cooper Black** typeface on the first line, with the letters curved and joined in an impressive logo directly underneath. **Cooper Black** was designed by Oswald Cooper. It's a member of the **Old Style Cooper** family he introduced in 1918. When he added **Cooper Black** in 1922, he stated that it was "for far-sighted printers with near-sighted customers." Note the unusual rounded serifs. Bitstream sells an updated version of the entire family.

12.5 The Davida typeface in its normal state (first line) and with the characters touching to create a logo.

12.6 The Image Club typeface in normal (top) and overlapping configurations.

MANY DISPLAY FACES
NEED LARGE POINT SIZES

Chapter 11 was devoted to blackletters. Well, in Figure 12.8 you can see one I didn't show you there, but am exhibiting now to make a point. This is Linotype's **Notre Dame,** designed by Karlgeorg Hoefer in 1992. This Textura design

12.7 Cooper Black (top) is distorted into a curved logo.

Myths of Beasts and Warriors

12.8 Notre Dame is most effective when used for display.

features beak and claw ornamentation on the capitals—an element that could easily be missed if you used it for text work or a small heading. Like many typefaces of all kinds that are intended primarily for display, it looks best in large point sizes where its various elements can be fully appreciated.

DISPLAY FACES YOU CAN USE

Figure 12.9 shows a group of display faces in a wide assortment of styles. Here you can see a tiny glimpse of the

ADOBE ROSEWOOD

BRENDEL DISCO

LETRASET PLAZA SWASH INLINE

Casady & Greene Epoque

IMAGE CLUB LYNZ

LETRASET SINALOA

Esselte Letraset COMPACTA LIGHT

Brendel Tabasco Twin

Brendel Japanette

Letraset Cabaret

Gill Sans Ultra

12.9 Useful display typefaces.

variety that's waiting for you at the type houses. I'll describe them all briefly.

Rosewood was discussed in Chapter 2.

Brendel's **Disco** and **Tabasco Twin** are ultra-modern designs developed in 1993 by B & P Graphics, Ltd., Dublin. In particular, **Disco** requires a large point size so the reader will be able to recognize the characters. I discussed **Japanet** in Chapter 2; Brendel's **Japanette** is a version of this design—good for Far East travel brochures or a menu in an Oriental restaurant.

Plaza was introduced in Chapter 9. The version of the Letraset family shown here—**Plaza Swash Inline**—is available from URW. The swash characters make it distinctive and very attractive.

Epoque from Richard A. Ware is an elaborate Art Nouveau design released in 1990 by Casady & Greene. This typeface definitely reflects this period in European fashion, but could also be used as a logo for a fine furniture store or the title of a fantasy tale.

Lynz, a 1991 Image Club design discussed in Chapter 1 was inspired by Aldo Novarese's **Stop,** shown in Chapter 9. In any event, it's appropriate for futuristic headings, but be careful in using letters with strokes missing, like the *B* in the figure.

Sinaloa, Compacta, and **Cabaret** are all Letraset designs. This company sells an outstanding assortment of display typefaces, many through its Fontek unit. **Sinaloa** is a 1974 design by Rosemarie Tissi; stripes are used to help identify characters in this striking contemporary work. **Compacta** was conceived by Fred Lambert in 1963—highly condensed but legible for headings or short paragraphs. **Cabaret** is the work of Alan Meeks; its internal shading gives this 1980 design a metallic look.

Gill Sans Ultra is one of the most popular members of the **Gill Sans** family released by Monotype in 1928–1930 and designed by Eric Gill. Note the unusual letter shapes in this weight and the off-center placement of the period on top of the lowercase *i*.

I'll show you a number of other display typefaces later in the book.

NOVELTY FACES—HANDLE WITH CARE!

You should approach novelty typefaces cautiously. In the first place, if you're considering buying one for your library, ask yourself how often you'd use it. Many of these are so distinctive and specifically targeted that you might select them for your documents once or twice. Furthermore, most are so detailed that you must reproduce them in a large size so they can be understood.

One of the best sources for novelty faces is Image Club. In Figure 12.10, you can buy all these designs from this one source: **Chrome Bumper, Image Club Neon, ICG Stamp Gray, Paper Clip, ICG Querty,** and **Rock A Billy.** They don't require much comment. **Chrome Bumper** looks like metal letters with a reflection. **Neon** imitates a neon sign. **Stamp Gray** has lettering that seems to have been produced with a rubber stamp. **Paper Clip** has a paper clip attached to each character. **Querty** offers all the characters on your keyboard so you can produce instructional manuals for the folks at work. **Rock A Billy** looks as if it were constructed from children's blocks.

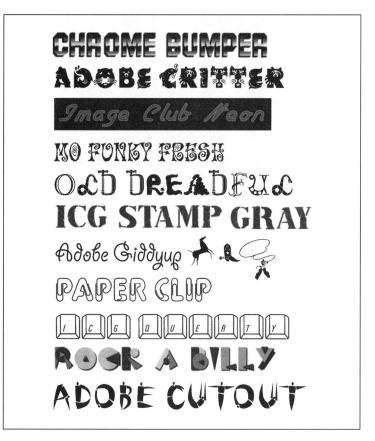

12.10 Novelty typefaces from several vendors.

The full name of **Old Dreadful** is **Old Dreadful No. 7**. It was manufactured at Bitstream in 1990 through the simple device of asking various employees each to design and contribute a letter. The resulting characters look like a snake, a clutching hand, a dinosaur, a cat seen from the rear, a blackletter initial capital, a C-clamp, and heaven knows what else. The name is apt.

Mo Funky Fresh is a Letraset design created by David Sagorski in 1993. This energetic work includes an alternate set of capitals, special symbols, and compatible spot drawings of summer fun—no lowercase.

In 1993 Adobe released its **Wild Type** collection, which includes the other designs shown in Figure 12.10. **Critter** has letters composed of animals, fish, and what not. It's the inspiration of Craig Frasier. The name of each critter shown actually starts with the letter used. For example, the T is a tiger. As for **Giddyup,** the characters are the loops of a lasso, conceived by Laurie Szujewska, and accompanied by appropriate cowboy drawings. **Cutout** is the work of Gail Blumberg; these human figures in odd positions were inspired by Matisse's paper cutouts, so she's in good company.

SPECIAL-PURPOSE TYPEFACES

You can find typefaces for almost any need. Figure 12.11 illustrates this statement with three examples. Interlogic sells **Bruce Classified,** a serif typeface specifically designed to be readable in small sizes for newspaper classified ads, and

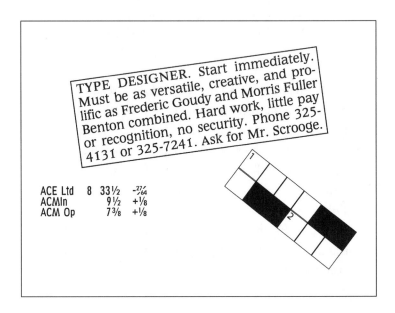

12.11 Special purpose typefaces for classified ads, stock market reports, and crossword puzzles.

Frame Stock, which provides all of the characters and symbols needed to print stock market quotations. Both were designed by Bruce Frame in 1993. You can buy the crossword puzzle typeface from Agfa; its name is **TF Crossword.** It comes with separate modules for presenting a puzzle and its solution and was developed for Treacyfaces in 1993.

Figure 12.12 shows still more special-purpose typefaces. First is **Stone Serif Phonetic,** designed by John Renner in 1992 to accompany Sumner Stone's **ITC Stone Serif** family.

12.12 More special purpose typefaces.

This typeface provides more than 300 symbols and markings used to record human speech, including those recommended by the International Phonetic Association. As you may have determined, the characters shown in the figure are symbols representing the words "the quick brown fox."

Let's move on down the figure. **Carta,** available from Adobe, presents symbols used in maps. **Astrology Pi** contains astrology symbols and is offered by Linotype-Hell, as are **Audio Pi**—audio symbols, **Warning Pi**—international warning symbols, and **Games Pi,** which has chess, dice, dominoes, and card-game symbols. Adobe's **Sonata** lets you write music on your computer.

KEEPING UP IS HARD TO DO

I could have devoted an entire book to display typefaces because there are thousands of them. You'll find them shown in nearly every chapter anyway, in connection with other subjects. Of course, this wealth of choices should be delightful news for you; you're likely to find exactly the right design for whatever subject you undertake. However, some inexperienced type users tend to become discouraged; they wonder how they'll ever master the field and learn about everything that's available.

The answer is that they won't. Artists create new typefaces every day; nobody's going to be able to keep up with all of them. But it doesn't matter. You can discover plenty of candidates for use in your projects simply by looking at type ads and articles in the computer magazines and by reading the catalogs and mailings from the companies that sell these useful products.

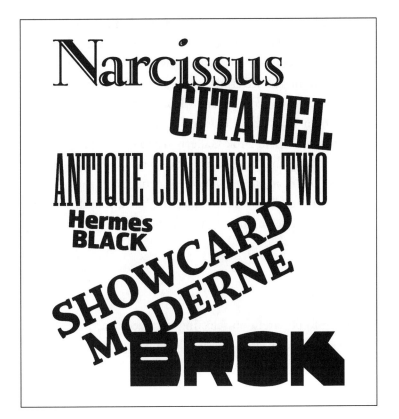

12.13 A few of the new Font Bureau display faces released by Agfa during one month in 1995.

Figure 12.13 provides a quick demonstration of the current activity in this area. Here you see less than half of the new display faces Agfa released in one month in 1995, *from one source alone*—the Font Bureau.

The top design is **Narcissus,** created by Brian Lucid and based on a set of ornamental inline capitals cut by Fournier about 1745. Tobias Frere-Jones drew **Citadel,** a different kind of Slab Serif that substitutes straight strokes for expected curves. **Antique Condensed Two** was inspired by nineteenth-century wood types and brought to life by Jim Parkinson. Matthew Butterick resurrected **Hermes Black** as part of a large family started in 1908 in Germany with a design by H. Hoffmann that was appropriate for factory printing chores. **Showcard Moderne** is a recreation by Jim Parkinson of the style of commercial lettering taught in the United States immediately after World War I. **Brok** first appeared as characters in a poster cut in wood by Chris Lebeau in 1925 to promote the Willem Brok Gallery in Holland; Elizabeth Holzman has transformed it into this black display face that can make use of *negative leading*—a reduction of the normal spacing between lines—to enhance the block-like shapes by matching the line spacing to the narrow spaces between letters.

SUMMARY

You want to be careful in selecting text faces; particularly if the block of text is large, you need to pick something that will not only be legible, but also not tire the reader. However, the selection problem is greater with display faces. They usually express more personality than their text counterparts, so it's easy to choose a design that reminds readers of the American Civil War when your subject is eighteenth-century France. Furthermore, they're called display faces because they were designed to be *big*. Therefore, any mistake you make is magnified tremendously, whether it's an error in style, kerning, tracking, or placement.

Familiarity is another difficulty. If the display face is memorable, readers will remember that you used it last week as well as this week. In particular, novelty faces are often really a "one-time gag." Once the reader has seen a humorous typeface that, perhaps, consists of characters composed of dogs in weird poses, he or she chuckles—and doesn't care to see that design again.

Until you acquire some sophistication in typeface selection, you might want to follow the rule used by numerous busy printers, which I mentioned in Chapter 2: Use a standard text typeface for your body copy, then use a simple sans-serif design for headings and titles. The result won't be spectacular, but you can avoid a lot of pitfalls and criticism. However, with a little experience, you'll enjoy discovering beautiful or clever new display types that will help you communicate and add sparkle to your documents.

13

Typeface Utilities and Special Effects

This chapter describes utilities that will help you insert special characters into your documents, manage your typefaces, and create some exciting special effects. Some of these utilities you should already have because they're included with your operating system software. However, you may not be aware that you have them. The others are inexpensive and can be very helpful.

INSERTING SPECIAL CHARACTERS IN WINDOWS 95

If you're running Windows 95—or a later version of Windows—you can use the Character Map utility to locate and copy special characters from any installed typeface into any application. Simply open the Start menu, select Programs, and from Programs select Character Map. The Character Map window will appear, resembling Figure 13.1. Click the arrow in the drop-down Font list if you want to change the font that's displayed and make another selection. The table below the list will show you every character that's available in the font. Click a character to add it to the Characters to Copy list in the upper right corner, then click the Copy button to copy it to the clipboard, and—from the

239

13.1 The Character Map utility in Windows 95.

application you're using—paste the character into your document at the spot where you want it. Unfortunately, you can't enlarge the Character Map window. However, if you press the left mouse button while the cursor is on a character, that particular character will be magnified for you.

As an alternative to using the copy and paste procedure, you can add a special character to your document by holding down the Alt key and typing the correct sequence of four numbers on your numeric keypad. (This technique won't work if you type the numbers from the keys along the top of your keyboard.) How do you know what the number sequence is for the character or symbol you want? When you highlight the character in Character Map, the correct keystroke combination will be displayed in the lower right corner of the window.

Some Windows applications have their own utilities for inserting special characters. Figure 13.2 shows you the Character Roll-Up utility included with Ventura Publisher. In this program, place the cursor at the point in your document where you want the character, then—from the Tools menu—select Character Roll-Up, select the font you want from the font box, and double-click the character in the Roll-Up table in order to insert it. The figure shows this table immediately after the final character has been inserted by this means into the name *René*.

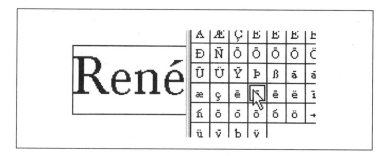

13.2 Inserting a special character in Ventura Publisher.

INSERTING SPECIAL CHARACTERS ON A MACINTOSH

For years Apple has included the Key Caps utility with its Macintosh operating system. You can pick this option from the Apple menu. A small menu will then appear at the top of your screen from which you can select a typeface to show and also copy any selected character to the clipboard for inserting into a document. Below the menu, a window will display the Mac keyboard in a reduced size. When you hold down a modifier key such as Shift, Option, or the Shift-Option combination, the little key tops in the window will show you the character you'll then get if you press any key. You select a character by clicking it with the pointer; it will appear in the box at the top of the window. For example, in Figure 13.3,

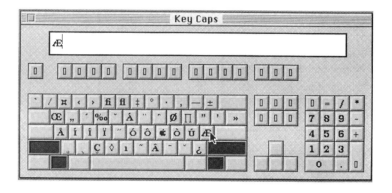

13.3 The Macintosh Key Caps utility.

with the Shift and Option keys held down, Æ was clicked to insert that ligature into the box, from which it could be copied through the clipboard into any open application.

Figure 13.4 shows Big Caps, a Dubl-Click Software utility provided free when you purchase some of the company's other products. After installation, you access Big Caps through the Apple menu, just as you do Key Caps. However, it's far more versatile. You can select from a variety of keyboard layouts, choose to have the utility fill your entire screen if you wish so you can really see those characters, make the characters any point size you want, add effects such as Bold or Outline to see how they look, open a typeface file that's not currently active in your system, and much more. In the figure, Big Caps is occupying the full screen on a 13-inch monitor and is showing the characters available in the **Auriol** typeface with the Option key pressed.

Auriol has an Art Nouveau style and was designed by Georges Auriol in 1901. It's sold wherever the Linotype-Hell library is available.

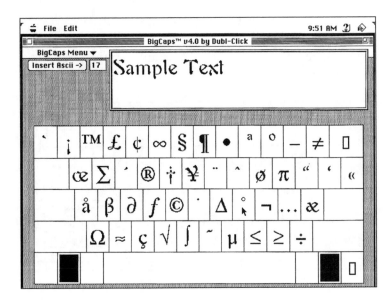

13.4 The Big Caps utility, from Dubl-Click Software.

The PopChar utility was written by Günther Blaschek. He lives in Austria and provides it free of charge through several font vendors in the United States and other countries. You can use it instantly while you're working in a document, without going through the clipboard. With PopChar installed, you can press a tiny square in the upper left corner of your screen to pop up a complete display of all the characters available in the currently selected typeface. You can then merely select a character with the pointer and it will appear immediately at the current entry position in the active document.

PopChar is a great convenience. However, it has three minor disadvantages. First, it displays the current typeface by using one of that face's installed bitmapped fonts. If you have only a 10-point bitmap in the font suitcase, PopChar will display the table of its characters in a reduced size that may be too small for you to read easily. On the other hand, if you have all of the bitmaps still in the suitcase that came with the typeface, PopChar can show you the characters in a large size.

Second, since PopChar shows only the contents of the typeface with which you're presently working, it's awkward to insert a character from, say, a separate expert set into the regular set that's in use. You'd have to select each of those two typefaces alternately, switching back and forth. On the other hand, the utilities I discussed previously let you work within the utility with a different typeface than the one selected in your current document.

The other disadvantage is that PopChar often does not display the contents of picture typefaces properly. In this case, you may have to use another utility.

Figure 13.5 shows PopChar displaying the characters in the casual typeface **ITC Kristen Not So Normal,** designed in 1994 by George Ryan of the Galápagos Design Group. When the pointer highlights any character, the keystroke

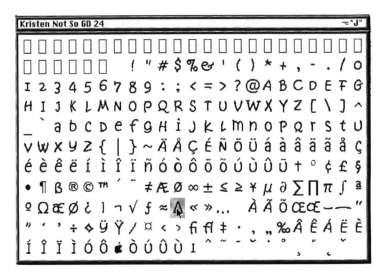

13.5 The PopChar utility shows all of the special characters in the currently selected typeface.

combination to produce the character is shown in the upper right corner of the PopChar window. This information is handy if you're going to use a special character frequently, since—as convenient as this utility is—it's still faster for a good typist to insert a character from the keyboard if the keystrokes are known.

PRINTING CHARACTER SETS

Several digital type foundries provide some kind of utility on their type CD-ROMs that will print a chart of all of the characters in a typeface and the key combinations required to access them. Of course, selecting a character from a chart is another way of discovering what special characters are available and the locations at which they're mapped on your keyboard. The difficulty here is that every time you need this information for a different design, you must stop what you're doing, load the utility, select the typeface, and wait for a new list to print out before you can continue working in your document. Figure 13.6 shows how the Adobe mapping utility prints out the character locations for **Pompeijana Roman,** a typeface created for Linotype by Adrian Frutiger in 1992, based on Roman inscriptions of the first century A.D. The Adobe utility is named KeyCap Utility; Adobe licenses it from Big Rock Software.

Pompeijana Roman

Key	None	Shift	Option	Opt-Shft	Key	None	Shift	Option	Opt-Shft
a	A	A	Å	Å	`	`	~	CC	˜
b	B	B	∫	1	1	1	!	¡	/
c	C	C	Ç	Ç	2	2	@	TM	¤
d	D	D	∂	Î	3	3	#	£	‹
e	E	E	CC	´	4	4	$	¢	›
f	F	F	f	Ï	5	5	%	∞	Fl
g	G	G	©	˜	6	6	^	§	FL
h	H	H	·	Ó	7	7	&	¶	‡
i	I	I	CC	ˆ	8	8	*	•	°
j	J	J	Δ	Ô	9	9	(	ª	·
k	K	K	¬	(apple)	0	0	)	º	‚
l	L	L	¬	Õ	-	-	_	–	—
m	M	M	µ	Â	=	=	+	≠	±
n	N	N	CC	˜	[	[	{	"	"
o	O	O	Ø	Ø	]	]	}	'	'
p	P	P	π	Π	'	'	"	Æ	Æ
q	Q	Q	Œ	Œ	;	;	:	…	Ú
r	R	R	®	‰	\	\			«	»
s	S	S	SS	Í	,	,	<	≤	¯
t	T	T	†	˝	.	.	>	≥	˘
u	U	U	CC	¨	/	/	?	÷	¿
v	V	V	√	◊					
w	W	W	Σ	„					
x	X	X	≈	´					
y	Y	Y	¥	Á					
z	Z	Z	Ω	˛					

1st Key	+ 2nd Key Composite Character						
	e	u	i	o	a	Spc	y,n
Option + `	È	Ù	Ì	Ò	À	`	
Option + e	É	Ú	Í	Ó	Á	´	
Option + u	Ë	Ü	Ï	Ö	Ä	¨	Ÿ
Option + i	Ê	Û	Î	Ô	Â	^	
Option + n				Õ	Ã	~	Ñ

13.6 A page printed with the Adobe utility for showing character keyboard combinations.

KeyCap Utility has advantages over a few of the similar utilities. First, after loading it and selecting the typeface to be used, you can view the character mapping on your screen without printing it, if you prefer. However, if you'll be using several special characters, you'll be in for a lot of switching back and forth between your document and KeyCap Utility. In addition, you can view the capital *A* from the selected typeface in an enlarged state if you wish, to analyze the design; you cannot select any individual character or copy any to the clipboard. Also, you have the option of adding a personalized footer to the printout, containing a brief comment of your own choosing. Finally, you can select a group of typefaces for printing as a batch.

ADOBE TYPE MANAGER

Adobe Type Manager is almost an essential for working with typefaces either in Windows or on a Macintosh. On both platforms, it uses the typeface printer file (sometimes called the *outline*) to generate a sharp screen font in any size you've selected. Without this utility, many typefaces may appear jagged on the screen. Furthermore, it lets you print PostScript typefaces with excellent quality on a printer that doesn't support the PostScript language.

Running under Windows 95—or an earlier or later version of Windows—ATM performs two additional functions: It will install PostScript typefaces for use with Windows—as explained in Chapter 2—and it will create Multiple Master typefaces. See this feature in action in Chapter 14. To generate Multiple Master typefaces on a Macintosh, you don't use ATM but, rather, a separate utility named Font Creator.

Figure 13.7 shows Adobe Type Manager running under Windows 95. As suggested in the figure by the cursor position,

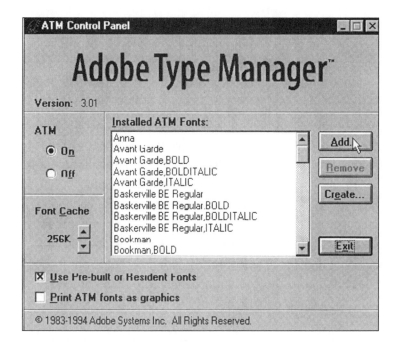

13.7 The Adobe Type Manager Control Panel, installed in Windows 95.

you click the Add . . . button to install a new typeface. Then you simply follow the directions on your screen. Incidentally, on both Windows and Macintosh computers, three dots in a row—called an *ellipsis*—are used at the end of command names to indicate that the command will not be executed immediately. Instead, when you select a command that includes an ellipsis, a *dialog box* appears—a special window in which you're expected to make additional choices.

ADOBE TYPE REUNION FOR MACINTOSH

If you're not using Adobe Type Reunion on a Macintosh, you'll find that each member of a type family will have a separate listing on the Font menu in most programs. For Mac users with many typefaces active, this means two things: The Font menu will become unbelievably long and you have to scroll through the whole thing to see how many weights are installed for, say, the **Palatino** family. **Palatino Bold** will show up on the menu alphabetically as *B Palatino Bold*, **Bold Italic** will be a separate alphabetical listing as *BI Palatino Bold Italic,* and so on, through light, roman, medium, bold, and black weights, plus their matching italics, plus small caps and Old Style figure sets—each a separate listing. However, with Adobe Type Reunion installed, it automatically collects those family members into a group, visible on a submenu.

Figure 13.8 shows you how Adobe Type Reunion works. Here you see the **Poppl-Laudatio** family, which you met in Chapter 12. To use a member of this family, all you have to do is highlight the name **Poppl-Laudatio** on the Font menu, where it appears only once; the submenu will pop up, from which you can highlight an entry to make your selection.

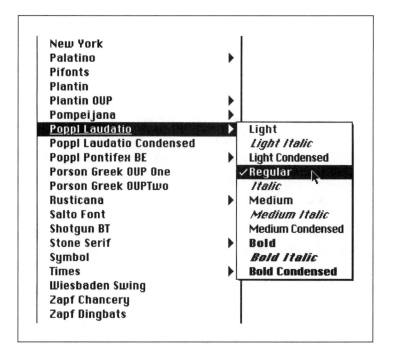

13.8 Adobe Type Reunion displays typefaces as families.

TYPEFACE MANAGEMENT
ON THE MACINTOSH

Read the instructions that accompany most typefaces for the Macintosh and you'll probably be told to install them by simply dragging their icons into your closed System folder. Under early versions of System 7, the typefaces will automatically be stored inside that folder. Under later versions of the system software, they'll automatically be stored in a special Fonts folder within the System folder. In either case, this method of installation works. Afterward, the faces will always appear on your Font menu and be ready for use. The more typefaces you have installed, the longer the Font menu will become—even with Adobe Type Reunion active. And, the more typefaces you have installed, the slower your Mac will operate, because the system software will have to plow through those typefaces again and again in performing other chores.

Yes, there is an easier way. Most professionals using a Mac rely on the Suitcase utility (sold by Symantec) to manage those typefaces. The only typefaces they have in their System folder are those used by the system software: **Chicago, Geneva, Monaco,** and **New York.** With Suitcase installed, you can store the rest of your typefaces anywhere you like—on any hard disk connected to your computer. Then you can organize the ones you use frequently into sets, naming the sets whatever you like, and activating or deactivating them according to your needs. For example, if you use certain typefaces only when you print a monthly report, you could group them into a set called Report. They would appear on your Font menu only when you wanted them and activated them through Suitcase.

There's more. You can manage desk accessories and even sounds with Suitcase too. You can renumber a typeface if

Suitcase tells you it has the same ID number as another one you're using. (Every typeface in your system has its own identification number; no two active typefaces can use the same number.) Furthermore, with Suitcase active, you can assign a modifier key so that, when that key is pressed (Shift, Command, or Option—or a combination of these) and you pull down the Font menu, the typeface names will appear in their actual designs.

You can create your own suitcases and combine typefaces in them as you choose. You can compress typefaces so they take up less space on your hard disk and are decompressed by Suitcase automatically when they're used. Figure 13.9 shows the Suitcase main window, giving you some idea as to how it's configured.

Figure 13.10 shows how a portion of the Font menu looks when the modifier key is pressed in Suitcase. The names all appear as they would look printed in their own typeface styles. This figure illustrates instantly why you

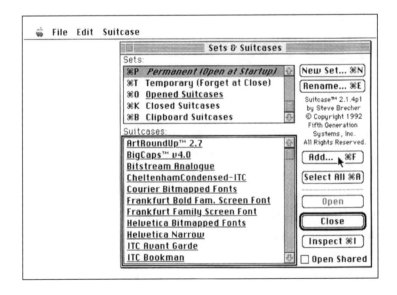

13.9 The Suitcase typeface management utility.

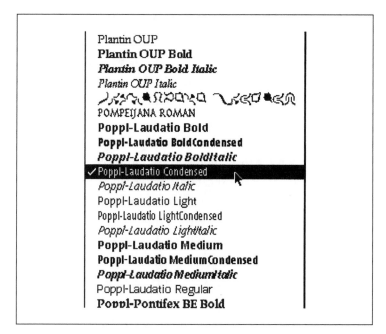

Plantin OUP
Plantin OUP Bold
Plantin OUP Bold Italic
Plantin OUP Italic
⟨ornamental glyphs⟩
POMPEIJANA ROMAN
Poppl-Laudatio Bold
Poppl-Laudatio BoldCondensed
Poppl-Laudatio BoldItalic
✓Poppl-Laudatio Condensed
Poppl-Laudatio Italic
Poppl-Laudatio Light
Poppl-Laudatio LightCondensed
Poppl-Laudatio LightItalic
Poppl-Laudatio Medium
Poppl-Laudatio MediumCondensed
Poppl-Laudatio MediumItalic
Poppl-Laudatio Regular
Poppl-Pontifex BE Bold

13.10 A portion of the Macintosh Font menu, with a modifier key pressed to show the actual appearance of the typefaces.

wouldn't want the actual designs displayed on the menu all the time. You'll note that the fifth line from the top consists of a series of fancy decorations. Actually, those decorations spell the name of this typeface composed of ornaments, if the actual letters of the alphabet were displayed instead of the ornaments attached to them. Therefore, if your menu had several of these ornamental or picture typefaces, you'd have little idea as to what was loaded—since you'd be seeing the result and not the name.

Another disadvantage to using a modifier key and showing actual designs instead of names is that Adobe Type Reunion won't work in this situation, so your menu will become much longer. If you have a very slow Macintosh, there's a third drawback. It will take longer for the complete menu to appear because you'll have to wait for the system to draw all those designs.

TYPEFACE MANAGEMENT IN WINDOWS

You can view typeface designs and manage your library in Windows too. For example, Figure 13.11 demonstrates that in Microsoft Word a little box at the lower right of the Font window will show you the actual design of any highlighted typeface.

More important to Windows users, however, is the ability to store your typefaces in sets and activate them only when you need them, as you can with Suitcase on the Macintosh. FontMinder, from Ares Software, will let you do this and more under Windows 95. It will group either TrueType or PostScript typefaces into sets called font packs, with the names you specify. You can even associate a font pack with a specific document so that you can double-click on the font pack to have FontMinder perform three tasks automatically: install the typefaces used, start the program in which the document was created, and open the document itself.

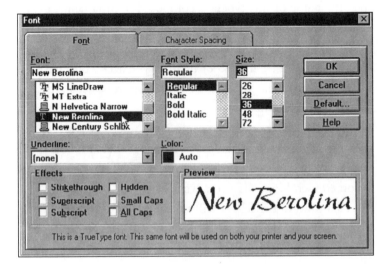

13.11 The Font window in Microsoft Word running under Windows 95.

This utility will print summaries of the typefaces installed, character charts, and type samples in several different forms. In Directory Mode, you can scan directories, preview fonts on screen, and print samples without installing the typefaces—or you can install any typeface viewed with a mouse click. On request, FontMinder will also rename typefaces and reset their family relationships.

Figure 13.12 shows the main window in FontMinder. On the left is a scrollable list of the typefaces available on your computer. Underneath this is a list box where any defined font packs are shown. On the right, you see the list of typefaces currently installed with the utility. To install another typeface, as illustrated in the figure, you highlight its name in the top left list box and click the Install Fonts button. As an alternative, you can simply drag the item into the right-hand box; this action will copy the typeface onto the active list.

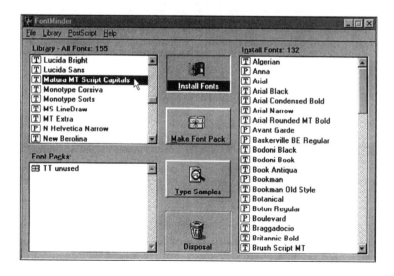

13.12 The main window in the FontMinder utility, running under Windows 95.

MANIPULATING TYPEFACES

You can perform several typeface-manipulation tricks in many Windows and Macintosh programs. You can rotate a font, skew or stretch words, and change colors, including creating white text on a black or colored background. Both PageMaker and QuarkXPress provide the capability to create a drop-cap effect in a paragraph automatically. Figure 13.13 shows how you can do this in Quark, by clicking the Drop Caps box; in this box you can specify how many characters you want to include in the drop and how many lines the dropped characters will occupy. The program resizes the selected number of characters at the beginning of the paragraph and produces the effect for you. Incidentally, the H & J item at the bottom of the Paragraph Formats box shown refers to hyphenation and justification.

13.13 Creating a drop-cap effect in QuarkXPress.

SPECIAL EFFECT UTILITIES

Even if you have very few typefaces, you can alter their
appearance radically with inexpensive special-effect utilities
available for both Windows and the Macintosh. You can
convert the characters into metallic letters, twist them into
new shapes, emboss or engrave them, or mount them inside
children's balloons—even mold a line of text into a circle.
Obviously, you don't want to get carried away by creating
strange images that make the words unintelligible or distract
from your message, but some of the alterations you can
achieve will freshen up your pages and fascinate your readers.
I'll show you a few of these utilities in this section of the
chapter.

Bitstream Mini-Makeup

Here's the ultimate software bargain for Windows users. How
about getting an unlocked CD-ROM full of 500 top-quality
typefaces for a mere $49.95? Doesn't excite you? What if I
tell you that the typefaces are from Bitstream and in both
PostScript and TrueType formats? Better, you say, but not
sensational? You're hard to please. Then consider this:
Included on the same CD-ROM is Bitstream Mini-Makeup.
This is a great special-effects utility—easily worth $49.95 in
itself and so simple to use that it's ridiculous.

Just look at the Mini-Makeup window displayed in Figure
13.14. All you have to do is select the typeface and style you
want at the top, type the characters to be shown, and click on
one of the shapes shown at the lower right. The text you typed
will instantly appear in the preview box at the lower left with
the special effect applied. You can then save this image to disk
or copy it through the clipboard directly into an application.
Other options let you include drop shadows stretching in any

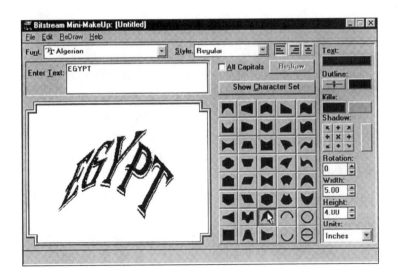

13.14 The Bitstream Mini-Makeup utility.

of six directions, align multiple lines of text, choose from 8 outline weights, and select from 16 colors, shades of gray, or fill patterns. In addition, you can adjust the size of the image and rotate it from 0 to 359 degrees.

One note of caution: Mini-Makeup doesn't work with Multiple Master typefaces. They can be easily identified on the Font menu because the letters *MM* are included in their names. So don't select them! And please see the next section on how to handle Mini-Makeup if you have either Adobe Acrobat or the Acrobat Reader installed on your PC.

Mini-Makeup and Adobe Acrobat

Adobe Acrobat is a utility that lets you create documents with a variety of typefaces and have them print correctly on computers that don't have those typefaces, provided the Adobe Acrobat Reader is installed there. This reader uses two special Multiple Master typefaces—**Adobe Sans** and **Adobe Serif**—to "recreate" an approximation of the original typefaces on systems where they don't exist. When you install the reader, it automatically adds these two Multiple Master typefaces to your list of available fonts.

Now here's the problem. When you load Mini-Makeup, it always opens by selecting and displaying the first typeface on its Font menu, in alphabetical order. Therefore, on a computer that has the Adobe Acrobat Reader installed, that first typeface is likely to be **Adobe Sans.** In this situation, since Mini-Makeup won't work with any Multiple Master typeface, it will crash immediately and not even finish loading.

What's the solution? Make sure there's some typeface installed in your computer with a name that comes *before* **Adobe Sans** alphabetically. Fortunately, on the same Bitstream CD-ROM that contains Mini-Makeup, you'll find a typeface called **Aachen.** It's a Slab Serif display face designed by Colin Brignall for Letraset in 1969 and it definitely precedes **Adobe Sans** alphabetically. If you have the Adobe Acrobat Reader installed, simply install **Aachen** before you try to load Mini-Makeup and the problem is solved.

Other "beginning of the alphabet" typefaces you could select that would appear before **Adobe Sans** include **Aardvark,** available from the Font Bureau; the **Aase** sans-serif family sold by Image Club; Monotype's **Abadi,** another sans-serif family; and, of course, **Adobe Caslon, Adobe Garamond**—or any other typeface with a name that begins with the word Adobe and ends with a word preceding Sans in the alphabet. You can view all the typefaces I've mentioned in the Specimens section of this book.

Letraset Envelopes

Letraset Envelopes is a plug-in for Adobe Illustrator and Macromedia Freehand that lets you twist type into shapes of your choosing, add perspective, and modify the results using Bézier control points. The plug-in offers more than 200 distortion effects. Figure 13.15 shows you some typical results. The illustrations are more Letraset DesignFonts drawings by Tom Lulevitch. The typefaces are all from the Font Bureau. The top example is **Showcard Gothic,** designed by Jim Parkinson in 1993 and based on showcard lettering of the 1920s and 1930s. Denyse Schmidt drew **Scamp,** the middle specimen, inspired by animated paper letter cutouts and completed in 1992. The bottom typeface is **Belucian Demi,** created by David Berlow in 1990 from a 1925 Lucian Bernhard design, at the request of *Smart* magazine; by 1994 it had been expanded into an upscale family suitable for text or display use.

Figure 13.16 shows another Envelopes example, with yet another DesignFonts drawing by Tom Lulevitch. The

13.15 Special effects produced with Letraset Envelopes.

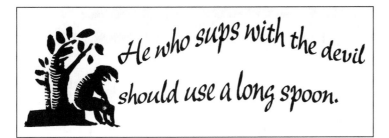

13.16 Another Envelopes example, using Monotype's New Berolina typeface.

typeface this time is **New Berolina,** from Monotype, a calligraphic script designed in 1965 by Martin Wilke.

Illustrator and Freehand Filters

Some drawing and paint applications provide their own built-in typeface special effects. Figure 13.17 shows the results of applying Adobe Illustrator's built-in filters to **Pilsner Black,** a member of the **Pilsner** family introduced to you in Chapter 9. The actual typeface is shown in the upper

13.17 Special effects created with Adobe Illustrator built-in filters.

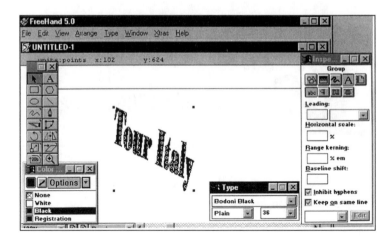

13.18 Text skewed and rotated within Freehand.

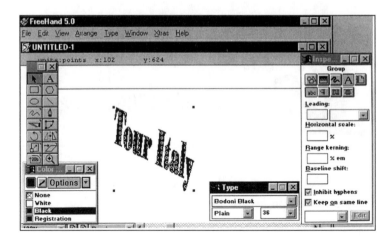

13.19 A spiral type effect produced by Macromedia Freehand.

left corner of the figure, where the word REPORT appears unmodified. All the other instances of the word have been dramatically altered.

Figure 13.18 shows the words *Tour Italy* skewed and rotated from within Freehand 5.0, running under Windows 95. You can accomplish this effect by merely selecting built-in tools and dragging a corner of the text object.

Figure 13.19 is a more interesting effect. This type spiral was achieved by using Freehand's Bind to Path command. The typeface is **Bookman Old Style,** a 1991 Monotype version of **Bookman** created by Ong ChongWah. Like the **Bookman** families from other vendors, its origins can be traced to an 1860 Scottish typeface designed by Alexander Phemister. The Monotype version has a smaller x-height than **ITC Bookman,** introduced in Chapter 1, and is closer in appearance to the nineteenth-century original.

Using Masking Effects in PageMaker

Adobe PageMaker has a masking capability you can use to create special type effects. In Figure 13.20, you can see what happened when I drew a star and used it to mask a block of text.

Type Twister

Adobe sells Type Twister in both Windows and Macintosh versions. It's very versatile. First of all, it comes with many typefaces of its own, which you'll see on its Font menu mixed alphabetically with those installed in your system. You can change colors, shapes, and effects by using preset options or you can create options of your own. You can choose from 50 full-color, extravagant settings for your text and you can modify those as well. In Figure 13.21 you see a type effect on the screen that was realized by setting the Effect list box to Multi Outline, the Font menu to **Showtime** (one of the built-in typefaces), the Shape list box to Double Convex, and the Colorset list box to Black and White.

13.20 Masking a block of type with a shape drawn in PageMaker.

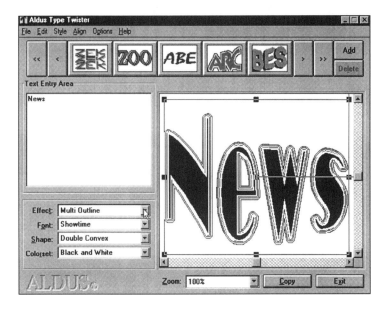

13.21 Type Twister running under Windows 95.

13.22 Text is imprinted on floating balloons in this Type Twister effect.

Figure 13.22 shows one of the standard effects provided. I added the text FLY; here's the result, using a built-in typeface. Obviously, this is one effect that you wouldn't use if you wanted to display two or three lines of text.

Another standard Type Twister effect employs curved lines of text in an Art Deco type style, as demonstrated in Figure 13.23. Each character casts a small shadow. You could modify this—or any other effect—by changing the typeface to one of your own or another built-in option, changing the path of the characters, using a different effect than the drop shadows, and so on. By default, most of the patterns are composed of bright and unusual color combinations—which I've converted to black-and-white or grayscale for duplication here.

This utility works through the clipboard, using either Windows or a Macintosh. You copy your completed effect to the clipboard, then paste it into an application—either for immediate use as part of a current document or to save it in a graphics format as a picture image.

TypeStyler

13.23 Another Type Twister effect uses an Art Deco type style.

Broderbund's TypeStyler is available only for the Macintosh. Like Type Twister, it provides many built-in effects and typefaces. You can customize the effects and use your own typefaces if you prefer. Unlike Type Twister, it will let you save the images you create in standard graphics formats. You can also create entire pages using different effects and save them as a single graphic, plus you can save any TypeStyler page or effect in the program's own format; this option lets you edit your work later if you wish, without duplicating the entire effort. Figure 13.24 shows the main TypeStyler window.

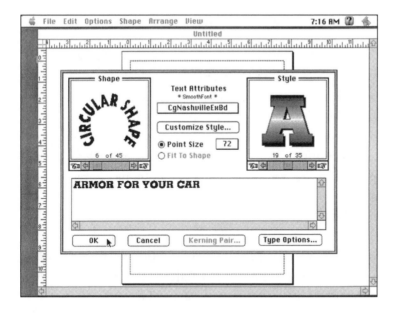

13.24 The main TypeStyler window.

TypeStyler has sophisticated kerning and tracking capabilities not available in Type Twister.

BUY TYPEFACES WITH SPECIAL EFFECTS BUILT IN

If you don't have any typeface special-effect utilities, there's another way you can use several special effects anyway. Buy a type CD-ROM from URW. This company provides effect versions of its typefaces along with the standard version you'd normally expect. For example, Figure 13.25 shows Letraset's **Edwardian** as sold by URW. You get the regular typeface—shown at the lower right—plus an outline version, two kinds of drop shadow effects, and an inline version (represented by the *W* with inner lines tracing its shape). There's even one more version not shown here that simply rounds the corners or all characters so you can use the typeface more easily in cutting out characters for use in signs.

13.25 URW provides special-effect versions of their typefaces.

MAKING BORDERS FOR YOUR TEXT

Many typefaces include ornaments you can use as borders. Other typefaces have been designed specifically as borders with separate side and corner elements so you can construct a frame any size you want. Unfortunately, most people who've made borders in this way have found that it was a tedious and time-consuming experience. Furthermore, in some programs, producing the vertical sides of a border frame can result in spacing nightmares.

Well, Letraset has a solution for these difficulties. It's a utility called BorderFonts. The program automatically constructs a border frame to the dimensions you specify, using any character you select from a series of border typefaces in different modern and historical styles. The characters are attractive, square-shaped, standalone designs. How much of the character will appear and repeat in your border depends upon the dimensions you've chosen—adding more variety to the results you can obtain. Moreover, you can use BorderFonts with characters from your regular typefaces. Now you're into real creativity—all painlessly.

Figure 13.26 illustrates all of these points. At the top of the figure, the circled design in the BorderFonts typeface is the character I selected from which to manufacture a border. Directly under this display you can see the result. Note that the program used only a small portion of the character to create the repeating pattern and then varied the design automatically to make the corners of the frame. Now the surprise! At the right of this BorderFonts-generated frame is another frame that could be used as a border for the menu at Gaston's French restaurant. At the top of this frame, I've replaced the repeating character with characters from a

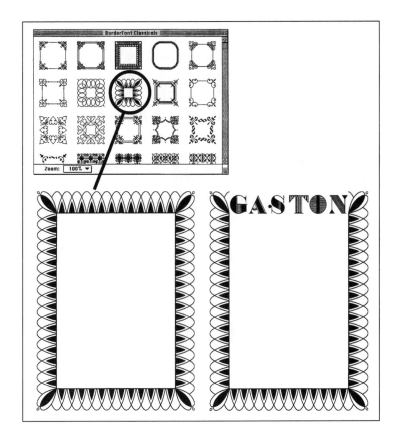

13.26 Using Letraset's BorderFonts utility to create decorative frames.

standard PostScript typeface in order to spell the name Gaston. As an alternative, I could have built an entire frame from the letter *G,* for example.

You can order BorderFonts through Fontek.

The typeface in the name Gaston is called **Bradley Initials.** It was designed in 1934 by Will Bradley. The style is Art Deco and alternate designs are included for each character. Glenda de Guzman drew the alternates added in a 1994 Font Bureau release.

SUMMARY

Some of the utilities I've shown you will enable you to create an almost endless series of variations on the typefaces you have. Of course, I hope you'll use this power wisely and not ruin your documents by adding special effects for their own sake. In addition, the character-insertion utilities will let you use interesting extra characters more easily that are already waiting for you in your type library.

However, I know that some people are never satisfied. Some readers are not going to be content with twisting and stretching characters. They'll want to make their own. So the next chapter is for everyone in this group.

14

Creating Your Own Characters and Typefaces

Don't skip this chapter because you think you're not a designer. Some of the programs I'll tell you about let you create a new typeface simply by sliding a few adjustment bars and saving the result. On the other hand, if you've always wanted to be a type designer, I'll introduce you to the programs the professionals use—welcome to the club!

I cover kerning here, too, but not the aspects you read about earlier. In addition to programs that let you manually adjust the spacing between two characters and/or kern all of the text for you by using the information in kerning tables built in to the typefaces, there are programs that let you modify existing kerning tables or build your own. Why would you want to do that? Well, some kerning tables that come with type are very small; they provide spacing information on only 50 or 100 character pairs. This means that other character combinations just won't be kerned. Some typefaces include no kerning table at all. Autologic usually provides its typefaces in this form because the principal customers for its type are newspapers that either don't want kerning or want to add their own tables.

First, let's explore the programs that let you create new typefaces from existing ones.

PROGRAMS THAT MODIFY TYPEFACES

It's usually easier to start with something and modify it to your needs than it is to build a masterpiece from scratch. For example, if you want a seriffed typeface with slightly wider, bolder characters than an existing design you admire, why design your own face character by character to achieve, perhaps, an inferior result? Why not use the existing design and make only the changes you want. Yes, there are programs that will let you do this.

Font Creator and Multiple Master Typefaces

I discussed Adobe Type Manager (ATM) in the previous chapter from the aspect of installing, displaying, and printing your type. The Windows version of ATM also includes Font Creator, the utility you use to create new variants from Multiple Master typefaces. If you're using a Macintosh, Font Creator is a separate utility that's provided with Multiple Master typefaces when you purchase them. Either way, the process is about the same.

To access Font Creator in Windows, you click a button in the main window of ATM. Then you'll see the Font Creator window shown in Figure 14.1. Here you first select a typeface from the list box at the top of the window, then change the coordinates directly underneath this box to achieve the effect you want. The changes you make are reflected in the sample box at the bottom of the window.

The exact changes you can make to a Multiple Master typeface are specified by the type designer. For example, a designer will select a weight range he deems acceptable without ruining his concept. He will probably also allow changes in character width, again, within limits. Some designers may let you alter the height of ascenders and

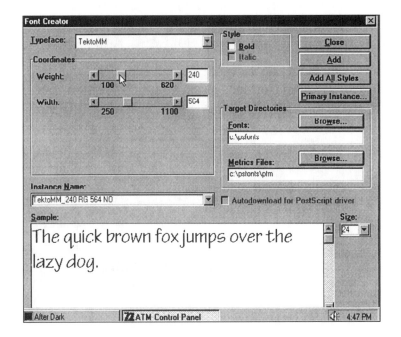

14.1 The Font Creator window within Adobe Type Manager, running under Windows 95.

descenders or change the slant of the characters. In Figure 14.1 height and character width are the two variables. The typeface is Adobe's **Tekton,** originally created by David Siegel and based on the handwriting of architect Frank Ching; the Adobe staff developed the Multiple Master version in 1993.

Now look at Figure 14.2. The sample box at the bottom of the Font Creator window shows a wider, bolder **Tekton** created by merely moving those sliders at the top of the window.

As mentioned in Chapter 2, you can use Multiple Masters to alter the width of characters slightly so they'll exactly fit into a certain space on a page without changing font sizes.

There is a down side to using Multiple Masters. The variation you create remains tied to its master. Its name is actually a combination of numbers and letters that constitute

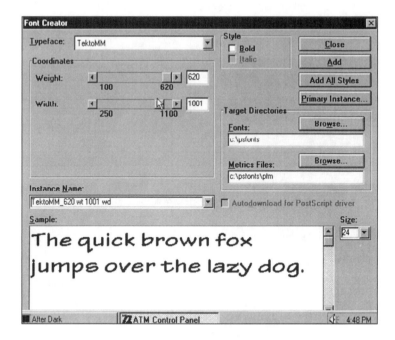

14.2 The Font Creator makes characters in the Tekton Multiple Master typeface wider and bolder.

the description of the slider settings that were used to create it. This fact may make it difficult for you to remember later what your variation actually looks like, without viewing it.

FontChameleon

Ares Software's FontChameleon is far more versatile. It, too, is available for both Windows and Macintosh, but lets you change weight, width, slant, tracking, x-height, numeral height, ascender and descender height, and capital height for any selected typeface. In addition, you can blend two of the program's master outlines together. This means you could take a serif typeface and mix it with a sans-serif, creating a new design half-way between the two. You can save your new creation as a *font descriptor*—a sort of tiny recipe for building the variation you made. This method of use lets you store many typefaces that require very little disk space and can be reconstituted for use as long as the FontChameleon program is available. As an alternative, you can save your new design in the standard PostScript Type 1 or TrueType formats and give it any name you choose. Figure 14.3 shows the main FontChameleon window, running under Windows 95.

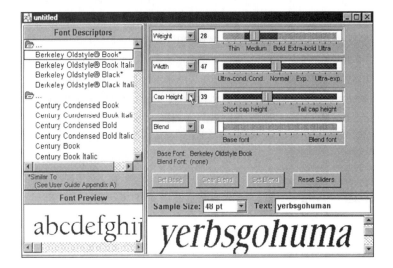

14.3 FontChameleon can alter or blend typefaces to create new ones.

DESIGNING YOUR OWN

The programs that let you design your own typefaces can be used for exactly that exalted purpose or, if you prefer, merely to add or modify a single character. You might pick the second alternative to add your company logo to the official corporate typeface or to add a foreign-language symbol that a type designer didn't provide. These applications are relatively easy to use, but I must warn you that designing an entire typeface—with all those characters—is a daunting task not to be undertaken lightly.

Ikarus M for the Macintosh

URW introduced the Ikarus system for developing digital typefaces in 1972. For years it was an expensive but accepted standard, requiring sophisticated special equipment. However, in 1989 Ikarus became available to many individual designers and companies with small budgets when the company introduced a version consisting entirely of software that would run on a Macintosh. With this program you can create either PostScript Type 1 or TrueType typefaces, including automatic generation of screen fonts and linking of family members. You can draw your design with a mouse or on a digitizing tablet, creating curves by marking points along the contour of a letter; the program will transmit the coordinate locations to the computer and calculate the correct arcs between the marked points. Other features include the capability of creating intermediate weights of a design automatically by interpolating between regular and bold weights. You can also save a design as a PostScript graphics file (EPS format). Figure 14.4 shows the main Ikarus window.

Fontographer

Fontographer is available both for Windows and the Macintosh. It originated on the Macintosh in 1986. Like Ikarus M, it will let you draw with a mouse or a digitizing tablet and create PostScript, TrueType, or EPS files. The program was developed by Altsys and later acquired by Macromedia. Both of these companies have updated Fontographer regularly and it has been adopted by many famous type designers as their primary design tool. One key advantage is its ability to import Freehand and Illustrator files, so designers can create a design in one of those programs if they wish and then complete the work and

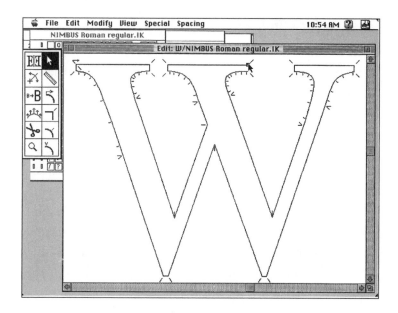

14.4 The Ikarus M typeface designing system.

generate the actual typefaces in Fontographer. The program will also trace scanned images automatically to create usable characters; morph two designs together; create Multiple Master typefaces; add automatic spacing, kerning, and hinting to any typeface produced; and it offers 101 levels of Undo and Redo. Figure 14.5 shows the main Fontographer window, running under Windows 95.

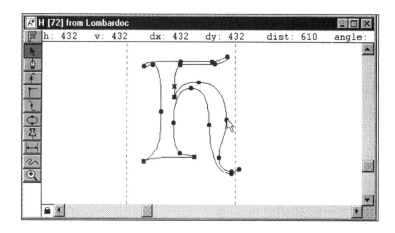

14.5 Modifying a character in Fontographer, under Windows 95.

FontLab for Windows

FontLab originated in Russia and was brought to the United States in 1994. It's fully professional and is the first typeface design program that was developed exclusively for Windows. Sold outside Russia by Pyrus North America, it has some enviable features. You can create a library of parts of characters for reuse, open up to 10 working windows plus 10 additional display windows at the same time, use multiple layers in creating a character, and move any point on a curve without using a node or control point. Like Fontographer, it supports scanned images, morphing, automatic kerning and hinting, and output in PostScript, TrueType, and EPS formats. The main window is shown in Figure 14.6.

Figure 14.7 shows one of the special effects built into FontLab. It has an extensive macro language that lets you develop your own special-effect routines. As of this writing,

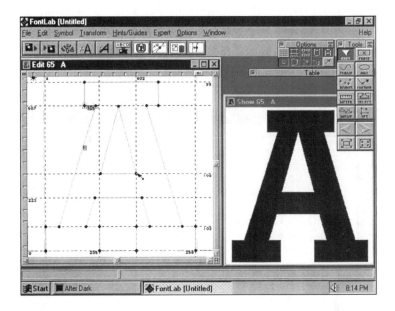

14.6 FontLab for Windows permits freehand drawing.

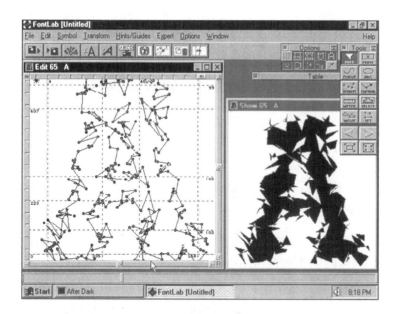

14.7 The result of applying FontLab's Broken Glass effect.

the program cannot create Multiple Master typefaces or open more than one typeface file at a time.

SPECIAL KERNING UTILITIES

If kerning is a major concern for you, special utilities can take care of your needs. Some typefaces contain no kerning table or a table limited to a few pairs. These practices made sense in the days when many programs had no support for kerning tables; in other words, if applications couldn't read the tables and adjust the spacing of character pairs accordingly, why bother to provide them? However, today many major programs do support kerning. Unfortunately, some support a maximum of 150 or even 500 kerning pairs. Sophisticated desktop publishing programs can handle up to 1,000 pairs or more, so major digital type foundries are creating products with kerning tables that large.

Keeping this background in mind, you might want to add a kerning table to a typeface that doesn't have one, replace an existing kerning table with one that's larger, or replace an existing table with one that offers tighter or looser kerning than the original. (In other words, with the characters placed closer together or further apart.)

Perhaps your needs are not that great. You've noticed only three pairs you use that are not kerned properly or at all. You want to correct those discrepancies. In either case, this section will profile two utilities that could help you.

Kernus for the Macintosh

Kernus is another URW utility that is available only for the Macintosh. This is a professional tool that sells for $495. However, before you hastily turn the page, let me tell you how to get Kernus for nothing. Simply buy one of the bargain URW CD-ROMs that contain 3,000 typefaces. These disks sell for $800 or $900 *and include Kernus free on the disk!*

With Kernus, you can set the point size for which a typeface was originally designed—if you know it, the target size for which you want to create a new version, how tight you want the kerning to be, and how many kerning pairs you want. If you select a number like 500 or less, Kernus does the kerning from special character-combination lists that include only the most important kerning pairs. In other words, the program won't start working from some giant list until it reaches the magic number of 500 and leave you with some obscure pairs kerned and some really important ones without any kerning at all because they appear later in the list.

Figure 14.8 shows the Kernus window ready to create a new version of Autologic's **Champfleury** typeface. As mentioned at the beginning of the chapter, Autologic

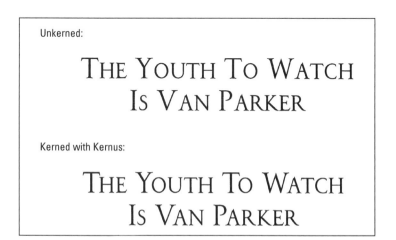

14.8 Kernus set up to add a kerning table to a PostScript typeface.

normally provides no kerning for its typefaces because its newspaper customers either don't want it or want to provide their own tables. I should add that the company will provide kerned typefaces on special request.

In Figure 14.9 you can see the difference the kerning table made by comparing the unkerned and kerned versions of **Champfleury.** Incidentally, this titling typeface was

Unkerned:

THE YOUTH TO WATCH IS VAN PARKER

Kerned with Kernus:

THE YOUTH TO WATCH IS VAN PARKER

14.9 A comparison of a typeface before and after kerning with Kernus.

designed by the Autologic staff in 1985, based on sixteenth-century lettering by Geoffroy Tory. The design doesn't lend itself to tight kerning, so the "before and after" contrast is not as great as it might otherwise be.

FontFiddler for Windows

Ares Software is the source for FontFiddler, an inexpensive Windows program that lets you change individual kerning pairs manually—as demonstrated in Figure 14.10—or add a new kerning table to a typeface that has none. Unfortunately, the feature that generates new kerning tables includes a table of only 200 pairs, which is inadequate for professional use. This utility also lets you change font names and their properties—how they're grouped in families and how they're handled in Windows. In addition, you can print out six different type sample charts, including a list of the kerning pairs, a chart of the typeface's character set, and a word list showing the kerned characters in use.

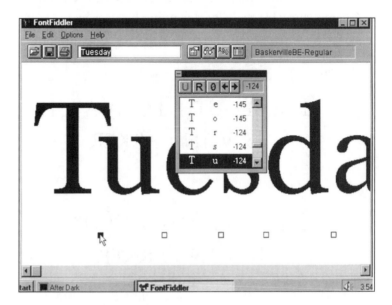

14.10 FontFiddler in the process of chaging the spacing for a kerning pair.

SUMMARY

As I indicated earlier, designing new typefaces is not an endeavor for everyone. However, if you're interested, this chapter has shown you that the tools are available for you to do just this. Almost any Macintosh or PC that can run Windows can handle the software and do the job.

Modifying a typeface, adding a character, or changing a kerning table are chores that interest many more people—particularly since most of these programs make the work easy. In any event, the options are there for you any time you become dissatisfied with the type you're using.

15

Using Type in Layouts

Once people are familiar with typeface categories and reliable choices they can make within those categories, they can still run into trouble when they start combining typefaces and using them in layouts, particularly in conjunction with artwork. In other words, welcome to the real world. If you've graduated from a design school employing instructors who know computers and actually practice what they preach, or if you work in an organization that has experts handy to advise you and critique your work, or if you've become an expert yourself through trial and error, you may have avoided or learned about most of the hazards. For those not experienced in design or with no guru power handy, this chapter may be essential reading. For everybody else, I think you'll pick up a few pointers and get acquainted with still more typefaces you might want to use.

WELDING TEXT TO CLIP ART

Figure 15.1 is the first example we'll investigate. First of all, it contains a portion of a well-known poem. By using the 1995 **Kennedy** typeface created by George Ryan of the Galápagos Design Group, I was able to add decorative touches to the

In Xanadu did Kubla Khan,
A stately pleasure dome decree:
Where Alph, the sacred river, ran,
Through caverns measureless to man,
Down to a sunless sea.

Coleridge

15.1 Fitting text to a parchment scroll.

text by substituting alternate characters with flourishes at the end of each line. However, the important factor here is the clip art—a drawing from Dubl-Click Software's Wet Paint collection. As you can see, the scroll the man is presenting to us is being held at a slight angle. Furthermore, at the bottom of the illustration, the parchment curves as it reaches the rolled-up portion. The trick is to make the text look as if it's actually printed on the parchment.

It would be irritating to the reader if the individual lines of the poem were to be placed at different angles. So I rotated all of the verse slightly to match the general tilt of the parchment. Then, since the author's name—Coleridge— appears lower on the scroll, close to the rolled-up portion, I angled it differently. Such subtle changes can be a big factor in having the viewer accept the joining of text to an unrelated piece of clip art.

COMBINING TYPEFACE SPECIAL EFFECTS WITH CLIP ART

With one piece of clip art, a typeface special-effects utility, and one actual typeface, you can create an infinite number of variations in design and in the placement of type and clip art in relation to each other. In this section of the chapter, I'll demonstrate a few.

15.2 Multiple copies of characters positioned to add emphasis.

The typeface I'll use is Linotype's **San Marco,** introduced in Chapter 11. The text will consist of two words: *Tour Europe.* The special-effects utility is Broderbund's TypeStyler. The artwork is a drawing of a castle on a mountain top, from the Metro library. First, in Figure 15.2, look at the text combined with a special-effect but without the clip art.

Here the words seem to leap out at the viewer because multiple copies of characters expand left and right from the center to impart an illusion of depth.

In Figure 15.3, you see the same text effect superimposed over the castle drawing—to provide visual reinforcement for the words. In this instance, I grayed out the black-and-white picture so the words would be clearly visible in front of it. You can accomplish the graying trick in most desktop-publishing programs or in image-editing applications such as Adobe Photoshop.

15.3 A grayed image is used as a background for the text.

I repositioned the drawing—in Figure 15.4—in its full black-and-white strength to the right of the text so that the text draws the eye toward the image. Now the words are shown in an inline format, with a single patterned duplicate added behind each character as a drop shadow to supply contrast to the original. Note that I've also gradually increased the height of the characters from left to right so that the

15.4 The text increases in size, emphasized by drop shadows, to draw the eye toward the drawing.

15.5 Metallic characters with drop shadows are grouped around the illustration.

15.6 In another rearrangement of the material, the characters appear in outline at the end of rays emitted from behind the castle.

word Europe is emphasized and the text leads more dramatically to the drawing.

In the next rendition (Figure 15.5), the characters become gray and metallic, with white highlights and black drop shadows, and are arranged around the drawing of the castle. Despite the changes in appearance, I haven't changed typefaces. The words are still displayed in Linotype's **San Marco** typeface.

In the final example (Figure 15.6) the characters are white, configured in an outline format, and arranged in an arc at the ends of rays emanating from behind the illustration. You can probably think of dozens of other ways to display this typeface in combination with the same drawing, often with little effort. After all, you can generate different effects and drag objects around on your screen until you like the effect produced.

A MOVIE POSTER RELIES ON ITS ELEMENTS

Sometimes the effectiveness of a layout relies heavily on the components you select. Figure 15.7 is a case in point. Here the illustration is dramatic. It's from the FargoFoto library and made more startling by being displayed upside down. The principal typeface is **Randumhouse,** from House Industries, created in 1994 by Bob Smartner; this unusual design is the

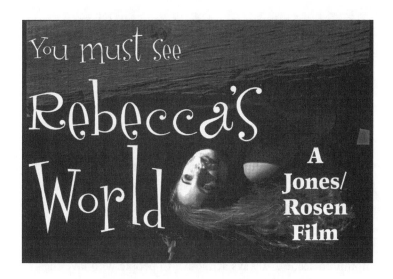

15.7 A movie poster combines an unusual photo with an innovative typeface.

other major factor contributing to the impact of the poster. The name of the production company—Jones/Rosen—is displayed in Friedrich Poppl's 1974 design, **Poppl-Pontifex Bold,** available through Adobe.

Because of its distance from the heading, the Jones/Rosen text balances with it, even though the heading is in much larger type. Using white type superimposed over the photo works better than relying on a more conventional layout, which would place black type beneath or around the photo.

USING WHITE SPACE

If you produce an ad of any kind, it'll be competing for the reader's attention with other ads in the same publication. As mentioned in Chapter 1, advertisers are always well aware of how much they're paying for advertising space and, regrettably, they often want to promote their product's features in every inch of that space. However, if they do this, they may well lose the reader entirely. An ad crammed full of small type doesn't look inviting and it tends to make the advertiser appear cheap and insignificant. A better strategy is to use your space primarily to attract the reader, then present a brief, simple message.

How do you attract the reader? *White space* is always helpful; leave part of your space empty—in a pleasing layout—and the novelty of this approach may keep the reader from turning to the next page. Another helpful tool is a good illustration. And yet another is using display type that is unique but appropriate for the subject matter. Figure 15.8 shows how all these factors can work together.

The photo in Figure 15.8 is from FargoFoto. A beautiful mountain scene is always attractive to people who love the outdoors. Of course, these are the people you'd want to reach if you were running a wilderness tours business. The short paragraph of text—the only "sell copy" in the ad—states concisely what the company offers and why it should be considered. No point would have been served by filling the area to the right of the photo with additional facts about the company that no one would read. The white space above and below the text makes it stand out.

The text typeface is **Maiandra Demibold,** created by Dennis Pasternak of Galápagos Design in 1994 and based on hand-lettering by Oswald Cooper for a 1909 ad. Cooper, in turn, derived these warm, irregular characters from his study of ancient Greek lettering. **Maiandra** is a complete family, with roman, demibold, black, and italic components. For the name of the tour company I used **ITC Digital Woodcuts,** a 1995 typeface designed by Timothy Donaldson and, certainly, fitting for an outdoor-related subject.

The layout has an asymmetrical balance. The positioning of the text block and the white space above and below it

Explore the back country with the mountain's most experienced guides. For 22 years we've been introducing families to the great outdoors.

FRED'S WILDERNESS TOURS
Phone 766-4211

15.8 An ad's readership is helped by white space, an interesting photo, and a unique typeface.

balances against the large photo and is given a solid base by the name of the tour company running across the bottom of the ad. The fact that the name is partially superimposed over the photo helps tie the elements together. From a psychological standpoint, the layout leads the eye first to the text block, then down through the photo to the name and phone number—exactly the sequence you'd want as an advertiser.

A WATERMARK AND A RUNAROUND

Figure 15.9 is an announcement for a mythical art gallery. The illustration is from the Image Club library. As you can see, the body copy wraps around the picture. This technique is called a *runaround* and, in this instance, helps tie the drawing to the text. The name of the gallery appears twice—once in big, black type at the bottom of the layout and again in a watermark effect behind the body copy. I produced this effect by merely rotating the word in PageMaker, then specifying a 10 percent tint on the lettering—which means that the normally black type was cut back to a pale gray.

The name of the gallery is shown in **ITC Matisse,** a 1995 design by Gregory Gray. The inspiration was paper cutout lettering created by the artist for a supplement to the *Figaro* newspaper in Paris that dealt with the work of Matisse. The

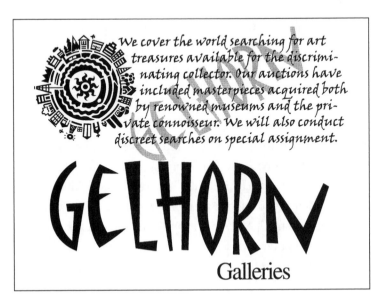

15.9 This announcement uses a runaround and a watermark as design elements.

lowercase positions in this typeface are occupied by alternate characters. If you're looking for a different display face, this might be the answer.

The word *Galleries* is in Monotype's **Times New Roman.** The body copy is **ITC Viner Hand,** a 1995 release based on the personal handwriting of its creator, British designer John Viner. This script is a welcome relief from others that have been overused.

The layout is basically symmetrical, although the word *Galleries* does balance against the heavy illustration in the upper left corner.

AN UNUSUAL TYPEFACE FAMILY USED TO THE FULLEST

Michael Johnson created the **Zeitgeist** family for Monotype in 1990. It's very large and unusual, in that it's based on the "stepping-stone," jagged effect seen in characters when you magnify low-resolution bitmapped typefaces. From this starting point, Johnson created swash characters, lowercase letters he calls "Crazy Paving," italics and condensed versions, and white-on-black lettersets he's named "Cameos." You can see several of these members of his happy family in Figure 15.10.

The illustration is a background from the Image Club library that I cropped in PageMaker. In the same program, I also skewed the word *Oblique* to provide a special effect that would tie in with the name of the theater. At the bottom of the poster, the entire word *The* is a ligature, as is the *fi* letter combination. The box office information at the lower right is surrounded by white space, which makes it balance against the large illustration at the upper left.

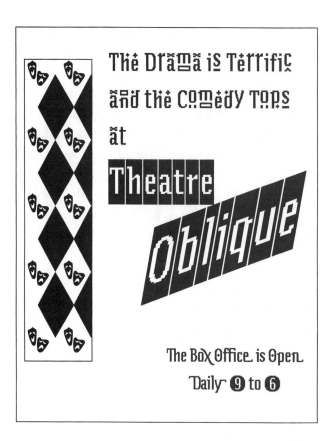

15.10 A theater poster uses members of the Zeitgeist typeface family.

TYPEFACES OF THE ERA MAKE THE DIFFERENCE

Figure 15.11 could be a page from a magazine. The subject of the article is British motion pictures of the 1930s and 1940s, so it would be nice to use typefaces that suggest the era. I did. Also note that there is no illustration. The entire page is type. However, the word *Film* repeated at an angle across the top of the page is actually used as a design element rather than for its information value. This typeface is **Metropolis,** created by W. Schwerdtner in 1932 and available from Image Club; it's a typical picturesque, heavy face of its period. Here's an important layout point: The fact that the line repeating the word *Film* is cut off in the middle of a character, both on the left and right, makes the reader understand instantly and subconsciously that the line *is* a design element and not something to be read carefully.

The display face used for the heading of this article is Letraset's **Burlington,** drawn by Alan Meeks in 1985. It deliberately reflects design conventions of the 1940s. The body copy was set in Letraset's **Charlotte Sans,** a Michael Gills design he created in 1992 as a companion to his **Charlotte** serif family. **Charlotte Sans** reminds us of the

British Movie Classics Still Merit Viewing

Many remain available on videotape and in art houses.

The British motion picture industry of the 1930s and 40s produced many magnificent films from scripts that really told a story and with actors who were not merely "screen personalities." They knew how to act.

Fortunately, through the magic of videotape, the general public can still enjoy a large percentage of these masterpieces. Also, cable channels such as Bravo and American Movie Classics run a select few with some regularity. Other movies of the era have never been transferred to the electronic medium—often due to legal squabbles over copyright ownership—but are occasionally seen in their original form in the cinema art houses that cater to film buffs. Unhappily, these circumstances leave many fans of this genre with nowhere to see certain titles except, perhaps,

in a handful of British theaters devoted to classic motion pictures. And some notable achievements have been lost forever. Numerous films have deteriorated because they were stored improperly; the negatives and prints of others have simply been lost.

Still, the videotape catalogs offer a rich feast. You can see the classic *Dead of Night*—a collection of short tales of fantasy and terror, featuring such memorable events as a ventriloquist's dummy taking over his master and a man becoming linked against his will to another time and place through a mirror in his bedroom. *Four Feathers* is an epic of adventure and redemption that warrants many reshowings. And H. G. Wells' *Things to Come* offers a fascinating vision of a future world with Art Deco spaceships and cities.

15.11 A layout for a magazine article uses typefaces from the right era.

humanist **Gill Sans** series, which was introduced as the 1930s began. Its characters look best with relatively loose tracking, a distinguishing element of types with this general style.

MAKING NOVELTY TYPEFACES WORK

A novelty typeface can be a real hazard. If it's not entirely appropriate for your subject—or if it's too hard to read—it would be better forgotten. Figure 15.12 is a fortunate exception to this dilemma. The subject is a Back to School sale for a clothing store, and the novelty face in the heading is what makes this ad delightful. The design is called **Tommy's Type** and was created in 1993 by Judith Sutcliffe. Each letter is a piece of wash hanging out to dry, with its own little piece of clothesline. Ms. Sutcliffe has provided

15.12 A Back to School ad uses a heading composed of wet laundry.

extra characters such a basket of laundry, a cat, several birds, and even a clump of weeds that you may place wherever you wish.

The unconventional typeface used for the body copy is **Janaki,** designed in 1993 by Mouli Marur. The name of the store appears in **Schwitters,** a 1995 design from David Quay and Freda Sack. (Karl Schwitters was a prominent avant-garde designer and typographer in the Germany of the 1920s.) This particular typeface is a geometric design based on rectangles. The "always in fashion" slogan appears in **Palatino Italic,** with very tight tracking. All the typefaces in the ad are available from Agfa.

As far as the layout is concerned, the black body-copy block is balanced by the store name and related text being placed in the lower right corner, surrounded by white space.

USING CONCENTRIC CIRCLES

Figure 15.13 is a layout developed around a background composed of light concentric circles. The background is from the Image Club clip-art library. The name *Talbot Center* is in **Narcissus,** which you encountered in Chapter 12. The remainder of the layout uses **Asphalt,** a very powerful Font Bureau display face designed in 1995 by Tobias Frere-Jones; it demands a tight letterfit. The layout draws your attention naturally from the name of the show at the top left to the vital "where and when" statistics balancing the name at the lower right and radiating from the center of one of those background circles. Below these elements, the list of attractions at the show provides a floor for the other type blocks, as well as further details for the viewer who wants more information.

15.13 A design that mixes heavy, black, contemporary display type with light, concentric circles.

IMPROVING YOUR WORD-PROCESSING DOCUMENTS

In addition to fine-tuning the obvious "artistic" work expected in ads, posters, and magazine articles, you can also improve the appearance of your lowly word-processing documents. Why should a report or even a business letter not be as attractive as possible? Furthermore, we all know that it's considered good form to try to write one-page business letters; be concise and don't burden your recipient with keeping track of multiple pages, right? However, when all of the necessary words won't quite fit onto one page, what do you do? Most computer users try tricks such as leaving three lines of spacing instead of four between the date and the name and address of the recipient, narrowing the margins, and—more than anything else—switching to a condensed typeface or a smaller point size.

My suggestion is to forget your word processor for your important letters and reports and produce them from within your desktop publishing program. Think how much more power you'd have. You could reduce the leading by a few points, bringing those lines of type slightly closer together. You could also tighten up the tracking, bringing the characters slightly closer together. With these changes, you might not have to switch to another typeface or a smaller point size—both very obvious and unappealing alterations. Furthermore, you could add illustrations with many more options and infinitely more control.

Another bonus: Most word processors still don't support automatic kerning. By using your desktop-publishing program instead, you'd get letters and reports with your type beautifully kerned.

"The problem," you might say, "is that I wouldn't have my spellchecker anymore. Now I'm a good speller, you know. But I make typos. How would I catch them?"

PageMaker, QuarkXPress, and Ready,Set,Go! all have built-in spellcheckers. Of course, they're not going to recognize words you've added to a personal dictionary belonging to your word processor. However, there's a solution for that problem, too. You can use an inexpensive, independent spellchecker. These products have definite advantages. Usually, they have a larger word base than the one that came with your word-processor; it's essential for them to offer more in order to compete. With one of these spellcheckers active, you can switch from program to program on your computer; each program will suddenly be aware of all the special spellings you added to your user dictionary from within the previous program. For example, Deneba Software sells a product of this sort for the Macintosh: Spelling Coach Professional; it'll work *within* your existing programs just as if it were built in to all of them, offers more features, and costs less than fifty bucks.

SUMMARY

I hope these layout examples have given you some ideas as to how to manage your own typeface strategies. At the very least, you may have discovered more typefaces you'd like to use.

Summarizing the rules you might deduce from reading this chapter: Don't use similar type designs together, don't be afraid of white space, feel free to use asymmetrical layouts, choose type appropriate for the subject, and make sure that your type and illustrations work well together.

16

Building a Library

Many computer users initially have only the typefaces that came with their hardware or with their copy of the latest version of Windows. Perhaps it's just as well that their selection is limited; until they learn more about how and when to use type, they might be tempted to include 25 different designs in the same document.

However, with time comes at least some knowledge. Maybe you've gained even more knowledge by reading this book; at any rate, that was my grand plan. So, now that you're ready to build a typeface library, where should you start and what should you buy?

SHAREWARE AND MAIL-ORDER

First of all, if money for type is impossible to find in your budget, you can locate some free typefaces. Most of them aren't very good. Some of them reflect surprising creativity. They're offered free or as shareware through computer bulletin boards. As you may know, *shareware* consists of software that you can download free of charge and try; if you like and use the software, then you're supposed to send some money to the person who created it. Regardless of the usual lack of quality, "type-starved" individuals get a thrill from the mere fact of seeing something different on their screens and issuing from their printers.

If you're going to travel this route, be sure you have some good virus-protection software first. One wonderful program for Windows users is Hilgraeve's HyperACCESS, a communications program that actually checks bulletin-board files for viruses *as you download them*. In fact, this program checks any data being received through your modem.

Another inexpensive source for type is the "*unbelievable*" offers you get in the mail or see in the computer magazines. You know, "5,000 fonts for $29.95." Most of these typefaces are poor copies of the real designs, sold under strange names.

It's easy to find either shareware or mail-order typefaces that will print badly or even hang up your system. In the long run, you're usually better off to buy from standard digital type houses or their authorized retailers than from an unknown source. They sell the work of recognized designers. Most professional designers have the training, experience, and development software to make certain that characters fit well together, are spaced properly, drawn beautifully, and follow the rules for either PostScript or TrueType typeface creation.

LOCATING SPECIAL TYPEFACES

You may have special typeface needs. Perhaps you want to publish documents in Japanese or Slavic languages such as Russian. Numerous vendors can handle your needs, including Adobe, Agfa, Casady & Greene (Cyrillic type only), and Linotype-Hell. If you need special math-related faces, you can contact Y & Y.

An excellent reference work that lists typeface vendors and their products is *Data Sources*, published by Information

Access Company, a Ziff-Davis company; this large reference work is sold only by subscription, is updated twice a year, and contains page after page of listings under its Fonts category. If you buy type for a large company, find out if your company is already a subscriber; many businesses order *Data Sources* to obtain information about other software categories or about hardware manufacturers. However, if you're an individual and thinking about subscribing, be aware that a one-year subscription (two issues) costs several hundred dollars.

GET A CD-ROM DRIVE

Provided your budget can stand it, before you start your typeface library, you should make sure you have a CD-ROM drive. These days a couple of hundred dollars will buy you an adequate performer for typeface use. If you also want to play fancy computer games, you may want the fastest drive available, at a higher price.

The reason you need a CD-ROM drive is that most of the real type bargains are actually quantity discounts. Buy a CD-ROM full of type and it'll cost you much less than buying the same faces one or two at a time.

The exception here is the *locked* CD-ROM. The purpose of these to let you have the convenience of ordering type from a vendor and immediately receiving unlocking codes so that the items you just bought are available to be copied to your hard disk within half an hour or so. You don't have to wait a day or two for a warehouse to fill the order, then for Federal Express or United Parcel Service to make the delivery. But the price you pay is usually full retail. And the installation, ordering, and unlocking processes can be tedious.

Some companies—Bitstream is one—no longer sell locked CD-ROMs at all. You either buy type from them on floppies or you buy in quantity on CD-ROM at your favorite computer software store for prices as low as $49.95 for 500 typefaces.

On balance, however, many typefaces are available only on locked CD-ROMs or on floppies that are delivered to you; so if you want those particular designs, you'll have to put up with the ordering and unlocking hassle or wait a few days for the delivery.

One recent change: An alternate way of buying typefaces is through the Internet. If you're considering downloading them which, of course, gives you instant access like unlocking type on a CD-ROM, be sure to figure in the cost per minute, based on what your particular Internet connection charges you.

WHERE TO BUY

Some designers sell their own typefaces. These are often one-person operations; they don't have enough product even to think about putting the files on a CD-ROM, so you must order floppies. You can obtain some of the latest, greatest work from these people.

Among the larger companies, each has its niche. For example, most of the Fontek library is great display faces developed by its parent company Esselte Letraset. That company has also developed some fine type-related products such as BorderFonts and Envelopes—both of which I've shown to you. Most of the Letraset text typefaces are sold under license by other vendors. Other vendors offer some of the display faces as well.

Monotype has been developing typefaces for nearly a hundred years—originally, for use on the Monotype hot metal type composing machine. Therefore, this firm controls countless classic designs. It continues to produce notable new faces.

Linotype-Hell has roots that go even slightly further back, based on developing typefaces for the Linotype machine. They own the rights to more famous-name designs than any other company. On their locked CD-ROMs—in addition to their own library and the Adobe library—they offer **Berthold** type and the entire output of Elsner + Flake, a German type design house that sells most ITC typefaces complete with small caps, lowercase figures, and alternate characters not provided by most vendors. Linotype has commissioned many memorable new designs as well—I've shown you several—and has made a major commitment to the GX technology.

Varityper is another company that was well-known for manufacturing a typesetting machine and related typefaces. Unfortunately, a few years ago the company went out of business. The Varityper typefaces were acquired and are now sold by PrePress Direct. A few outstanding ones are included in this book.

Agfa acquired the Compugraphic Corporation typefaces. Many were copies of designs originally released by other type houses and are no longer sold, since Agfa now sells the originals—many included in the Adobe library. However, Agfa still offers other Compugraphic type, including **Garth Graphic,** an excellent serif family named after one of the Compugraphic founders, Bill Garth; you saw it in Chapter 4. In addition, Agfa now aggressively markets typefaces created by talented artists and small design groups around the world and has developed an admirable library.

URW was a pioneer in the production of digital typefaces and has had numerous famous designers under contract. As mentioned previously, this company also developed Ikarus, one of the first type design systems, as well as other type-related programs. It sells bargain unlocked CD-ROM collections of name-brand designs, including modified forms of each, incorporating special effects.

Bitstream was created to produce digital type. The noted designer Matthew Carter was one of the founders. This company sells many historic typefaces and new designs that you can't find elsewhere.

Of course, Adobe is the company that developed the PostScript language and other computer-industry innovations. The programs it has either developed or purchased and upgraded include Illustrator, Photoshop, and PageMaker, among others. Its type staff has designed many new, high-quality faces and families. Its type library is also sold by Monotype, Agfa, Linotype-Hell, and others, and includes designs owned by these organizations.

Image Club has been purchased by Adobe, but continues to operate independently. This Canadian-based mail-order concern has established an enviable reputation for selling licensed name-brand typefaces at low prices, in addition to many exclusive faces that have been created by the company's own designers. Image Club will send you type on floppies or on locked or unlocked CD-ROMs. As mentioned in earlier chapters, Image Club also has a large clip-art library.

I've discussed some of the smaller type companies as I've presented their products to you. I'd love to talk about each and every one of them here in detail, but there simply isn't room in the book.

A CHANGING INDUSTRY

This industry has changed radically. There was a time when most typefaces were created by designers on staff at large metal-type foundries and at companies manufacturing typesetting machines. When digital type became a factor, this tradition of staff type designers continued. However, economic considerations have since caused most companies to restrict their staff operations. They now acquire most of their new designs through distribution agreements with individuals or small design houses—a practice that greatly reduces their overhead.

Although these large companies are fine sources for type, no one company has a monopoly. After looking at an Adobe brochure, you might be tempted to say, "I see where the Adobe library includes the typefaces from Monotype, Agfa, and Linotype, so I'll just buy everything I need from Adobe." You could certainly buy all your type from Adobe—a top company, but they don't offer the entire contents of their competitors' libraries. For example, you can purchase only about a fourth of the Monotype library from Adobe; if you want Monotype's other designs, you'll have to order them from Monotype itself.

As for those designers that used to be on staff with the big type companies, many have formed small operations of their own. And most of the famous independent designers—including some who've always been independent—now earn impressive incomes creating logos and corporate-identity packages for major companies. A few do this to the extent that they rarely design typefaces for public consumption anymore.

ITC is another matter that requires discussion. Originally, International Typeface Corporation created new typefaces and acquired distribution rights to others, marketing them all with the ITC name attached, through licensed vendors. You didn't buy the type directly from ITC. However, the vendors could pick and choose as to the specific ITC typefaces they wanted to sell; they could even select which variations within a typeface they wanted to stock. That's why you can buy small caps and lowercase figures for many ITC typefaces through Linotype in the Elsner + Flake library and not from most other vendors; most vendors have thought their customers wouldn't want those extra characters.

These ITC designs have been of beautiful quality, although nearly all adhered to the philosophy of the ITC founders, who had worked in advertising: Use a large x-height and a tight letterfit. As I've remarked, this policy caused them to issue versions of some classic designs that bear little resemblance to the original. This is not necessarily a criticism. You may prefer the larger x-height and the tight letterfit and you may not care about the origins of a design.

Now ITC is changing, too. As mentioned earlier in the book, it's now owned by Esselte Letraset. Some of the designs produced for ITC don't have the large x-height or the tight letterfit anymore. Two examples shown in this book are **ITC Golden Type** and **ITC Bodoni.** ITC licensees can still offer any ITC type they choose, but the company is also selling many of its typefaces direct.

WHAT TO BUY

I've probably preached enough already in previous chapters, so I'll just repeat some essentials here.

- First, it's wise to buy PostScript typefaces if you think some of your work might be going to a service bureau in preparation for professional printing or, of course, if you already know that's your situation.
- Avoid extremes in design—such as the wild novelty faces—unless you're sure you'll have a continuing need for them (such as on the cover of a chatty monthly newsletter).

- When you buy a typeface that's part of a family, buy the entire family if you can afford it. You never know when a slightly different version of the design—a different weight or different width or an inline variation—may be exactly what you need in a particular spot on a page.

- Consider readability before design brilliance. If the typeface looks fantastic, but you can't read the characters, you've made a bad choice.

SUMMARY

You'll find phone numbers in the Sources Appendix for vendors who sell the type designs I've shown you. Throughout the chapters, I've mentioned either sources I knew offhand or the actual source from which I obtained a product myself. Other companies may sell the same typefaces. You can browse through hundreds of additional designs in the Specimens section of the book—also with sources—then look up the phone number you need in the appendix.

As computer users become more sophisticated, they are demanding extra characters. Therefore, the so-called expert sets and small caps/lowercase figures packages are becoming popular. Another trend is the growing interest in the designers themselves. Increasingly, companies now include this information in their catalogs.

The Type Specimens

This section contains nearly 400 type specimens. On the accompanying CD-ROM, you can see alphabets, numerals, a few special characters, plus the sample sentence to demonstrate typefaces that may interest you. This is not a complete display of every design available; there are thousands of them. It's not even a display of all members of the families represented; there are too many of those, too, so I've chosen representative members.

Every typeface is shown in the same point sizes. Therefore, if the type looks much smaller in one example than another, that's because it *is* smaller in relation to its specified point size. Obviously, if you buy the typeface, you can use it in any size you wish.

A source for each typeface is given to the right of its name, in parenthesis. In most cases, this is not the only source. It's simply the name of one company from which you can order the design.

Typefaces are listed alphabetically by the name of the design, not the name of the company providing it. For example, **ITC Bodoni** is listed alphabetically under Bodoni, not ITC.

Now—about that sample sentence. I'm sure you're familiar with the sentence that begins, "The quick brown fox . . ." Somebody wrote this to demonstrate type styles because it includes all the letters of the alphabet. But I was tired of it. So I created a new one for this section: "Quickly the Paul Yusef zebra vented its wrath on groom Jack Knox." I must confess that I've never met anyone named Paul Yusef, nor do I know whether he owns a zebra or not. I don't even know if "groom Jack Knox" is a man who just got married or a man who grooms zebras. And I certainly don't know why the zebra turned on him. You'll have to figure out the answers for yourself. Enjoy.

Aachen Bold (Fontek)

Quickly the Paul Yusef zebra vented its wrath on groom Jack Knox

Aardvark Regular (Font Bureau)

QUICKLY THE PAUL YUSEF ZEBRA VENTED ITS WRATH ON GROOM JACK KNOX

Aase Regular (Image Club)

Quickly the Paul Yusef zebra vented its wrath on groom Jack Knox

Abadi Condensed Regular (Monotype)

Quickly the Paul Yusef zebra vented its wrath on groom Jack Knox

Advertiser's Gothic Light (Agfa)

Quickly the Paul Yusef zebra vented its wrath on groom Jack Knox

Agency Black (Font Bureau)

Quickly the Paul Yusef zebra vented its wrath on groom Jack Knox

Agency Black Wide (Font Bureau)

Quickly the Paul Yusef zebra vented its wrath on groom Jack Knox

Agency Bold (Font Bureau)

Quickly the Paul Yusef zebra vented its wrath on groom Jack Knox

Agency Bold Compressed (Font Bureau)

Quickly the Paul Yusef zebra vented its wrath on groom Jack Knox

Agency Bold Extended (Font Bureau)

Quickly the Paul Yusef zebra vented its wrath on groom Jack Knox

Agency Light Condensed (Font Bureau)

Quickly the Paul Yusef zebra vented its wrath on groom Jack Knox

Agency Regular (Font Bureau)

Quickly the Paul Yusef zebra vented its wrath on groom Jack Knox

Agency Regular Wide (Font Bureau)

Quickly the Paul Yusef zebra vented its wrath on groom Jack Knox

Agency Thin Extended (Font Bureau)

Quickly the Paul Yusef zebra vented its wrath on groom Jack Knox

Agrafie (Linotype-Hell)

quickly the Paul Yusef zebra vented its wrath on groom Jack Knox

Airstream, ITC (ITC)

Quickly the Paul Yusef zebra vented its wrath on groom Jack Knox

URW Alcuin (URW)

Quickly the Paul Yusef zebra vented its wrath on groom Jack Knox

URW Alcuin DisCaps (URW)

QUICKLY THE PAUL YUSEF ZEBRA VENTED ITS WRATH ON GROOM JACK KNOX

Aleksei Disturbed (Agfa)

Quickly the Paul Yusef zebra vented its wrath on groom Jack Knox

Alhambra (Font Bureau)

QUICKLY THE PAUL YUSEF ZE-BRA VENTED ITS WRATH ON GROOM JACK KNOX

Annlie (Linotype-Hell)

Quickly the Paul Yusef zebra vented its wrath on groom Jack Knox

URW Antiqua (URW)

Quickly the Paul Yusef zebra vented its wrath on groom Jack Knox

Antique Condensed 2 (Agfa)

Quickly the Paul Yusef zebra vented its wrath on groom Jack Knox

Apolline Regular (Agfa)

Quickly the Paul Yusef zebra vented its wrath on groom Jack Knox

Apollo (Monotype)

Quickly the Paul Yusef zebra vented its wrath on groom Jack Knox

Arabia Felix (Agfa)

Quickly the Paul Yusef zebra vented its wrath on groom Jack Knox

Arepo Roman (Agfa)

Quickly the Paul Yusef zebra vented its wrath on groom Jack Knox

Aritus Extra Bold (URW)

Quickly the Paul Yusef zebra vented its wrath on groom Jack Knox

Arriba (Fontek)

Quickly the Paul Yusef zebra vented its wrath on groom Jack Knox

Bitstream Arrus (Bitstream)

Quickly the Paul Yusef zebra vented its wrath on groom Jack Knox

Ashley Crawford (Agfa)

QUICKLY THE PAUL YUSEF ZEBRA VENTED ITS WRATH ON GROOM JACK KNOX

Asphalt Black (Agfa)

Quickly the Paul Yusef zebra vented its wrath on groom Jack Knox

Athenæum (Agfa)

Quickly the Paul Yusef zebra vented its wrath on groom Jack Knox

Auriol (Linotype-Hell)

Quickly the Paul Yusef zebra vented its wrath on groom Jack Knox

Balder (Linotype-Hell)

QUICKLY THE PAUL YUSEF ZEBRA VENTED ITS WRATH ON GROOM JACK KNOX

Baskerville Old Face (Linotype-Hell)

Quickly the Paul Yusef zebra vented its wrath on groom Jack Knox

ITC Beesknees PosterType (URW)

QUICKLY THE PAUL YUSEF ZEBRA VENTED ITS WRATH ON GROOM JACK KNOX

Behemoth (Agfa)

Quickly the Paul Yusef zebra vented its wrath on groom Jack Knox

Belizio (Font Bureau)

Quickly the Paul Yusef zebra vented its wrath on groom Jack Knox

Bell (Monotype)

Quickly the Paul Yusef zebra vented its wrath on groom Jack Knox

Belucian Book (Font Bureau)

Quickly the Paul Yusef zebra vented its wrath on groom Jack Knox

Bembo (Monotype)

Quickly the Paul Yusef zebra vented its wrath on groom Jack Knox

Benguiat Frisky (Agfa)

Quickly the Paul Yusef zebra vented its wrath on groom Jack Knox

Berliner Grotesk (URW)

Quickly the Paul Yusef zebra vented its wrath on groom Jack Knox

Bigband Terrazzo (Linotype-Hell)

Quickly the Paul Yusef zebra vented its wrath on groom Jack Knox

Black Rocks (Agfa)

Quickly the Paul Yusef zebra vented its wrath on groom Jack knox

Black Tents (Agfa)

Quickly the Paul Yusef zebra vented its wrath on groom Jack knox

Blado (Monotype)

Quickly the Paul Yusef zebra vented its wrath on groom Jack Knox

Boberia Light (Linotype-Hell)

Quickly the Paul Yusef zebra vented its wrath on groom Jack Knox

Bauer Bodoni (Adobe)

Quickly the Paul Yusef zebra vented its wrath on groom Jack Knox

Bodoni (Benton version) (Adobe)

Quickly the Paul Yusef zebra vented its wrath on groom Jack Knox

Berthold Bodoni Antiqua (Adobe)

Quickly the Paul Yusef zebra vented its wrath on groom Jack Knox

Berthold Bodoni Old Face (Adobe)

Quickly the Paul Yusef zebra vented its wrath on groom Jack Knox

ITC Bodoni Brush (ITC)

Quickly the Paul Yusef zebra vented its wrath on groom Jack Knox

ITC Bodoni Seventy-Two Bold (ITC)

Quickly the Paul Yusef zebra vented its wrath on groom Jack Knox

ITC Bodoni Twelve Book OS (ITC)

Quickly the Paul Yusef zebra vented its wrath on groom Jack Knox

Bradley Initials (Font Bureau)

QUICKLY THE PAUL YUSEF ZEBRA VENTED ITS WRATH ON GROOM JACK KNOX

Broadpen (Varityper)

Quickly the Paul Yusef zebra vented its wrath on groom Jack Knox

Brok (Agfa)

QUICKLY THE PAUL YUSEF ZE-BRA VENTED ITS WRATH ON GROOM JACK KNOX

Bulmer Display (Monotype)

Quickly the Paul Yusef zebra vented its wrath on groom Jack Knox

Cabaret (Fontek)

Quickly the Paul Yusef zebra vented its wrath on groom Jack Knox

PMN Caecilia, Old Style figures (Linotype-Hell)

Quickly the Paul Yusef zebra vented its wrath on groom Jack Knox

Caflisch Script Swash (Adobe)

Quickly the Paul Yusef zebra vented its wrath on groom Jack Knox

FB Californian (Font Bureau)

Quickly the Paul Yusef zebra vented its wrath on groom Jack Knox

Calligrapher (Varityper)

Quickly the Paul Yusef zebra vented its wrath on groom Jack Knox

Camellia (Linotype-Hell)

Candice (Linotype-Hell)

Quickly the Paul Yusef zebra vented its wrath on groom Jack Knox

Capone Light (Agfa)

Quickly the Paul Yusef zebra vented its wrath on groom Jack Knox

Carver (Image Club)

Quickly the Paul Yusef zebra vented its wrath on groom Jack Knox

Adobe Caslon (Adobe)

Quickly the Paul Yusef zebra vented its wrath on groom Jack Knox

Camelia (Image Club)

Quickly the Paul Yusef zebra vented its wrath on groom Jack Knox

Bitstream Carmina (Bitstream)

Quickly the Paul Yusef zebra vented its wrath on groom Jack Knox

Bitstream Cataneo (Bitstream)

Quickly the Paul Yusef zebra vented its wrath on groom Jack Knox

Catull (Adobe)

Quickly the Paul Yusef zebra vented its wrath on groom Jack Knox

Caxton Book (Adobe)

Quickly the Paul Yusef zebra vented its wrath on groom Jack Knox

Celestina Roman (Autologic)

Quickly the Paul Yusef zebra vented its wrath on groom Jack Knox

Centaur (Monotype)

Quickly the Paul Yusef zebra vented its wrath on groom Jack Knox

Champfleury Titling (Autologic)

QUICKLY THE PAUL YUSEF ZEBRA VENTED ITS WRATH ON GROOM JACK KNOX

Charlotte (Fontek)

Quickly the Paul Yusef zebra vented its wrath on groom Jack Knox

Charter, ITC (Bitstream)

Quickly the Paul Yusef zebra vented its wrath on groom Jack Knox

Bitstream Chianti (Bitstream)

Quickly the Paul Yusef zebra vented its wrath on groom Jack Knox

Chic (Agfa)

QUICKLY THE PAUL YUSEF ZEBRA VENTED ITS WRATH ON GROOM JACK KNOX

Chilada Cuatro (Image Club)

Quickly the Paul Yusef zebra vented its wrath on groom Jack Knox

Chilada Uno (Image Club)

Quickly the Paul Yusef zebra vented its wrath on groom Jack Knox

Chiller (Fontek)

Quickly the Paul Yusef zebra vented its wrath on groom Jack Knox

Cirkulus (Linotype-Hell)

quickly the paul yusef zebra vented its wrath on groom jack knox

Citadel Inline (Agfa)

Quickly the Paul Yusef zebra vented its wrath on groom Jack Knox

Clearface Gothic Regular (Linotype-Hell)

Quickly the Paul Yusef zebra vented its wrath on groom Jack Knox

Codex (Linotype-Hell)

Quickly the Paul Yusef zebra vented its wrath on groom Jack Knox

Colonna (Monotype)

Quickly the Paul Yusef zebra vented its wrath on groom Jack Knox

Columbus (Monotype)

Quickly the Paul Yusef zebra vented its wrath on groom Jack Knox

Comic Book (Image Club)

QUICKLY THE PAUL YUSEF ZEBRA VENTED ITS WRATH ON GROOM JACK KNOX

Commerce Fat (Font Bureau)

Quickly the Paul Yusef zebra vented its wrath on groom Jack Knox

Conference (Linotype-Hell)

Quickly the Paul Yusef zebra vented its wrath on groom Jack Knox

Cortez (Linotype-Hell)

Quickly the Paul Yusef zebra vented its wrath on groom Jack Knox

Crackhouse (House Industries)

Quickly the Paul Yusef zebra vented its wrath on groom Jack Knox

Crane (Agfa)

Quickly the Paul Yusef zebra vented its wrath on groom Jack Knox

Crillee Italic (Linotype-Hell)

Quickly the Paul Yusef zebra vented its wrath on groom Jack Knox

Croissant (URW)

Quickly the Paul Yusef zebra vented its wrath on groom Jack Knox

Crucible Medium (Psy/Ops Type Foundry)

QUICKLY THE PAUL YUSEF ZEBRA VENTED ITS WRATH ON GROOM JACK HNOX

Cycles (Stone Type Foundry)

Quickly the Paul Yusef zebra vented its wrath on groom Jack Knox

Dante (Monotype)

Quickly the Paul Yusef zebra vented its wrath on groom Jack Knox

Debbie (Varityper)

Quickly the Paul Yusef zebra vented its wrath on groom Jack Knox

Demos Medium (Linotype-Hell)

Quickly the Paul Yusef zebra vented its wrath on groom Jack Knox

Derek Italic (Agfa)

Quickly the Paul Yusef zebra vented its wrath on groom Jack Knox

Deville Thruster Deluxe One (Psy/Ops Type Foundry)

Quickly the Paul Yusef zebra vented its wrath on groom Jack Knox

Linotype Didot (Linotype-Hell)

Quickly the Paul Yusef zebra vented its wrath on groom Jack Knox

Digi Grotesk N (Linotype-Hell)

Quickly the Paul Yusef zebra vented its wrath on groom Jack Knox

Digital Woodcuts, Open, ITC (ITC)

QUICKLY THE PAUL YUSEF ZEBRA VENTED ITS WRATH ON GROOM JACK KNOX

Dizzy Regular (Font Bureau)

quickly the paul yusef zebra vented its wrath on groom Jack Knox

Dom Diagonal (Linotype-Hell)

Quickly the Paul Yusef zebra vented its wrath on groom Jack Knox

Dynamo Medium (Linotype-Hell)

Quickly the Paul Yusef zebra vented its wrath on groom Jack Knox

Dynamo Bold Shadow (Linotype-Hell)

Quickly the Paul Yusef zebra vented its wrath on groom Jack Knox

Bureau Eagle Book (Font Bureau)

Quickly the Paul Yusef zebra vented its wrath on groom Jack Knox

Eaglefeather Bold (Agfa)

Quickly the Paul Yusef zebra vented its wrath on groom Jack Knox

Eaglefeather Regular Small Caps (Agfa)

QUICKLY THE PAUL YUSEF ZEBRA VENTED ITS WRATH ON GROOM JACK KNOX

East Bloc Closed Alternate (Image Club)

QUICKLY THE PAUL YUSEF ZEBRA VENTED ITS WRATH ON GROOM JACK KNOX

East Bloc Open (Image Club)

QUICKLY THE PAUL YUSEF ZEBRA VENTED ITS WRATH ON GROOM JACK KNOX

Eclipse (Agfa)

QUICKLY THE PAUL YUSEF ZEBRA VENTED ITS WRATH ON GROOM JACK KNOX

Edison Book (Linotype-Hell)

Quickly the Paul Yusef zebra vented its wrath on groom Jack Knox

ITC Edwardian Script Bold (ITC)

Quickly the Paul Yusef zebra vented its wrath on groom Jack Knox

ITC Edwardian Script Bold Alternate (ITC)

Quickly the Paul Yusef zebra vented its wrath on groom Jack Knox

Egliziano (Agfa)

Quickly the Paul Yusef zebra vented its wrath on groom Jack Knox

ITC Élan Medium (Linotype-Hell)

Quickly the Paul Yusef zebra vented its wrath on groom Jack Knox

Electra Small Caps & OS Figs. (Linotype-Hell)

QUICKLY THE PAUL YUSEF ZEBRA VENTED ITS WRATH ON GROOM JACK KNOX

Elefont (Linotype-Hell)

QUICKLY THE PAUL YUSEF ZEBRA VENTED ITS WRATH ON GROOM JACK KNOX

El Grande (Font Bureau)

QUICKLY THE PAUL YUSEF ZEBRA VENTED ITS WRATH ON GROOM JACK KNOX

Ellington (Monotype)

Quickly the Paul Yusef zebra vented its wrath on groom Jack Knox

Elysium (Fontek)

Quickly the Paul Yusef zebra vented its wrath on groom Jack Knox

Entebbe (Linotype-Hell)

QuickLY the paul Yusef zeBra venteD its wrath on grOOM Jack knOx

Equinox (Fontek)

Quickly the Paul Yusef zebra vented its wrath on groom Jack Knox

ITC Esprit Medium (Linotype-Hell)

Quickly the Paul Yusef zebra vented its wrath on groom Jack Knox

Fairfield (Linotype-Hell)

Quickly the Paul Yusef zebra vented its wrath on groom Jack Knox

Fajita Mild (Image Club)

QUICKLY THE PAUL YUSEF ZEBRA VENTED ITS WRATH ON GROOM JACK KNOX

Fajita Picante (Image Club)

QUICKLY THE PAUL YUSEF ZEBRA VENTED ITS WRATH ON GROOM JACK KNOX

Fiedler Gothic Bold (Agfa)

Quickly the Paul Yusef zebra vented its wrath on groom Jack Knox

Figural (Fontek)

Quickly the Paul Yusef zebra vented its wrath on groom Jack Knox

Fina (Image Club)

Quickly the Paul Yusef zebra vented its wrath on groom Jack Knox

Flamenco Inline (Fontek)

Quickly the Paul Yusef zebra vented its wrath on groom Jack Knox

Fobia (Font Bureau)

Quickly the Paul Yusef zebra vented its wrath on groom Jack Knox

Folio Extra Condensed (Linotype-Hell)

Quickly the Paul Yusef zebra vented its wrath on groom Jack Knox

Fournier (Monotype)

Quickly the Paul Yusef zebra vented its wrath on groom Jack Knox

Fragile (Image Club)

quickly the paul yusef zebra vented its wrath on groom jack knox

Franklin Gothic (Adobe)

Quickly the Paul Yusef zebra vented its wrath on groom Jack Knox

Franklin Gothic Small Caps Book Condensed (Linotype-Hell)

QUICKLY THE PAUL YUSEF ZEBRA VENTED ITS WRATH ON GROOM JACK KNOX

Frutiger (Linotype-Hell)

Quickly the Paul Yusef zebra vented its wrath on groom Jack Knox

Futura Book (Adobe)

Quickly the Paul Yusef zebra vented its wrath on groom Jack Knox

Futura Maxi Light (Agfa)

Quickly the Paul Yusef zebra vented its wrath on groom Jack Knox

Galliard, ITC (Adobe)

Quickly the Paul Yusef zebra vented its wrath on groom Jack Knox

Adobe Garamond (Adobe)

Quickly the Paul Yusef zebra vented its wrath on groom Jack Knox

Garamond No. 5 Bold (Linotype-Hell)

Quickly the Paul Yusef zebra vented its wrath on groom Jack Knox

Garth Graphic (Agfa)

Quickly the Paul Yusef zebra vented its wrath on groom Jack Knox

Geometrica Titling (Autologic)

QUICKLY THE PAUL YUSEF ZEBRA VENTED ITS WRATH ON GROOM JACK KNOX

Gilgamesh Book (Fontek)

Quickly the Paul Yusef zebra vented its wrath on groom Jack Knox

Gillies Gothic Light (Linotype-Hell)

Quickly the Paul Yusef zebra vented its wrath on groom Jack Knox

Gill Sans Ultra Bold (Monotype)

Quickly the Paul Yusef zebra vented its wrath on groom Jack Knox

ITC Giovanni Small Caps Book (Linotype-Hell)

QUICKLY THE PAUL YUSEF ZEBRA VENTED ITS WRATH ON GROOM JACK KNOX

Glastonbury (Fontek)

Quickly the Paul Yusef zebra vented its wrath on groom Jack Knox

Gnomad B Gauge (Psy/Ops Type Foundry)

Quickly the Paul Yusef zebra vented its wrath on groom Jack Knox

ITC Golden Type (URW)

Quickly the Paul Yusef zebra vented its wrath on groom Jack Knox

Gothic Extra Light Extended (Agfa)

Quickly the Paul Yusef zebra vented its wrath on groom Jack Knox

Goudy Handtooled DisCaps (URW)

QUICKLY THE PAUL YUSEF ZEBRA VENTED ITS WRATH ON GROOM JACK KNOX

Goudy Old Style (Adobe)

Quickly the Paul Yusef zebra vented its wrath on groom Jack Knox

Graffiti (Font Bureau)

Quickly the Paul Yusef zebra vented its wrath on groom Jack Knox

Graffitto Condensed (Galápagos)

QUICKLY THE PAUL YUSEF ZEBRA VENTED ITS WRATH ON GROOM
JACK KNOX

Grafilone Semi Bold (Linotype-Hell)

Quickly the Paul Yusef zebra vented its wrath on groom Jack Knox

Gravura (Fontek)

*Quickly the Paul Yusef zebra vented its wrath on groom Jack
Knox*

Greeting Monotone (Agfa)

Quickly the Paul Yusef zebra vented its wrath on groom
Jack Knox

Groschen (Image Club)

Quickly the Paul Yusef zebra vented its
wrath on groom Jack Knox

Bureau Grotesque One Five (Font Bureau)

Quickly the Paul Yusef zebra vented its wrath on groom Jack Knox

Habitat Decorated (Agfa)

**Quickly the Paul Yusef zebra vented
its wrath on groom Jack Knox**

Handel Gothic Medium (Linotype-Hell)

Quickly the Paul Yusef zebra vented its wrath on groom Jack Knox

Hawthorn (Linotype-Hell)

Quickly the Paul Yusef zebra vented its wrath on groom Jack Knox

Heraldus (Linotype-Hell)

Quickly the Paul Yusef zebra vented its wrath on groom Jack Knox

Highlight (Linotype-Hell)

Quickly the Paul Yusef zebra vented its wrath on groom Jack Knox

Hindenburg (Agfa)

Quickly the Paul Yusef zebra vented its wrath on groom Jack Knox

Hip Hop Demi (Font Bureau)

Quickly the Paul Yusef zebra vented its wrath on groom Jack Knox

Hip Hop Inline (Font Bureau)

Quickly the Paul Yusef zebra vented its wrath on groom Jack Knox

Hiroshige Book (Adobe)

Quickly the Paul Yusef zebra vented its wrath on groom Jack Knox

Hogarth Script (Linotype-Hell)

Quickly the Paul Yusef zebra vented its wrath on groom Jack Knox

Hollander (Linotype-Hell)

Quickly the Paul Yusef zebra vented its wrath on groom Jack Knox

Holland Title (Agfa)

Quickly the Paul Yusef zebra vented its wrath on groom Jack Knox

Horatio Medium (Linotype-Hell)

Quickly the Paul Yusef zebra vented its wrath on groom Jack Knox

Horndon (Linotype-Hell)

QUICKLY THE PAUL YUSEF ZEBRA VENTED ITS WRATH ON GROOM JACK KNOX

Ho Tom (Linotype-Hell)

Quickly the Paul Yusef zebra vented its wrath on groom Jack Knox

Housemix (House Industries)

QUICKLY THE PAUL YUSEF ZEBRA VENTED ITS WRATH ON GROOM JACK KNOX

Imprint Shadow (Monotype)

Quickly the Paul Yusef zebra vented its wrath on groom Jack Knox

Improv (Image Club)

Quickly the Paul Yusef zebra vented its wrath on groom Jack Knox

Interstate Regular (Font Bureau)

Quickly the Paul Yusef zebra vented its wrath on groom Jack Knox

Ironmonger Black (Font Bureau)

QUICKLY THE PAUL YUSEF ZEBRA VENTED ITS WRATH ON GROOM JACK KNOX

Ironmonger Extended (Font Bureau)

QUICKLY THE PAUL YUSEF ZEBRA VENTED ITS WRATH ON GROOM JACK KNOX

Ironmonger Extra Condensed (Font Bureau)

QUICKLY THE PAUL YUSEF ZEBRA VENTED ITS WRATH ON GROOM JACK KNOX

Ironmonger Inlaid (Font Bureau)

QUICKLY THE PAUL YUSEF ZEBRA VENTED ITS WRATH ON GROOM JACK KNOX

Ironmonger Three D (Font Bureau)

QUICKLY THE PAUL YUSEF ZEBRA VENTED ITS WRATH ON GROOM JACK KNOX

Italia (Adobe)

Quickly the Paul Yusef zebra vented its wrath on groom Jack Knox

Monotype Italian Old Style (Monotype)

Quickly the Paul Yusef zebra vented its wrath on groom Jack Knox

Jacoby Condensed Black (Image Club)

Quickly the Paul Yusef zebra vented its wrath on groom Jack Knox

Jacoby Light (Image Club)

Quickly the Paul Yusef zebra vented its wrath on groom Jack Knox

Janson Text (Linotype-Hell)

Quickly the Paul Yusef zebra vented its wrath on groom Jack Knox

Jazz (Fontek)

Quickly the Paul Yusef zebra vented its wrath on groom Jack Knox

Jenson Old Style Bold Condensed (Linotype-Hell)

Quickly the Paul Yusef zebra vented its wrath on groom Jack Knox

Joanna Solotype (Agfa)

Quickly the Paul Yusef zebra vented its wrath on groom Jack Knox

Julia Script (URW)

Quickly the Paul Yusef zebra vented its wrath on groom Jack Knox

Kago (Linotype-Hell)

Quickly the Paul Yusef zebra vented its wrath on groom Jack Knox

Kaixo (Psy/Ops Type Foundry)

Quickly the Paul Yusef zebra vented its wrath on groom Jack Knox

Kapitellia Bold (Linotype-Hell)

Quickly the Paul Yusef zebra vented its wrath on groom Jack Knox

Kennedy Book (Galápagos)

Quickly the Paul Yusef zebra vented its wrath on groom Jack Knox

Kennedy Book Small Caps (Galápagos)

QUICKLY THE PAUL YUSEF ZEBRA VENTED ITS WRATH ON GROOM JACK KNOX

Knightsbridge (Linotype-Hell)

Quickly the Paul Yusef zebra vented its wrath on groom Jack Knox

Koloss (Linotype-Hell)

Quickly the Paul Yusef zebra vented its wrath on groom Jack Knox

Kristin Not So Normal, ITC (ITC)

QUICKLY tHE PAUL YUSEF zebra venteD its wratH on groom Jack Knox

Kufi Script (Agfa)

Quickly the Paul Yusef zebra vented its wrath on groom Jack Knox

Lafayette Extra Condensed (Agfa)

Quickly the Paul Yusef zebra vented its wrath on groom Jack Knox

Lambada (Fontek)

Quickly the Paul Yusef zebra vented its wrath on groom Jack Knox

Lindsay (Linotype-Hell)

Quickly the Paul Yusef zebra vented its wrath on groom Jack Knox

Latienne Swash (URW)

Quickly the Paul Yusef zebra vented its wrath on groom Jack Knox

Latin Bold (Agfa)

Quickly the Paul Yusef zebra vented its wrath on groom Jack Knox

Lazybones (Linotype-Hell)

Quickly the Paul Yusef zebra vented its wrath on groom Jack Knox

Le Griffe (Linotype-Hell)

Quickly the Paul Yusef zebra vented its wrath on groom Jack Knox

Lightline Gothic (Linotype-Hell)

Quickly the Paul Yusef zebra vented its wrath on groom Jack Knox

Lubalin Graph Medium Condensed (Linotype-Hell)

Quickly the Paul Yusef zebra vented its wrath on groom Jack Knox

Lucida Blackletter (Bigelow & Holmes)

Quickly the Paul Yusef zebra vented its wrath on groom Jack Knox

Lucida Bright (Bigelow & Holmes)

Quickly the Paul Yusef zebra vented its wrath on groom Jack Knox

Lucida Calligraphy Italic (Bigelow & Holmes)

Quickly the Paul Yusef zebra vented its wrath on groom Jack Knox

Lucida Sans (Bigelow & Holmes)

Quickly the Paul Yusef zebra vented its wrath on groom Jack Knox

Ludovico Smooth (Agfa)

Quickly the Paul Yusef zebra vented its wrath on groom Jack Knox

Ludovico Woodcut (Agfa)

Quickly the Paul Yusef zebra vented its wrath on groom Jack Knox

Lynz (Image Club)

QUICKLY THE PAUL YUSEF ZEBRA VENTED ITS WRATH ON GROOM JACK KNOX

Mad Zine Whip (Linotype-Hell)

Quickly the Paul Yusef zebra vented its wrath on groom Jack Knox

Magnus (Linotype-Hell)

Quickly the Paul Yusef zebra vented its wrath on groom Jack Knox

Maiandra Roman (Galápagos)

Quickly the Paul Yusef zebra vented its wrath on groom Jack Knox

Maltby Antique (Agfa)

Quickly the Paul Yusef zebra vented its wrath on groom Jack Knox

Mandarin (URW)

QUICKLY THE PAUL YUSEF ZEBRA VENTED ITS WRATH ON GROOM JACK KNOX

Mantinia (Carter & Cone)

QUICKLY THE PAUL YUSEF ZEBRA VENTED ITS WRATH ON GROOM JACK KNOX

Marconi (Linotype-Hell)

Quickly the Paul Yusef zebra vented its wrath on groom Jack Knox

Mariage (URW)

Quickly the Paul Yusef zebra vented its wrath on groom Jack Knox

Mateo Bold (Linotype-Hell)

Quickly the Paul Yusef zebra vented its wrath on groom Jack Knox

Matisse, ITC (ITC)

QUICKLY THE PAUL YUSEF ZEBRA VENTED ITS WRATH ON GROOM JACK KNOX

Matra (Agfa)

QUICKLY THE PAUL YUSEF ZEBRA VENTED ITS WRATH ON GROOM JACK KNOX

Matthia (Linotype-Hell)

Quickly the Paul Yusef zebra vented its wrath on groom Jack Knox

Melencolia Titling (Autologic)

QUICKLY THE PAUL YUSEF ZEBRA VENTED ITS WRATH ON GROOM JACK KNOX

Meno Roman (Font Bureau)

Quickly the Paul Yusef zebra vented its wrath on groom Jack Knox

Méridien (Linotype-Hell)

Quickly the Paul Yusef zebra vented its wrath on groom Jack Knox

Mesa Bold, Tall Caps (Font Bureau)

QUICKLY THE PAUL YUSEF ZEBRA VENTED ITS WRATH ON GROOM JACK KNOX

Mesopotamia (Agfa)

Quickly the Paul Yusef zebra vented its wrath on groom Jack Knox

Metronome Gothic (Agfa)

Quickly the Paul Yusef zebra vented its wrath on groom Jack Knox

Metropolis (Image Club)

Quickly the Paul Yusef zebra vented its wrath on groom Jack Knox

Metropolitaines (URW)

QUICKLY THE PAUL YUSEF ZEBRA VENTED ITS WRATH ON GROOM JACK KNOX

Mezzo (Image Club)

Quickly the Paul Yusef zebra vented its wrath on groom Jack Knox

Minion (Adobe)

Quickly the Paul Yusef zebra vented its wrath on groom Jack Knox

Minister (Linotype-Hell)

Quickly the Paul Yusef zebra vented its wrath on groom Jack Knox

Mirarae (Bitstream)

Quickly the Paul Yusef zebra vented its wrath on groom Jack Knox

Bitstream Mr. Earl (Bitstream)

Quickly the Paul Yusef zebra vented its wrath on groom Jack Knox

Modern Extended (Monotype)

Quickly the Paul Yusef zebra vented its wrath on groom Jack Knox

Modernique (Agfa)

Quickly the Paul Yusef zebra vented its wrath on groom Jack Knox

Modern No. 216 Medium (Linotype-Hell)

Quickly the Paul Yusef zebra vented its wrath on groom Jack Knox

Modified Gothic (Linotype-Hell)

Quickly the Paul Yusef zebra vented its wrath on groom Jack Knox

Monanti Regular (Linotype-Hell)

Quickly the Paul Yusef zebra vented its wrath on groom Jack Knox

Motter Corpus (Adobe)

Quickly the Paul Yusef zebra vented its wrath on groom Jack Knox

Musketeer (Agfa)

Quickly the Paul Yusef zebra vented its wrath on groom Jack Knox

Myriad (Adobe)

Quickly the Paul Yusef zebra vented its wrath on groom Jack Knox

Nadianne (Agfa)

Quickly the Paul Yusef zebra vented its wrath on groom Jack Knox

Napoleon Roman (Linotype-Hell)

Quickly the Paul Yusef zebra vented its wrath on groom Jack Knox

Narcissus (Agfa)

Quickly the Paul Yusef zebra vented its wrath on groom Jack Knox

Neo Neo (Fontek)

Quickly the Paul Yusef zebra vented its wrath on groom Jack Knox

Neuland Star (Linotype-Hell)

QUICKLY THE PAUL YUSEF ZEBRA VENTED ITS WRATH ON GROOM JACK KNOX

Niagara Engraved (Font Bureau)

Quickly the Paul Yusef zebra vented its wrath on groom Jack Knox

Niagara Light Engraved Small Caps (Font Bureau)

QUICKLY THE PAUL YUSEF ZEBRA VENTED ITS WRATH ON GROOM JACK KNOX

Niagara Solid (Font Bureau)

Quickly the Paul Yusef zebra vented its wrath on groom Jack Knox

Niagara Thin (Font Bureau)

Quickly the Paul Yusef zebra vented its wrath on groom Jack Knox

Nikis Light (Linotype-Hell)

Quickly the Paul Yusef zebra vented its wrath on groom Jack Knox

Nofret Regular (Adobe)

Quickly the Paul Yusef zebra vented its wrath on groom Jack Knox

Nueva (Adobe)

Quickly the Paul Yusef zebra vented its wrath on groom Jack Knox

Numskill Bold (Font Bureau)

Quickly the Paul Yusef zebra vented its wrath on groom Jack Knox

Nutcracker (Font Bureau)

Quickly the Paul Yusef zebra vented its wrath on groom Jack Knox

Oculus Regular (Psy/Ops Type Foundry)

Quickly the Paul Yusef zebra vented its wrath on groom Jack Knox

Odilia (Agfa)

Quickly the Paul Yusef zebra vented its wrath on groom Jack Knox

Odin (URW)

Quickly the Paul Yusef zebra vented its wrath on groom Jack Knox

Olympia Light (Linotype-Hell)

Quickly the Paul Yusef zebra vented its wrath on groom Jack Knox

Bitstream Oranda (Bitstream)

Quickly the Paul Yusef zebra vented its wrath on groom Jack Knox

Bitstream Oz Handicraft (Bitstream)

Quickly the Paul Yusef zebra vented its wrath on groom Jack Knox

Paddington (Linotype-Hell)

Quickly the Paul Yusef zebra vented its wrath on groom Jack Knox

Peignot (Linotype-Hell)

Quickly the Paul Yusef zebra vented its wrath on groom Jack Knox

Penumbra (Adobe)

QUICKLY THE PAUL YUSEF ZEBRA VENTED ITS WRATH ON GROOM JACK KNOX

Phalanx Regular (Psy/Ops Type Foundry)

Quickly the Paul Yusef zebra vented its wrath on groom Jack Knox

Perpetua (Monotype)

Quickly the Paul Yusef zebra vented its wrath on groom Jack Knox

Piccadilly (Linotype-Hell)

QUICKLY THE PAUL YUSEF ZEBRA VENTED ITS WRATH ON GROOM JACK KNOX

Pilsner (Agfa)

Quickly the Paul Yusef zebra vented its wrath on groom Jack Knox

Poetica Chancery II (Adobe)

Quickly the Paul Yusef zebra vented its wrath on groom Jack Knox

Poison Flowers (Linotype-Hell)

QUICKLY THE PAUL YUSEF ZEBRA VENTED ITS WRATH ON GROOM JACK KNOX

Poliphilus (Monotype)

Quickly the Paul Yusef zebra vented its wrath on groom Jack Knox

Poppl-Pontifex (Adobe)

Quickly the Paul Yusef zebra vented its wrath on groom Jack Knox

Post-Mediæval (Adobe)

Quickly the Paul Yusef zebra vented its wrath on groom Jack Knox

Praxis Regular (Linotype-Hell)

Quickly the Paul Yusef zebra vented its wrath on groom Jack Knox

Proforma Book (Font Bureau)

Quickly the Paul Yusef zebra vented its wrath on groom Jack Knox

Quay Sans Book (Linotype-Hell)

Quickly the Paul Yusef zebra vented its wrath on groom Jack Knox

Quicksans Accurate Solid (Image Club)

Quickly the Paul Yusef zebra vented its wrath on groom Jack Knox

Quicksans Fast Regular (Image Club)

Quickly the Paul Yusef zebra vented its wrath on groom Jack Knox

Quaint Roman (Agfa)

Quickly the Paul Yusef zebra vented its wrath on groom Jack Knox

Quirinus Bold (Agfa)

Quickly the Paul Yusef zebra vented its wrath on groom Jack Knox

Radiant EF Text Book (Linotype-Hell)

Quickly the Paul Yusef zebra vented its wrath on groom Jack Knox

Railroad Gothic (Linotype-Hell)

QUICKLY THE PAUL YUSEF ZEBRA VENTED ITS WRATH ON GROOM JACK KNOX

Renault Light (Linotype-Hell)

Quickly the Paul Yusef zebra vented its wrath on groom Jack Knox

Republik Serif One (Image Club)

QUICKLY THE PAUL YUSEF ZEBRA VENTED ITS WRATH ON GROOM

Republik Serif Two (Image Club)

QUICKLY THE PAUL YUSEF ZEBRA VENTED ITS WRATH ON GROOM JACK KNOX

Republik Serif Three (Image Club)

QUICKLY THE PAUL YUSEF ZEBRA VENTED ITS WRATH ON GROOM JACK KNOX

Repro Script (Varityper)

Quickly the Paul Yusef zebra vented its wrath on groom Jack Knox

Ritmo Bold (Agfa)

Quickly the Paul Yusef zebra vented its wrath on groom Jack Knox

Robust Regular (Image Club)

Quickly the Paul Yusef zebra vented its wrath on groom Jack Knox

Rockwell (Monotype)

Quickly the Paul Yusef zebra vented its wrath on groom Jack Knox

Romana Book (Linotype-Hell)

Quickly the Paul Yusef zebra vented its wrath on groom
Jack Knox

Rosewood (Adobe)

QUICKLY THE PAUL YUSEF ZEBRA VENTED ITS
WRATH ON GROOM JACK KNOX

Rotis Sans Serif (Agfa)

Quickly the Paul Yusef zebra vented its wrath on
groom Jack Knox

Rotis Semisans (Agfa)

Quickly the Paul Yusef zebra vented its wrath on
groom Jack Knox

Rotis Semiserif (Agfa)

Quickly the Paul Yusef zebra vented its wrath on
groom Jack Knox

Rotis Serif (Agfa)

Quickly the Paul Yusef zebra vented its wrath
on groom Jack Knox

Rubino Solid (Image Club)

Quickly the Paul Yusef zebra vented its wrath on
groom Jack Knox

Runa Serif (Agfa)

Quickly the Paul Yusef zebra vented its wrath on groom Jack Knox

Rundfunk (Fontek)

Quickly the Paul Yusef zebra vented its wrath on groom Jack Knox

Sabon (Linotype-Hell)

Quickly the Paul Yusef zebra vented its wrath on groom Jack Knox

Salut (Agfa)

Quickly the Paul Yusef zebra vented its wrath on groom Jack Knox

San Marco (Linotype-Hell)

Quickly the Paul Yusef zebra vented its wrath on groom Jack Knox

Scherzo (Agfa)

Quickly the Paul Yusef zebra vented its wrath on groom Jack Knox

Schneidler Mediæval DisCaps (URW)

QUICKLY THE PAUL YUSEF ZEBRA VENTED ITS WRATH ON GROOM JACK KNOX

Schnitz (Linotype-Hell)

Quickly the Paul Yusef zebra vented its wrath on groom Jack Knox

Skiffledog Scratch (Psy/Ops Type Foundry)

Quickly the Paul Yusef zebra vented its wrath on groom Jack Knox

Scotty Normal (Agfa)

Quickly the Paul Yusef zebra vented its wrath on groom Jack Knox

Section Bold Condensed (Agfa)

QUICKLY THE PAUL YUSEF ZEBRA VENTED ITS WRATH ON GROOM JACK KNOX

Serpentine Medium (Adobe)

Quickly the Paul Yusef zebra vented its wrath on groom Jack Knox

Shannon Extra Bold (Agfa)

Quickly the Paul Yusef zebra vented its wrath on groom Jack Knox

Shelley (URW)

Quickly the Paul Yusef zebra vented its wrath on groom Jack Knox

Showcard Moderne (Agfa)

Quickly the Paul Yusef zebra vented its wrath on groom Jack Knox

Silica Regular (Stone Type Foundry)

Quickly the Paul Yusef zebra vented its wrath on groom Jack Knox

Sinah Black (Linotype-Hell)

Quickly the paul yusef zebra vented its wrath on groom Jack Knox

Skidoos (URW)

Quickly the Paul Yusef zebra vented its wrath on groom Jack Knox

Skjald (Agfa)

Quickly the Paul Yusef zebra vented its wrath on groom Jack Knox

Slag Irregular (Psy/Ops Type Foundry)

Quickly the paul yusef zebra vented its wrath on groom Jack Knox

Slogan (Linotype-Hell)

Quickly the Paul Yusef zebra vented its wrath on groom Jack Knox

Sloop Script One (Font Bureau)

Quickly the Paul Yusef zebra vented its wrath on groom Jack Knox

Sloop Script Two (Font Bureau)

Quickly the Paul Yusef zebra vented its wrath on groom Jack Knox

Sloop Script Three (Font Bureau)

Quickly the Paul Yusef zebra vented its wrath on groom Jack Knox

Snell Roundhand Black Script (Linotype-Hell)

Quickly the Paul Yusef zebra vented its wrath on groom Jack Knox

Spanner B Gauge (Psy/Ops Type Foundry)

QUICKLY THE PAUL YUSEF ZEBRA VENTED ITS WRATH ON GROOM JACK

Sprint (Linotype-Hell)

Quickly the Paul Yusef zebra vented its wrath on groom Jack Knox

Squire (URW)

Quickly the Paul Yusef zebra vented its wrath on groom Jack Knox

Stentor (Linotype-Hell)

Quickly the Paul Yusef zebra vented its wrath on groom Jack Knox

Stereo (Font Bureau)

QUICKLY THE PAUL YUSEF ZE-BRA VENTED ITS WRATH ON GROOM JACK KNOX

Stigmata (Psy/Ops Type Foundry)

QUICKLY THE PAUL YUSEF ZE-BRA VENTED ITS WRATH ON GROOM JACK HNOX

Stone Informal Medium Old Style Figs. (Stone Type Foundry)

Quickly the Paul Yusef zebra vented its wrath on groom Jack Knox

Stone Print Roman (Stone Type Foundry)

Quickly the Paul Yusef zebra vented its wrath on groom Jack Knox

Stone Sans Small Caps Semibold (Stone Type Foundry)

QUICKLY THE PAUL YUSEF ZEBRA VENTED ITS
WRATH ON GROOM JACK KNOX

Stone Serif Medium (Stone Type Foundry)

Quickly the Paul Yusef zebra vented its
wrath on groom Jack Knox

Stop (Linotype-Hell)

QUICKLY THE PAUL YUSEF ZEBRA VENTED ITS
WRATH ON GROOM JACK KNOX

Stratford Bold (Agfa)

Quickly the Paul Yusef zebra vented its wrath on
groom Jack Knox

Strayhorn Extra Bold Italic (Monotype)

*Quickly the Paul Yusef zebra vented its wrath
on groom Jack Knox*

Strayhorn Regular (Monotype)

Quickly the Paul Yusef zebra vented its wrath on
groom Jack Knox

Streamline Light (Agfa)

Quickly the Paul Yusef zebra vented its wrath on groom Jack Knox

Stylus (Galápagos)

Quickly the Paul Yusef zebra vented its wrath on groom Jack Knox

Stymie DisCaps (URW)

QUICKLY THE PAUL YUSEF ZEBRA VENTED ITS WRATH ON GROOM JACK KNOX

Swift (Linotype-Hell)

Quickly the Paul Yusef zebra vented its wrath on groom Jack Knox

Syllogon Hard (Image Club)

Quickly the Paul Yusef zebra vented its wrath on groom Jack Knox

Syllogon Soft (Image Club)

Quickly the Paul Yusef zebra vented its wrath on groom Jack Knox

Talon (Font Bureau)

Quickly the Paul Yusef zebra vented its wrath on groom Jack Knox

Tarragon (URW)

Quickly the Paul Yusef zebra vented its wrath on groom Jack Knox

Tech Land (Linotype-Hell)

QUICKLY THE PAUL YUSEF ZEBRA VENTED ITS WRATH ON GROOM JACK KNOX

Throhand Ink Roman (Agfa)

Quickly the Paul Yusef zebra vented its wrath on groom Jack Knox

Throhand Pen Roman (Agfa)

Quickly the Paul Yusef zebra vented its wrath on groom Jack Knox

Trillium Gilded (Psy/Ops Type Foundry)

QUICKLY THE PAUL YUSEF ZEBRA VENTED ITS WRATH ON GROOM JACK KNOX

Trump Mediaeval (Linotype-Hell)

Quickly the Paul Yusef zebra vented its
wrath on groom Jack Knox

Tube (Agfa)

Quickly the Paul Yusef zebra vented its wrath on
groom Jack Knox

Utopia Black (Adobe)

**Quickly the Paul Yusef zebra vented its
wrath on groom Jack Knox**

Van Dijck (Monotype)

Quickly the Paul Yusef zebra vented its wrath on
groom Jack Knox

Vario (Linotype-Hell)

**Quickly the Paul Yusef zebra vented its wrath on
groom Jack Knox**

Vendôme (Image Club)

Quickly the Paul Yusef zebra vented its wrath on groom Jack Knox

Village Italic (Font Bureau)

*Quickly the Paul Yusef zebra vented its wrath on
groom Jack Knox*

Village Roman Titling (Font Bureau)

Quickly the Paul Yusef zebra vented its
wrath on groom Jack Knox

Viner Hand, ITC (ITC)

Quickly the Paul Yusef zebra vented its
wrath on groom Jack Knox

Virile (Agfa)

Quickly the Paul Yusef zebra vented its wrath on groom Jack Knox

Viva Extra Extended (Adobe)

Quickly the Paul Yusef
zebra vented its
wrath on groom Jack
Knox

Viva Regular Condensed (Adobe)

Quickly the Paul Yusef zebra vented its wrath on
groom Jack Knox

Volta Medium (Linotype-Hell)

**Quickly the Paul Yusef zebra
vented its wrath on groom Jack
Knox**

Wessex Roman (Font Bureau)

Quickly the Paul Yusef zebra vented its wrath on groom Jack Knox

Whassis Calm (Image Club)

Quickly the Paul Yusef zebra vented its wrath on groom Jack Knox

Whassis Frantic (Image Club)

Quickly the Paul Yusef zebra vented its wrath on groom Jack Knox

Windsor Bold Outline (Linotype-Hell)

Quickly the Paul Yusef zebra vented its wrath on groom Jack Knox

Windsor Elongated (Linotype-Hell)

Quickly the Paul Yusef zebra vented its wrath on groom Jack Knox

Windsor Ultra Heavy (Linotype-Hell)

Quickly the Paul Yusef zebra vented its wrath on groom Jack Knox

Woodblock (Agfa)

QUICKLY THE PAUL YUSEF ZEBRA VENTED ITS WRATH ON GROOM JACK KNOX

Zaragoza (Fontek)

Quickly the Paul Yusef zebra vented its wrath on groom Jack Knox

Zebrawood (Adobe)

QUICKLY THE PAUL YUSEF ZEBRA VENTED ITS WRATH ON GROOM JACK KNOX

Zeppelin (Agfa)

Quickly the Paul Yusef zebra vented its wrath on groom Jack Knox

Appendix A: Sources

This appendix lists sources for the products mentioned in the book.

Adobe Systems, Inc.
Mountain View, CA
(415) 961-4400
(800) 521-1976

Agfa Division, Bayer Corp.
Wilmington, MA
(508) 658-5600
(800) 424-8973

Ares Software
Foster City, CA
(415) 578-9090

Autologic, Inc.
Thousand Oaks, CA
(805) 498-9611
(800) 457-8973

Bitstream, Inc.
Cambridge, MA
(617) 497-6222
(800) 522-3668

Brendel Type, Inc.
La Grange, IL
(708) 579-0552

Broderbund Software, Inc.
Novato, CA
(415) 382-4700

Carter & Cone Type, Inc.
Cambridge, MA
(617) 576-0398
(800) 952-2129

Casady & Greene
Salinas, CA
(408) 484-9228

Corel Corporation
Ottawa, Ontario, Canada
(613) 728-3733

**Digital Typeface
Corporation**
Eden Prairie, MN
(612) 944-9264

Dubl-Click Software, Inc.
Bend, OR
(503) 317-0355
(800) 266-9525

Dynamic Graphics, Inc.
Peoria, IL
(309) 688-8800

Fargo Electronics, Inc.
Eden Prairie, MN
(800) 258-2974

The Font Bureau, Inc.
Boston, MA
(617) 423-8770

Fontek, Letraset USA
Paramus, NJ
(201) 845-6100
(800) 343-8973

Galápagos Design Group, Inc.
Littleton, MA
(508) 952-6200

House Industries
Wilmington, DE
(302) 888-1648
(800) 888-4390

Image Club Graphics
Calgary, Alberta, Canada
(403) 262-8008
(800) 661-9410

International Typeface Corp.
New York, NY
(212) 371-0699
(800) 425-3882

Lari Software, Inc.
Chapel Hill, NC
(919) 968-0701

Linotype-Hell Co.
Hauppauge, NY
(516) 434-2000
(800) 799-4922

Macromedia, Inc.
San Francisco, CA
(415) 252-2000
(800) 326-2128

Manhattan Graphics Corporation
Hartsdale, NY
(914) 725-2048

Metro Creative Graphics, Inc.
New York, NY
(212) 947-5100
(800) 223-1600

Monotype Typography, Inc.
Chicago, IL
(312) 855-1440
(800) 666-6897

PhotoDisc
Seattle, WA
(206) 441-9355
(800) 528-3472

PrePress Direct, PrePress Solutions
East Hanover, NJ
(201) 887-8000
(800) 631-8134

Psy/Ops
San Francisco, CA
(415) 285-8820

Pyrus North America
Millersville, MD
(800) 435-1960

Quark, Inc.
Denver, CO
(303) 344-3491
(800) 788-7835

Stone Type Foundry, Inc.
Palo Alto, CA
(415) 324-1870
(800) 557-8663

Symantec Corporation
Cupertino, CA
(408) 253-9600
(800) 441-7234

URW America
Nashua, NH
(603) 882-7445
(800) 229-8791

Y & Y
Concord, MA
(508) 371-3286
(800) 742-4059

Index

About the CD-ROM

The hybrid PC/Macintosh CD-ROM included with this book contains a collection of font libraries, utilities, demos and software for font creation, management and organization.
The CD-ROM includes:

FONT LIBRARIES

- **Image Club Clip Art Images and Fonts**
- **Bitstream Arrus typeface family** (Bitstream© Arrus™)
- **The Font Bureau**
- **Autologic Signa typeface Regular**
- **URW Antigua Medium typefaces**
- **Type specimens from Galapagos Design Group** for the PC and Macintosh.

SOFTWARE

- **Fontographer and Freehand Demos** for the PC and Macintosh.
- **Tryout versions of:**
  - **Adobe Illustrator™**
  - **Adobe Acrobat™ Reader**

A-1

- **Adobe After Effects™**
- **Adobe Dimentions™**
- **Adobe Fetch™**
- **Adobe Gallery Effects™**
- **Adobe Pagemaker™**
- **Adobe Photoshop™**
- **Adobe Premier™**
- **Adobe Streamline™**
- **Adobe Texturemaker™**
- **Demo version of FontChameleon** for the PC and Macintosh.
- **Demos of Ikarus-M and Linus-M**
- **FontLab 2.5 demo for Windows**
- **PMN Cæcilia™ 55 and HotMetal Borders 1 Font** for PC and Macintosh
- **GX Type Expo**

Image Club clip art and fonts are used with express permission, Adobe© and Image Club Graphic Inc.™ are trademarks of Adobe Systems Incorporated.

All Macromedia product names are trademarks or registered trademarks of Macromedia, Inc. Other product names are trademarks of their respective owners, as indicated.

Adobe, Adobe Illustrator, Adobe Acrobat Reader, Adobe After Effects, Adobe Dimentions, Adobe Fetch, Adobe Gallery Effects, Adobe Pagemaker, Adobe Photoshop, Adobe Premier, Adobe Streamline, and Adobe Texturemaker are trademarks of Adobe Systems Incorporated or its subsidiaries, and may be registered in certain jurisdictions. All other product and company names are the trademarks of their respective holders.

Demo version of FontChameleon 00© 1995 Ares Software Corporation. All rights reserved.

Type specimens from Galapagos Design Group© 1995 Galapagos Desing Group, Inc.
    All rights reserved.

PMN Caecilia™ 55 and HotMetal Borders 1 Font© 1991, 1992 Adobe Systems.
    PMN Cæcilia is a trademark of Linotype-Hell AG and/or its subsidiaries.

GX Type Expo© 1994 Linotype-Hell AG

Chapter 4   Funny Pages

Chapter 5   Covers

Chapter 6 The Four Seasons

JESSICA ABEL © 1995

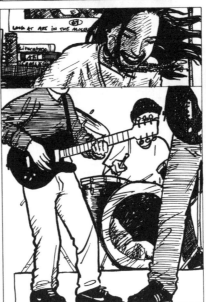

3

last one out close the door and shut off the lights—
Jessica Abel @ 1993

4

3:47 PM — THE CLOCK STOPS ON DIVISION ST.

JESSICA ABEL © 1995

CLOUDS HEAVY WITH THE THREAT OF RAIN HAD BEEN LYING IN WAIT FOR US ALL DAY.

DAMN.

WE HAD KNOWN IT WAS COMING, BUT WE WERE BEHIND ON THE JOB, SO WE WENT TO WORK ANYWAY. IT WAS GOING TO BE A **DOWNPOUR.** ANYBODY COULD SEE THAT.

a true story by jessica abel © 1995

mile marker

BURR! IT'S RAINING! LET'S GET PACKED UP!

7

"I CAN'T FIND THE RIDER."

THERE WERE TWO OF 'EM.

WE LOOKED EVERYWHERE — THE DITCHES, EVEN BACK IN THE TREES... NOTHING.

AND THEN, ALL AT ONCE, THE THREE OF US TURNED... AND LOOKED BACK.

THEY LOOKED LIKE RAG DOLLS THAT HAD BEEN WADDED UP AND THROWN DOWN.

THEY WERE DEAD, OF COURSE.

8

I KNOW THAT LOOK.

$'64 QUESTION

J.ABEL©92

IT'S THE SAME LOOK I GET WHEN I'M TOUCHING WHAT I MOST WANT, BUT CAN'T HAVE.

I SLIDE MY EYES PAST YOUR GAZE, TRYING TO AVOID MEANINGFUL GLANCES, PRETENDING I DON'T NOTICE, BUT I DO.

I ONLY WONDER WHETHER YOU LOVE ME BECAUSE I DON'T WANT YOU, OR I DON'T WANT YOU BECAUSE YOU LOVE ME.

10

11

Pass it on...

as told to David Greenberger by Neil Henderson. Art by Jessica Abel © Jan. 1995

THROUGH MY LIFE I'VE NOT GOTTEN EXCITED, BECAUSE IT'S THE WRONG THING TO DO, YOU HURT YOURSELF.

MY EXPERIENCE THROUGH LIFE HAS BEEN FRIENDSHIP BACK AND FORTH.

SKRITCH SCRATCH

SCRATCH SCRATCH

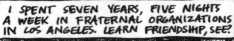

I SPENT SEVEN YEARS, FIVE NIGHTS A WEEK IN FRATERNAL ORGANIZATIONS IN LOS ANGELES. LEARN FRIENDSHIP, SEE?

THAT'S A GREAT THING.

FROM OUT OF YOUR HEART BANISH EVERY UNKIND THOUGHT.

WOULDN'T IT BE WONDERFUL TODAY IF PEOPLE THOUGHT THAT WAY AND PRACTICED THAT WAY. WHY CAN'T WE TEACH EACH OTHER TO BE GOOD AND HONEST?

Welcome to BOSNIA Have a Nice Day!

PEOPLE HAVE BEEN GOOD TO ME ALL MY LIFE, AND I TRY TO PASS IT ON.

12

IT ALL STARTED SO INNOCENTLY. I SAW HIM AT A SHOW; HE WAS TRYING TO ROLL A CIGARETTE, BUT HIS HAIR KEPT FALLING IN HIS

FACE. EVERY TIME HE PUSHED IT AWAY, IT JUST SLID RIGHT BACK DOWN IN FRONT OF HIS EYES. HE LOOKED CONFUSED. I JUST— LOOKED. WHEN HE CLOSED HIS EYES AND LICKED THE PAPER, I HAD TO LEAVE THE ROOM. I TOLD MY FRIEND, AND SHE JUST SAID, "WHO, THAT JUNKIE?" "YEAH," I SAID,

PART ONE ©1992 BY JESSICA ABEL

MY NAME IS COURTNEY CLARE, AND THIS STORY IS ALMOST TRUE.

I SAID "ALMOST"!!

YOU KNOW HOW IT IS — YOU SCOPE SOMEONE OUT AND YOU FIGURE, OK, HERE'S THIS GUY, I BETTER JUST TAKE A GOOD _LONG_ LOOK, BECAUSE I'LL NEVER SEE HIM AGAIN. OH WELL. NO BIG DEAL, RIGHT? BUT SOMETIMES, IF YOU HAPPEN TO LIVE ON HIS BUS ROUTE OR SOMETHING, THEN MAYBE YOU START TO SEE HIM AROUND, AND MAYBE YOU MIGHT START TO FIND OUT STUFF ABOUT HIM... LIKE HIS NAME, AND WHERE HE WORKS, AND WHERE HE GETS HIS GROCERIES... ALMOST LIKE IT'S INVOLUNTARY, EXCEPT YOU'RE TRYING SO HARD. SO THAT'S HOW IT WAS. LIKE THE NEXT TIME I SAW HIM, HE WAS IN THE KOPY KAVE, YOU KNOW, THAT HIP NEW CAFE/COPY CENTER? I SAW HIM THROUGH THE WINDOW; HE WAS BENT OVER A MACHINE.

I DRAGGED MY ROOMMATE, DAWN, EVEN THOUGH I KNEW SHE HATES ROCK SHOWS. I KNEW SHE'D LOVE THE JUNKIE.

THIS IS HORRIBLE. YOU BETTER BE RIGHT ABOUT THIS GUY.

TRUST ME.

EARPLUGS

HEY BABY...

THANKS — WE'RE CRUDE... STICK AROUND FOR PINK PEARL.

Pink Pearl

Fried eggs.

HEY, COURTNEY?

YEAH?

IS THAT HIM?

YEAH.

AFTER THAT, I SAW HIM EVERYWHERE.

EVEN WHEN HE WASN'T AROUND.

16

ONE SUNDAY AFTERNOON, I WAS IN CITY CAFÉ HAVING BREAKFAST WHEN HE WALKED IN LOOKING NOT GOOD (—IF SUCH CAN BE SAID...)

HAHAHA! LOOKIT THE BIG ROCK STAR! SHIT, JOHNNY, YOU LOOK LIKE HELL. YOU'RE TWO HOURS LATE, YOU KNOW.

I KNOW... I'LL COVER FOR YOU ON TUESDAY.

DON'T WORRY ABOUT IT. JUST PUT ME ON THE LIST FOR YOUR NEXT SHOW.

—EXCUSE ME...

SURE... SHIT, MY EYES HURT. DO YOU THINK BRIAN WILL GET PISSED IF I WEAR MY SUNGLASSES TODAY?

EXCUSE ME... MISS? EXCUSE ME, WOULD YOU LIKE SOME MORE COFFEE?

HUH?

WITHIN FIVE MINUTES, I WAS A REGULAR.

PACKAGE FOR JOHN FABER?

YO.

ANOTHER PANTY-OF-THE-MONTH CLUB DELIVERY SO SOON, JOHNNY?

NAME: JOHN FABER

CLIP and SAVE FOR YOUR "OBSESSION ROL-O-DEX"

HEY JOHNNY! HAPPY BIRTHDAY!

HEY LIZ!

BIRTHDAY: JULY 15

AGE: 24

OK... SO ... YEAH. WE'LL MEET AT MY PLACE AT NINE. YOU KNOW WHERE I LIVE?

CAFÉ LA
• CAPPUCIN
• DOUBLE C
• ESPRESSO
• DOUBLE E
• CAFÉ AU

ADDRESS: 234 ROLLINS 3rd FLOOR

17

I KNEW HIS WHOLE SCHEDULE, AND SOMETIMES I'D SHOW UP ON WEEKNIGHTS, BUT I WAS THERE EVERY SUNDAY LIKE CLOCKWORK

UM— I'll have coffee, and, um... a bagel — toasted, with cream cheese ...

Coffee, plain bagel, toasted, with cream cheese

coffee and a bagel

Coffee and a bagel?

Yeah, thanks.

The usual?

Thanks.

How ya doin?

oh, fine, you?

Hey—

ONE TIME, HE WAS TRYING TO BALANCE A BUNCH OF STUFF AND HAND ME A CUP OF COFFEE AT THE SAME TIME. I TOOK IT FROM HIS HAND AND WE ACCIDENTALLY TOUCHED. I THINK HE STARTED, THO IT MIGHT HAVE JUST BEEN ME...

AFTER A WHILE, WHEN I SAW HIM ON THE STREET, WE'D SORTA ACKNOWLEDGE EACH OTHER.

HEY.

HEY.

I THINK IT WAS SOMETIME IN AUGUST WHEN I WAS SITTING OUTSIDE J AND J FINER FOODS AND HE WALKED BY.

HEY COURTNEY— WHAT'S UP? I'M WORKING TONITE, THINK YOU'LL BE BY?

contact.

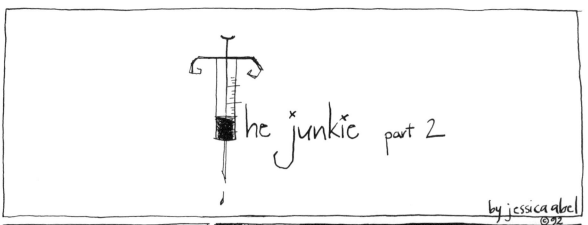

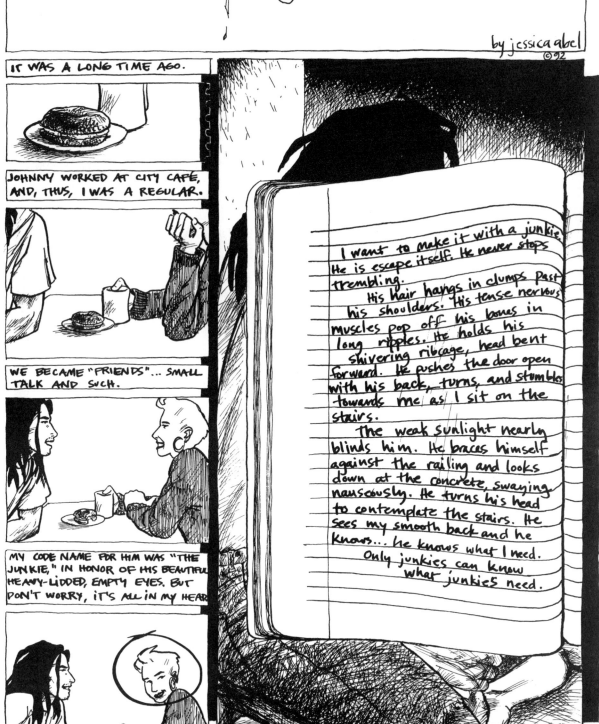

He steps down next to me and lifts my hair away from my face. His trembling, ice-cold lips brush the back of my earlobe. I turn, gently, to look at him - at his eyes.
His eyes. They're

Black.   and

Electric.

Every five seconds, a spark goes off in his eyes.

He is fucking PLUGGED IN.

No one has ever looked at me like that. I mean, that's how he probably looks at everyone, but right now, he's only looking at me like that.

Jesus.

The object of desire.

and...?

And we screw each other's brains out. I mean, no pretenses here. This is not "making love."
This is need.
This is symbiotic.

shiver to here

21

10mm Gut Wrench

CHICAGO'S NEWS & ARTS WEEKLY | FREE | MAY 4-MAY 10, 1995

NEWCITY

PUNK PILGRIMAGE

Jessica Abel eavesdrops on the Fireside chatter, Page 8.

Pro bowling's new world order • Around The Coyote suffers a shakeup

AT HER READING, ELIZABETH WURTZEL STATED THAT THE PRINCIPAL AIM OF *PROZAC NATION*, WHICH, DESPITE ITS TITLE, IS ABOUT NEITHER "NATION" NOR, FOR THE MOST PART, PROZAC, IS TO DESCRIBE AND DEROMANTICIZE THE MENTAL ILLNESS OF DEPRESSION. WURTZEL WISHES US TO RECOGNIZE THAT DEPRESSION IS *DEBILITATING* AND A VERY *REAL* ILLNESS. AS SHE OFTEN INSISTS IN THE BOOK, I AM SICK, I NEED HELP. (AND IT'D BE NICE IF IT CAME IN THE FORM OF PSYCHOACTIVE DRUGS.)

HOWEVER, THE BOOK LARGELY FAILS IN THAT GOAL. WURTZEL'S CONTINUAL INSISTENCE THAT SHE WAS PERSISTENTLY MISUNDERSTOOD, AND EVEN MISTREATED, BY FAMILY, FRIENDS, AND DOCTORS, SMOOTHES OUT INTO ONE LONG OBSESSIVE WHINE. THIS ASSESSMENT MAY BE A TAD UNFAIR, AS WURTZEL CERTAINLY PURSUES A NOBLE GOAL, BUT ONE CAN'T HELP FEELING THAT SHE'S GOT A CHIP ON HER SHOULDER, NOT A SCIENTIFIC THESIS.

HAVE YOU EVER SPENT ANY TIME WITH "RECOVERING ALCOHOLICS" — THAT IS, PEOPLE WHO HAVE A PROBLEM WITH ALCOHOL, BUT HAVE GOTTEN SOBER THROUGH AA? THOUGH AA APPARENTLY FROWNS ON IT, MANY OF THEM TELL "WAR STORIES," A FORM OF ONE-UPSMANSHIP DESIGNED TO SHOW HOW WILD, HOW DEBAUCHED, HOW VERY FAR GONE THEY WERE. YOU CAN EASILY UNDERSTAND WHY THEY WOULD DO THIS. IN OUR SOCIETY, IT'S HARD TO BE "HARD" — TO BE REALLY COOL — WITHOUT THE BENEFIT OF BEING REALLY OUT-OF-CONTROL AND FUCKED-UP. YOU CAN ALSO EASILY UNDERSTAND WHY AA WOULD DISCOURAGE THIS PRACTICE.

PROZAC NATION IS A LITTLE BIT LIKE THAT. ITS COVER LOOKS LIKE A PHOTO LAYOUT IN *SASSY* MAGAZINE. DEPRESSION ALONE ISN'T TOO GLAMOROUS, SO WE GET SELF-MUTILATION, DRUG AND ALCOHOL ABUSE AND OVERDOSES (THOUGH SHE "LACK[S] THE GERM, THE TENDENCY TOWARD CHEMICAL DEPENDENCY"), CRYING FITS, AND LOTS OF DETAILS ABOUT HER PRECOCIOUS, AND YET PREDICTABLE, MUSICAL TASTES. YOU'VE GOT YOUR VELVET UNDERGROUND, YOUR PATTI SMITH, JONI MITCHELL AND BOB DYLAN. SHE DESCRIBES HER HABIT OF TELLING ALL HER PROBLEMS TO NEAR-STRANGERS AND WE CONCLUDE THAT SHE HAS RUN OUT OF NEAR-STRANGERS.

30

SOMEONE SAID ADAM IS "THE ULTIMATE FAN"... APPARENTLY, HE TRADES BANDS TAPES OF THEIR SHOWS IN EXCHANGE FOR BEING ALLOWED TO TAPE THEM. AN ARTICLE ABOUT ADAM ONCE CALLED HIM "MR. ARCHIVES ~ SO I GUESS THIS SHOW HAS JUST ENTERED THE ANNALS OF HISTORY.

STANLEY'S JOYFUL NOISE "FROM CHICAGO, ILLI-NOISE!"

ANDREW: "I WAS A LATE ROCKER. MY FIRST SHOW WAS CIRCUS LUPUS AT THE 950 CLUB IN D.C. WHEN I WAS 18."

TIM: " OUR BAND'S PHILOSOPHY IS TO BE SO PHAT THAT WE HAVE TO GO ON DIETS !"

DAN: " MY PERSONAL PHILOSOPHY? 'FOR THE GRACE OF GOD.'"

"STANLEY ISN'T ANYBODY. WELL, ACTUALLY HE'S MY BROTHER, BUT IT DOESN'T MEAN ANYTHING."

IT'S A LITTLE WEIRD TO SEE A FEW PEOPLE ACTUALLY TAKING ADVANTAGE OF THE LANES DURING A BAND. ON THE OTHER HAND, MOST HAVE QUICKLY ADAPTED TO SITTING IN "BOWLER'S SETTEES" (OFFICIAL TERM FOR THOSE BENCHES ACCORDING TO THE AJBC*), NOT TO BOWL, BUT TO WATCH THE SHOW.

* AMERICAN JUNIOR BOWLING CONGRESS.

I STARTED DOING THIS WHEN I WAS 19 AND NOW I'M 26. I'VE SEEN SO MANY BANDS... I DON'T EVEN KNOW WHAT'S GOOD ANYMORE. SOMEONE ASKS ME HOW I LIKE SOME BAND, I GO, "MMM... TOO MUCH TREBLE."

Do you work for a poetry magazine?

?!

ELLIOT, SOUND GUY

AH, THE HENTCHMEN. LAST TIME I SAW THEM, I WAS DANCING UNSTEADILY AT A FRIEND'S WEDDING RECEPTION. APPARENTLY, THERE ARE PHOTOS.

MY FIRST ROCK CONCERT WAS CHEAP TRICK AND REO SPEEDWAGON WHEN I WAS 13. NO, I DIDN'T BOWL TONIGHT.

I THINK THE ROCK IS A GOOD ADDITION TO BOWLING, THOUGH I BOWLED TERRIBLY TONIGHT. I'M HERE BECAUSE I HEARD THE LAST BAND WAS GREAT. MY SISTER MINDY TOLD ME.

"THE 'T' IN 'HENTCH' IS THERE BECAUSE A LOT OF SIXTIES BANDS WERE CALLED HENCHMEN, AND WE DIDN'T WANT TO GET IN TROUBLE WITH COPYRIGHTS. SO NO, IT'S NOT JUST MISSPELLED. BUT A LOT OF PEOPLE MISSPELL HENTCHMEN AND IT MAKES US MAD."

YOU SHOULD TALK TO MINDY AND HER FRIENDS. THEY ARE ALL 17 OR 18 AND DROVE 150 MILES FROM BLOOMINGTON. NORMAL FOR THIS SHOW!

TOM, 31, OF CHICAGO

KIM, 28, OF CHICAGO

end. J.A. 5/2/95

31

UPSTAIRS IN THE TREE-VIEWING AREA:

WE JUST CAME TO SEE THE TREE. WE USED TO EAT, BUT NOW IT'S TOO CROWDED.

I LIKE THE WINDOWS AT FIELD'S BEST. I'M ASKING FOR CDS FOR XMAS.

I WANT THE NEW SMASHING PUMPKINS.

JERRY   LUKE   DANNY

MY FAMILY COMES EVERY YEAR. WE'RE WAITING TO MEET THEM. NO, I DON'T SHOP IN THE LOOP. TOO CHAOTIC.

LIZ   KRIS

FIELD'S USED TO CRANE IN A REAL TREE WITH REAL CANDLES ~ AND THEY WOULD PAY A FIREMAN TO JUST SIT THERE ALL DAY AND WATCH THE TREE TO MAKE SURE IT DIDN'T CATCH FIRE.

FAKE HEDGE.

TWO GIRLS PLAYING OUTSIDE THE DINING ROOM.

(SO WHAT'S THE DEAL WITH THE "MIRACLE" TREE?)

OH, HA HA! THE STAFF JOKE AROUND ABOUT THE BLIND GUY, THE CRIPPLED WOMAN, WHO SITS BY THE TREE...

...AND THEN SHE WALKS OUT!! AND HE CAN SEE!!

CORPORATE CHEF TERRENCE BRAXTON

PEOPLE WOULD DO ANYTHING, SAY ANYTHING, NOT TO WAIT IN LINE.

WHAT THEY DON'T REALIZE IS THAT THE STAFF IS TOO AFRAID OF PROVOKING THE CROWD TO RIOT TO FALL FOR ANY TRICKS!!

CHEF DAVE: "I REALLY RESPECT THE PEOPLE WHO WILL WAIT 3 HOURS TO EAT HERE. I TRY TO DO A LITTLE EXTRA FOR THEM. MAKE IT NICER."

(WOULD YOU DO IT?)

"HEH. I GUESS I WOULDN'T WAIT 3 HOURS FOR ANY-THING. I'M TOO IMPATIENT."

JA 12/2/95

BY JESSICA ABEL
© 1995

I CAUGHT A RARE GLIMPSE OF LIFE THROUGH THE EYES OF A G-FAN WEEKEND-BEFORE-LAST AT THE SECOND ANNUAL G-CON OUT IN ARLINGTON HEIGHTS.

THE SUITS WEIGH CLOSE TO 100 lbs. AND CAN CAUSE ACTORS TO LOSE UP TO 5 lbs. OF WATER A DAY. ACTORS CAN'T STAY IN THE SUITS LONGER THAN 20 MINUTES AT A TIME. PURISTS FEEL THAT GODZILLA CAN'T BE ANIMATED...

...HE HAS TO BE A GUY IN A SUIT.

RADIOACTIVE RAY

(GODZILLA)

ALEX, MY GUIDE, IS THE REAL McCOY; HE OWNS SEVERAL THOUSAND GODZILLA TOYS AND SPEAKS JAPANESE.

THE ORIGIN OF GODZILLA: 1954.

NUCLEAR TESTS

AWAKEN GODZILLA FROM SEA FLOOR

THIS "COMBAT JOE" WITH GODZILLA SUIT IS WORTH $750.00

THE ORIGIN OF GODZILLA: 1995.

NUCLEAR TESTS

MUTATE PREHISTORIC HOLD-OVER "GODZILLASAURUS" ON SOUTH SEA ISLAND.

I'VE SEEN ALL THE OLD ONES— "GODZILLA VS. SMOG MONSTER", "DESTROY ALL MONSTERS"...

"DESTROY ALL MONSTERS" RULES!

YEAH, THAT'S WHAT GOT ME HOOKED.

DAVID

ROBERT

SORDID SCENE OF NAKED COLLECTOR LUST:

I... I HATE TO ASK, BUT HOW MUCH IS THAT "QUISP"?

$150.00

OH, NOT AS BAD AS I FEARED... IT'S JUST... SO ...PERFECT!

CARESSING AIR OVER CASE

UP UNTIL ABOUT 1965, GODZILLA WAS A BAD GUY, AND DESTROYED TOKYO.

SWAT

AROUND 1966, GODZILLA BECAME A GOOD GUY, AND FOUGHT OFF BAD MONSTERS, ACCIDENTALLY DESTROYING TOKYO DUE TO HIS SIZE

OOPS!

HAH! MISSED!—

CRUSH CRUMBLE

"OH NO! THERE GOES TOKE-EE-OH! GO GO GODZILLA!"

I PREFER THE EARLIER MOVIES... STRONGER VILLAIN = MORE CONFLICT = BETTER MOVIE

ZILLA

UNGCC

UNITED NATIONS GODZILLA COUNTER-MEASURE CENTER (ACTUAL PROP)

ED

THE END...I HOPE. THANKS ALEX WALD.

3

41

42

44

48

49

WE SPENT A LOT OF TIME — AND A LOT OF UNCLE SAM'S MONEY — TOGETHER. TURNS OUT THAT THE FRENCH FAMILY SHE LIVED WITH WAS WELL-CONNECTED IN THE COLLABORATOR GOVERNMENT, SO I COULD HAVE MY CAKE AND EAT IT — IF ONLY SHE WOULD HELP ME OUT A LITTLE...

I EXPLAINED THE WHOLE THING TO HER, ABOUT HOW I NEEDED INFORMATION FROM HER "FAMILY."...

SHE PROMISED TO HELP ME, BUT THE WEEKS WENT BY, AND THEN, DECEMBER 7, WELL, IT STEPPED UP THE PRESSURE...

... NOW I WAS IN ENEMY TERRITORY. I WASN'T GETTING ANYTHING, I WASN'T EVEN FOLLOWING ANY LEADS; I COULDN'T TEAR MYSELF AWAY FROM HER FOR LONG ENOUGH TO DO ANYTHING. FINALLY, I WAS DESPERATE. THE INFORMATION SHE WAS GIVING ME WAS PRACTICALLY COMMON KNOWLEDGE. IF I DIDN'T GET SOMETHING SOON, THEY WERE GOING TO SEND ME HOME.

AT LAST, SHE PROMISED ME A BIG ONE.

A WEAPONS CACHE, A HEADQUARTERS. MY SUPERIORS WERE REAL PLEASED. THEY SENT IN A BATTALLION~

A WHOLE BATTALION~

THOSE POOR BOYS.

IT WAS A MASSACRE. AN AMBUSH. A SET-UP. ONLY THING I COULDN'T FIGURE OUT WAS— HOW COULD SHE DO THIS TO HER COUNTRY? TO **ME**.

I LOOKED ALL OVER FOR HER AND FINALLY FOUND HER AT THE STATION WITH A TALL, BLOND GERMAN— GESTAPO. AT FIRST I THOUGHT HE'D ARRESTED HER AND WAS GETTING SET TO TAKE A SHOT AT HIM WHEN SHE LOOKED ME STRAIGHT IN THE EYE AND THEN KISSED HIM. RIGHT IN FRONT OF ME.

THEN SHE LAUGHED. I STOOD THERE WATCHING AS THEY CLIMBED ABOARD THE PARIS TRAIN. WHAT COULD I DO? HE WAS GESTAPO, FOR CHRIST'S SAKE.

AND I CAN'T HELP THINKING THAT IF I HADN'T MET HER IN NICE

AND COME ALIVE FOR THE FIRST TIME ~

I WOULDN'T FEEL SO DEAD NOW THAT I'M ALONE IN SENEGAL.

SHE IS MY LIFE, AND SHE'S GONE.

4
Funny Pages

SHE PUTS THE "ARTY" IN "PARTY"...

HI!

WOW! HOW DID YOU GET BRIGHT BLUE DREADS?

DO YOU LIKE IT?

YEAH!

I DIPPED MY HAIR IN "ROBIN'S EGG" LATEX INTERIOR WALL PAINT!

YIKE

SHE'S—ARTBABE!

58

59

1 *Six Degrees of Separation* — a play by John Guare, and a movie directed by Fred Schepisi.

2 Steve Albini — a well-known Chicago producer (or, as he prefers, engineer) for numerous "alternative" bands, such as The Jesus Lizard and Nirvana.

3 The Whitewater scandal came to a head around the time the *Six Degrees of Separation* movie came out, and President Clinton dismissed certain connections of his by commenting that, in Arkansas, it's more like two degrees of separation.

4 Phil Spector — legendary pop music producer.

5 An example of Mr. Albini's reported tendency to have little good to say about anyone.

6 John La Grou, "Recording the Acoustic Combo," *Mix* June 1994; p. 33. (Industry magazine for engineers; mostly ads and endorsements rather than editorial content.)

7 Steve Albini, "The Problem With Music," *The Baffler* no. 5 (1993); p. 33. (Noting extreme distaste for such terms as "punchy" and "warm," when used in reference to music.)

8 An argument in the recording industry analogous to the argument among music consumers over the value of vinyl records versus compact discs.

9 The poor schmuck certainly meant to say an Otari 8-track.

10 Urge Overkill — a Chicago band, once good friends with Mr. Albini, now inimical.

11 Mix Magazine. See 6 Above.

12 Two degrees of separation means, if you live in Chicago, you know someone who knows someone who knows Steve Albini. Count on it. It's just like that around here.

IT'S "BOYS' ADVENTURE" TRYING TO BE "GREAT BOOKS"...

IT'S FRAZIER THOMAS TRYING TO BE ALISTAIR COOKE...

IT'S SUNDAY AFTERNOON, TIME FOR...

NOTE TO NON-CHICAGOANS: THIS IS ABOUT A T.V. SHOW THAT RAN OLD ADVENTURE MOVIES LIKE "ALI BABA AND THE FORTY THIEVES" AND STUFF, BUT THEY ALMOST ALWAYS SEEMED TO TAKE PLACE ON BOATS, SOMEHOW. ALI BABA ON BOATS? I DON'T KNOW. ANYHOW, EVERYONE WATCHED IT, IT WAS THE ONLY THING ON, BUT EVERYONE ALSO SEEMED TO HATE IT...

63

64

65

67

She puts the "arty" in "party" — She's Artbabe!!

71

JESSICA ABEL ©1995
11/29/95

BREAKDOWN

comics magazine number 2 fall 1989

artbabe

no 2 $1.50

Jessica Abel © '93

artbabe 4

$1 50

JESSICA ABEL © 1995

The Four Seasons

The HEART of a TURTLE

JESSICA ABEL © 1995

WHAT HAPPENED?

YOU RAN OVER A BIG WHEEL.

OH.

GOD, I FEEL BAD.

SOME POOR KID IS GOING TO BE PRETTY BUMMED.

YEAH.

MAN, LOOK AT ALL THAT TRASH UP IN THAT TREE.

SOMEBODY GOT T.P.'d.

IT LOOKS LIKE SPANISH MOSS...

...HA HA... LISTEN, I'VE GOT TO TELL YOU ABOUT THIS WEIRD THING THAT HAPPENED TO ME A COUPLE OF YEARS AGO WHEN I WAS DOWN IN LOUISIANA VISITING MY BROTHER.

HE WAS WORKING IN WHAT, DOWN THERE, THEY CALL THE "OIL PATCH", NEAR LAFAYETTE, FOR A YEAR OR SO. I GUESS SOME BAD-WEIRD SHIT WAS GOING ON IN HIS HEAD, AND HE JUST HAD TO DO SOMETHING PRETTY FUCKED-UP AT THAT POINT IN HIS LIFE, YOU KNOW?

ANYWAY, HE HAD A BUNCH OF MONEY 'CAUSE ROUSTABOUTS MAKE LIKE FIFTEEN DOLLARS AN HOUR AND IT DOESN'T COST MUCH TO LIVE IN LAFAYETTE, AT LEAST, NOT THE WAY HE WAS LIVING. HE FLEW ME DOWN FOR HIS BIRTHDAY.

HE WAS LIVING IN THIS SHACK WITH LIKE FIVE GUYS, AND HAVING FUCKED-UP PARTIES EVERY NIGHT. I WAS DRUNK OR JUST FUCKING OUT OF IT THE WHOLE TIME... AND IT WAS HOTTER THAN HELL, TOO, WHICH DIDN'T HELP MUCH. I WAS BATHED IN SWEAT AND I JUST FELT LIKE SHIT.

IT WAS FUCKING DEPRESSING SEEING HIM LIKE THAT, YOU KNOW?

WELL, ANYWAY... SO THIS ONE DAY, MY BROTHER SENT ME TO TOWN FOR SOME FOOD OR SOMETHING. THE SUN WAS SHINING, THE GREY SPANISH MOSS DRIPPING, AND THE HEAT JUST SHIMMERING OFF THE ROAD. IT WAS SO WET, YOU FELT LIKE YOU COULD **SEE** THE AIR. ON THE WAY BACK, I STARTED COMING UP ON THIS RED PICKUP.

IT KEEPS STOPPING, SO I'M COMING UP ON IT FAST.

AS I GET CLOSER, I REALIZE THAT THERE IS A WOMAN DRIVING THE TRUCK AND THAT EACH TIME SHE STOPS, SHE GETS OUT AND PICKS A TURTLE OFF THE ROAD AND PUTS IT SAFELY IN THE GRASS.

NOW, DOWN THERE, THERE IS A LOT OF WILDLIFE CROSSING THE ROAD, BUT IT'S NOT ALL TURTLES, YOU KNOW? THERE'RE SNAKES AND SHIT, RATS, WHATEVER, SO THIS WAS WEIRD.

IT STARTED TO FEEL LIKE A DREAM OR SOMETHING, YOU KNOW? LIKE THE HEAT WAS GETTING TO ME.

WHEN I CAUGHT UP TO HER, I CRUISED SLOWLY BEHIND RATHER THAN PASS HER.

89

I GUESS SHE WAS PROBABLY 45 OR SO, BUT SHE WAS SO BEAUTIFUL, AND I GUESS I HAD THIS FEELING LIKE I REALLY KNEW HER, LIKE I HAD INSTANTANEOUSLY BECOME AWARE OF THE WHOLE STORY OF HER LIFE AND OF WHAT KIND OF PERSON SHE REALLY WAS.

SHE WAS TOTALLY UNAWARE OF ME. I FELT THIS GREAT DISTANCE BETWEEN US, BUT IT WAS LIKE I LOVED HER.

WELL, WHAT HAPPENED?

I CALLED OUT TO HER NEXT TIME SHE STOPPED AND ASKED HER OUT. SHE WOULDN'T TALK TO ME. SHE MUMBLED SOME-THING ABOUT DAMN YANKEES, SHERMAN BURNING ATLANTA, AND DROVE OFF.

IS THAT TRUE?

HAH HAH, NO... ACTUALLY I JUST TOOK MY TURNING AND NEVER SAW HER AGAIN. HAH HAH, WHAT A TRIP.

HEH. YEAH. SOUNDS PRETTY WEIRD.

END. 12/14

90

THE ANT
& THE GRASSHOPPER

©1996 JESSICA ABEL

91

"...I JUST WISH YOU'D BE A LITTLE CAREFUL—IT LOOKS LIKE YOU'RE HEADED FOR A FALL..."

DEC 6

KNOCK KNOCK KNOCK

7:30 A.M. SATURDAY

GRASSHOPPER?!

I GOT KICKED OUT OF MY PLACE. CAN I SLEEP ON YOUR COUCH?

OF COURSE! OH, GRASSHOPPER, THAT'S SO AWFUL! TO LOSE YOUR HOME! YOU MUST BE VERY UPSET.

OH, YEAH. I HATE LOOKING FOR AN APARTMENT. BUT A GUY I MET A FEW HOURS AGO TOLD ME I COULD MOVE IN WITH HIM, SO MAYBE I'LL DO THAT.

OH, WAIT... SHIT! I FORGOT TO GET HIS NUMBER!

A FEW WEEKS LATER...

I CAN'T TAKE IT ANYMORE! SHE NEVER WASHES THE DISHES, SHE COMES IN AT 4 A.M. EVERY NIGHT, SHE EATS ALL MY FOOD, AND, TO TOP IT OFF, SHE'S FLIRTING WITH CHARLES AND HE'S FLIRTING BACK! I CAN'T LET HER STEAL MY BOYFRIEND TOO!

MAN, YOU'VE JUST GOT TO SHAPE UP! YOU DON'T HAVE TO TAKE THAT KIND OF SHIT; KICK THE BITCH OUT! SHE HAS ALWAYS BEEN THAT WAY. SHE WON'T EVER CHANGE.

YEAH, YOU'RE RIGHT! HELL YEAH! SHE'S OUT ON HER "SKINNY ASS!"

THAT'S THE SPIRIT! YOU GO GIRL!

93

THE END. (AAH!)

IT'S A BIG WEATHER DAY. A BAD CTA DAY.

JACK LONDON

JESSICA ABEL ©1996

SITTING IN THE OVER-WARM, CROWDED TUBE, INCHING ITS WAY TO EVANSTON, READING A BOOK...

...I'M SHOCKED INTO STARING WHEN I CHANCE TO LOOK OUT THE WINDOW; I CAN BARELY DISCERN ENOUGH LANDMARKS TO FIGURE OUT WHAT STOP WE'RE AT ON A ROUTE I'VE TAKEN TWICE A DAY FOR A YEAR AND A HALF AND MAYBE A BIT LESS OFTEN FOR MY WHOLE LIFE.

I DON'T MIND THE SLOW RIDE. IT'S SORT OF EXHILARATING, BEING WRAPPED IN ALL THAT BIGNESS.

AND NO ONE CAN BLAME ME FOR BEING LATE TO WORK; MY EXCUSE IS BATTERING AT EVERYONE'S WINDOWS.

NOT THAT ANYONE EVER SAYS ANYTHING ANYWAY.

COURTNEY, YOU'RE HERE- GREAT. LOOK, I'M OFF TO A BOARD MEETING. CAN YOU TYPE THIS MEMO AND GET IT OUT? OH, AND THE BROCHURE LAYOUTS ARE IN, SO COULD YOU GET STARTED ON PROOFING?

SURE. DO YOU THINK THEY'LL SHOW UP?

306

WHO'LL SHOW UP?

THE BOARD. BECAUSE OF THE SNOW.

OH! HA HA, I HOPE SO!

FEB

THE SNOW HAS BEEN HOWLING DOWN SINCE LAST EVENING...

...AND IT'S PILED IN DRIFTS WHERE YOU CAN SINK TO YOUR KNEE.

ITS TEXTURE IS ALMOST LIKE BREAD DOUGH, SQUOOSHY AND MALLEABLE. THE SNOW HAS COATED EVERYTHING SO THICKLY THAT EVEN THE STREETS ARE HARDLY GREY.

ALL THE PEOPLE STAND HUDDLED AROUND WAITING ON BUSES LOOKING LIKE, DEPENDING ON HOW GENEROUS I FEEL, EITHER MINIATURE PIKE'S PEAKS OR ENORMOUS FROSTED FLAKES.

IT LOOKS, OUTSIDE, LIKE THE PICTURES THE AD AGENCIES PULL OUT EVERY FALL OF THE BLIZZARD OF '79 TO SCARE CHICAGOANS INTO BUYING NEW SNOW TIRES, OR COATS, OR INSURANCE.

AND IT'S LATE FEBRUARY, FOR GOD'S SAKE. NO ONE THOUGHT IT WOULD SNOW AGAIN THIS YEAR. AT LEAST NOT LIKE THIS.

COURTNEY! YOU DONE WITH THAT PROOFING? I WANT JIM TO GIVE IT THE ONCE-OVER.

DESPITE ITS REPUTATION, CHICAGO IS NOT GENERALLY A VERY SNOWY TOWN. COLD, GOD YES. BUT NOT SO DEEP IN SNOW. I REMEMBER THE ONE WINTER I SPENT IN MINNESOTA, NOTICING IN NOVEMBER THAT THE CITY HAD JUST GONE AROUND AND MADE ALL THE STOP SIGNS TALLER, TO ACCOUNT...

ACTUALLY, TO BE CONSISTENT, I SHOULD POINT OUT THAT I HATE THE WINTER. I HATE TO BE COLD, I HATE THE WIND, I HATE ALL THE BULKY CLOTHES AND THE GREY SKY AND THE MONOTONY.

BUT SOMETIMES IT GIVES ME A THRILL, LIKE WHEN IT'S 40 DEGREES BELOW ZERO, I FEEL LIKE JACK LONDON. WE ARE A CITY FULL OF ARCTIC PIONEERS, BONDED BY THE HARSH CONDITIONS.

IT'S REALLY ONLY ON DAYS THAT ARE THAT COLD, OR THIS SNOWY, BUT SOMETIMES THE WHOLE CITY FEELS LIKE IT'S CELEBRATING ITS RESILIENCE TOGETHER.

HOW OFTEN CAN YOU TRADE GRIMLY PROUD SMILES WITH THE TOTAL STRANGERS YOU RUN INTO IN THE SAFETY OF THE GROCERY STORE OR GAS STATION, JUST BECAUSE YOU WERE ALL VIRTUOUS AND TOUGH ENOUGH TO MAKE IT TO THE STORE OR GAS STATION?

COLOR COPIE $1.00

YOU TALK TO MORE STRANGERS AT TIMES LIKE THAT.

COLOR COPIES

THERE'S A SENSE THAT WE'RE ALL IN THIS TOGETHER.

HOT WEATHER DOES IT TOO, A LITTLE BIT, BUT PEOPLE ARE A LOT MORE LIKELY TO MUG YOU OR SHOOT YOU IN THE HOT WEATHER. IT'S NOT JUST THE TOUGH, VIRTUOUS ONES WHO MAKE IT OUT.

Dec/Jan:
FACILITIES ----- 3805
MATERIALS|

num lock

ON THE OTHER HAND, I ESPECIALLY LIKE TO BE AT HOME ALL DAY WHEN IT'S REALLY COLD. I SORT OF FOOL MYSELF INTO THINKING I'M TRAPPED AND I MUST BE ORGANIZED AND INDUSTRIOUS TO KEEP MYSELF SAFE. I BUNDLE UP AND WALK AROUND THE EMPTY HOUSE CLEANING THINGS UP AND WORK PROJECTS. ING ON LOT OF I MAKE A THINK TEA AND WITH ABOUT THINGS A SERIOUS BUT PLEASANT OUTLOOK...

...MAYBE I CALL MY FRIENDS, BUT MAYBE THE PHONES ARE OUT! AN ADVENTURE. AS LONG AS I DON'T HAVE TO GO OUT AND TORTURE MYSELF WITH THE COLD. I'M A COUCH JACK LONDON.

COURTNEY, ARE YOU DONE WITH THE REPORT?

NO, UH, GIVE ME ABOUT 5 MINUTES!

100

DOUG? HERE IT IS—

THANKS.

OH, COURTNEY, CAN WE TALK FOR A MOMENT?

SURE~

I'M A LITTLE CONCERNED ABOUT YOUR PERFORMANCE LATELY.

I KNOW YOU'VE HAD SOME DIFFICULTIES LATELY, AND I'M SORRY, BUT I REALLY NEED YOU TO...

...TODAY, I COULDN'T SEE THE LAKE FROM ONLY A HUNDRED YARDS AWAY. THE SKY AND THE LAND AND THE WATER WERE ALL EQUALLY WHITE, WITH ONLY A FEW SCRAGGLY TREES, TORN BY THE WIND, TO MARK A PALE GREY DIVISION. I CAN HEAR IT, THOUGH.

IT IS POUNDING AND ROARING LIKE IT IS THE OCEAN. IT'S AMAZING TO ME THAT IT CAN MAKE SO MUCH NOISE, AND YET BE INVISIBLE. THE ONLY THING I'M SORRY ABOUT IN THE PLACE THAT I LIVE IS THAT I CAN'T GET TO THE LAKE SO EASILY. I SPENT WHOLE SUMMERS THERE WHEN I WAS YOUNGER, AND NOW IT'S BEEN TWO YEARS SINCE I EVEN STEPPED ON TO THE SAND, JUST A MILE OR SO OFF.

...SO I HOPE YOU'LL GIVE IT YOUR BEST EFFORT. YOU THINK WE CAN WORK TOGETHER ON THIS?

102

VIVA!
BY JESSICA ABEL
©1996

...AND SO HE'S LIKE, "HOW CAN SHE GO OUT WITH DAVID? HE'S LIKE 15 YEARS OLDER..." AND I SAY, I DUNNO, IT SEEMS OKAY, AND HE GOES, "I'M SO OVER IT, I'M SO OVER THIS SHIT. I JUST WANT TO BE *FRIENDS* WITH HER..."

NGUUUGH... YOU *KNOW* HE'S NOT OVER HER WHEN HE SAYS THAT!

I KNOW! FUCK! IT'S KILLING ME!

I MEAN, AT THIS POINT, I *NEVER* WANT TO SEE HIM! IT'S JUST TOO HARD. BUT I CAN'T RESIST THE TEMPTATION...

YOU HAVE GOT TO TALK TO HIM.

NO! NO, YOU KNOW HOW HUNG UP ON EVA...

"...EVIL..."

NO, COME ON, IT'S NOT HER FAULT. BUT I CAN'T RISK MESSING UP OUR FRIENDSHIP OVER SOME BAD-KARMA SEX SHIT AND NOT BEING ABLE TO SEE HIM AT ALL.

BUT YOU ALL HAVE BEEN FRIENDS FOR SO LONG — THAT COULDN'T HAPPEN!

UGH! UGH! I CAN'T TALK ABOUT THIS ANYMORE, I'M GOING NUTS! AND I JUST GOT THE COVER ART FOR THE NEXT *SHEBA* FROM BETTINA, AND IT SUCKS! MY LIFE IS SHIT!

GIRL, YOU NEED A COCKTAIL.

NO SHIT. I NEED A BOURBON, AND I NEED IT NOW.

ALLOW ME — CASEY! EMERGENCY BOURBON!

GOOD EVENING, LADIES. WHAT SEEMS TO BE THE PROBLEM?

TOP SECRET. REQUIRES "BOOKERS."

OOH, SOUNDS SERIOUS —

MAKE IT A DOUBLE.

103

105

OH YEAH — *

I'M, UH, GOING TO GET A DRINK. YOU WANT ONE?

NO, I'M FINE.

I GOTTA GET OUT OF HERE.

YOU O.K.?

YEAH. CALL ME TOMORROW.

YOU SURE?

YEAH! FUCK I AM SUCH A FUCKING MORON — GOD DAMNIT — TOO FUCKING DRUNK TO GET MY RIDICULOUS ASS HOME —

CAN'T EVEN FUCKING — MOTHER FUCKER!! — WISH I HAD JUST STAYED HOME — SONOFABITCH, I AM NOT GOING TO CRY!...

HEY!

...HUH? ...